The

# True Story

of

# Fake News

## Mark Dice

**The Resistance**
San Diego, CA

# Table of Contents

# Introduction

Just one week after the 2016 presidential election, when tens of millions of Hillary supporters were still in absolute shock that Donald Trump actually beat her — and while many Trump supporters were in a similar state of surprise since he was the long-awaited anti-establishment underdog — the term "fake news" became the talk of the town and quickly turned into one of the most loaded and controversial labels in America. It wasn't just a topic that circulated in a week-long news cycle. It was an issue that got more polarizing and more complex as the weeks and months went on; and with seemingly every day that passed the 'fake news' conspiracy got deeper and darker.

Fake news stories have been around for centuries, although they had usually just been called disinformation, propaganda, yellow journalism, conspiracy theories, or hoaxes; but this modern incarnation was different. All of a sudden it was supposedly everywhere, and just cost Hillary Clinton the election.

Democrats were so shocked at Hillary's defeat that they couldn't come to grips with the fact that despite all the polls and media coverage painting a picture that Trump would surely lose — he didn't. With headlines like "Think Trump has a chance to snag GOP nomination? Analysis gives him just 1%,"[1] and "Our pollster polls model gives Hillary Clinton a 98.1% chance of winning

---

[1] CNN "Think Trump has a chance to snag GOP nomination? Analysis gives him just 1%" by Daniella Diaz (July 9th 2015)

the presidency,"[2] Hillary supporters thought her victory would be a sure thing. In a now-famous clip, Bill Maher's audience burst out in laughter at Ann Coulter on his HBO show when she predicted Donald Trump had the best chance of winning early on in the race.

Instead of accepting the fact that voters wanted a non-politician in the White House for a change, and that they wanted the illegal immigration problem fixed, Obamacare overhauled, and a conservative Supreme Court Justice to replace Antonin Scalia who had recently died — Democrats started playing the blame game, and their reasons for Hillary's defeat kept getting longer and more bizarre by the day.

First, they pointed the finger at FBI director James Comey for amending his testimony about the investigation into Hillary Clinton's email scandal when classified material sent from her was later found on Anthony Weiner's computer (then-husband of Huma Abedin, her campaign's vice chairman).[3] Then they blamed white supremacists and the KKK, or the "whitelash" against a black president as CNN's Van Jones famously cried about on election night.[4] They went on to blame Islamophobia, xenophobia, and sexism, saying that people just didn't want a "woman president." But then they came up with their most creative excuse ever. An excuse that would serve as a massive umbrella under which all other excuses could be tied together into one grand unified excuse: "Fake News."

---

[2] https://twitter.com/huffpost/status/795663593689808896?lang=en

[3] New York Times "Hillary Clinton Blames F.B.I. Director for Election Loss" by Amy Chozick (November 12th 2016)

[4] CNN "'This was a whitelash': Van Jones' take on the election results" by Josiah Ryan (November 9th 2016)

People must have been duped into not trusting or disliking Hillary Clinton because they read lies about her on Facebook, they concluded. The culprit? Not ordinary right-wing news sites highlighting the reasons why Hillary was wrong for the job, or documenting her history of corruption and scandals. No. It was supposed "fake news" articles that were posted on little-known websites and then spread virally through Facebook by people sharing them.

*The Washington Post* led the charge and sounded the alarm with a headline reading, "Facebook fake-news writer: 'I think Donald Trump is in the White House because of me.'"[5] An avalanche of accusations followed, causing a moral panic in the mainstream media as they tried to warn the world about this newly discovered 'danger.' *Rolling Stone* magazine immediately echoed this new battle cry with the headline, "How a Fake Newsman Accidentally Helped Trump Win the White House."[6] CBS's *60 Minutes* declared, "In this last election the nation was assaulted by imposters masquerading as reporters. They poisoned the conversation with lies [and] many did it to influence the outcome."[7]

*The Washington Post* pointed out a few of the most popular (actual) fake news articles, and named the man behind them — Paul Horner, a 38-year-old Internet

---

[5] Washington Post "Facebook fake-news writer: 'I think Donald Trump is in the White House because of me" by Caitlin Dewey (November 17th 2016)

[6] Rolling Stone "How a Fake Newsman Accidentally Helped Trump Win the White House" by Erik Hedegaard (November 29th 2016)

[7] CBS 60 Minutes "What's "fake news"? 60 Minutes producers investigate" (March 26th 2016)

entrepreneur who ran CNN.com.de, CBSnews.com.co, NBC.com.co, ABCnews.com.co, and other fake news websites which were designed to look like actual news sites and used similar URLs. Stories posted on these sites were really satire, not technically fake news. But an article about anti-Trump protesters being paid duped Eric Trump and Trump campaign manager Corey Lewandowski, who both tweeted about it thinking it was proof of another George Soros plot, since he had been giving tens of millions to Black Lives Matter front groups so they could fan the flames of civil unrest.[8]

Paul Horner and his fake CNN, ABC, and NBC websites weren't part of a plot to hurt Hillary Clinton, or help Donald Trump in the 2016 election — they were just satire, which should be obvious to anyone who read past the first two or three sentences of the stories. And Horner's motivation wasn't political; it was financial.

Most fake news and satire websites simply want to make money from the web traffic their articles bring to the sites. The way most website advertising works is that Google Ad Sense (or other ad companies) pay them per page visit, so if the site can create sensational headlines and get lots of people to post links to their articles on Facebook it will drive a lot of traffic to their site and they get paid. While a few fake news websites did produce some viral stories during the 2016 election, as you will see, these stories had no measurable effect on voters.[9]

The liberal media, however, seized on 'fake news' publisher Paul Horner's admissions and his viral success,

---

[8] Washington Times "George Soros funds Ferguson protests, hopes to spur civil action" by Kelly Riddell (January 14th 2015)

[9] Stanford News "Stanford study examines fake news and the 2016 presidential election" by Krysten Crawford (January 18th 2017)

4

and used his stories as if they were the smoking gun in a huge conspiracy to spread disinformation about Hillary Clinton hoping to prevent people from voting for her, despite his stories being satire and designed to actually make fun of Trump supporters.

A few of the most viral fake news stories about the election were that "Pope Francis Shocks World, Endorses Donald Trump for President," "The Amish in America Commit Their Vote to Donald Trump; Mathematically Guaranteeing Him a Presidential Victory," "FBI Agent Suspected in Hillary Email Leaks Found Dead in Apartment Murder-Suicide," and "Donald Trump Sent His Own Plane to Transport 200 Stranded Marines."[10]

While these stories were designed to bolster Donald Trump and demonize Hillary, fake news is a two way street. The mainstream media was framing the issue as if all fake news articles were written to smear Hillary Clinton, but there were plenty of viral fake stories and memes with fake quotes attributed to Donald Trump that were made to smear him as well.

For example, one of the most popular memes of the entire election was one with a fake quote of Donald Trump that cited a non-existent interview with *People* magazine which claimed he said, "If I were to run, I'd run as a Republican. They're the dumbest group of voters in the country. They believe anything on Fox News. I could lie and they'd still eat it up. I bet my numbers would be terrific."[11]  It started circulating in October of 2015

---

[10] CNBC "Read all about it: The biggest fake news stories of 2016" by Hannah Ritchie (December 30th 2016)

[11] BuzzFeed "No, Trump Never Told People Magazine That Republicans Are "The Dumbest" Voters" by Ishmael N. Daro (July 21st 2016)

shortly after Trump announced his run for president and despite being easily debunked, people kept spreading it around for over a year and it would regularly show up on Facebook and Twitter from liberals who kept posting it, thinking it was real.

Some of the fake news trying to smear Trump was far more sophisticated than a fabricated quote made into a meme, and far more dirty. BuzzFeed published details about a 'Russian dossier' which claimed that Donald Trump had been caught on video getting golden showers (being peed on) by Russian hookers.[12] A lot of idiots on the Internet believed the story even though it was just part of a disinformation campaign designed to smear Donald Trump, and publishing the story ultimately led to BuzzFeed getting sued for defamation.[13]

In another carefully orchestrated smear campaign a fraudulent lawsuit was actually filed against Donald Trump claiming he raped a 13-year-old girl.[14] Most Trump-hating liberal mainstream media outlets wouldn't even report on the frivolous lawsuit because they knew it was a vicious hoax to defame him, but a few did, including *The New York Daily News* and *People* magazine. Word of the lawsuit circulated on Twitter and Facebook when unscrupulous websites published the allegations, knowing such an inflammatory headline

---

[12] CNN "Vladimir Putin dismisses Donald Trump dossier claims as 'rubbish'" by Angela Dewan and Milena Veselinivic (January 18th 2017)

[13] New York Times "Russian Executive Sues BuzzFeed Over Unverified Trump Dossier" by Eli Rosenberg (February 4th 2017)

[14] Politico "Woman suing Trump over alleged teen rape drops suit, again" by Josh Gerstein (November 4th 2016)

would get them some web traffic.[15]   Rosie O'Donnell even tweeted about it to her one million Twitter followers multiple times, along with the hashtag #TrumpRape, either believing it to be true, or just trying to spread the story around hoping to hurt him.[16]

The person behind the lawsuit was later identified by the London *Guardian* as a former producer for the *Jerry Springer* show, who has a history of being accused of making sensational and false claims about celebrities in order to get media attention.[17]   But despite carefully crafted fake news stories designed to smear Donald Trump, like the 13-year-old girl rape hoax and the Russian hookers golden showers dossier, the liberal media kept claiming that 'fake news' about Hillary Clinton spread through social media had ruined the 2016 presidential election, in effect, 'stealing' it from her.

It wasn't just people who were writing satirical articles that some gullible people may have thought were true, or completely fake stories on obscure websites which hoped to hurt Hillary Clinton that were the culprits. Instead, a new scandal erupted claiming the Russians were behind the new fake news phenomenon as part of a plot to install Trump as their "puppet president."   One of the biggest liberal newspapers in the country, *The Washington Post*, which was dedicated to stopping Donald Trump from becoming president, came out with an article two weeks after the election titled, "Russian

---

[15] The Guardian "Woman accusing Trump of raping her at 13 cancels her plan to go public" by Rory Carroll (November 3rd 2016)

[16] https://twitter.com/Rosie/status/793873581314891776
https://twitter.com/Rosie/status/788924850597396480

[17] The Guardian "Rape lawsuits against Donald Trump linked to former TV producer" by John Swaine (July 7th 2016)

Propaganda Effort Helped Spread 'Fake News' During Election, Experts Say," which claimed that the fake news stories about Hillary Clinton were part of a disinformation operation launched by the Russians in order to help Donald Trump win.[18]

Their article started off saying, "The flood of 'fake news' this election season got support from a sophisticated Russian propaganda campaign that created and spread misleading articles online with the goal of punishing Democrat Hillary Clinton, helping Republican Donald Trump and undermining faith in American democracy, say independent researchers who tracked the operation."[19]

President Obama's advisor Dan Pfeiffer tweeted a link to the article and asked, "Why isn't this the biggest story in the world right now?"[20] This new angle on the 'fake news conspiracy' now focusing on "the Russians" quickly ballooned out of control, going beyond the McCarthyism panic of the 1940s and 50s when Senator Joseph McCarthy thought there were secret Communists in Congress around every corner working to undermine the United States. A new war against fake news was just beginning that would raise important concerns about censorship and the secret agendas of mainstream media corporations, social media giants, and Internet search engines.

---

[18] Washington Post "Russian propaganda effort helped spread 'fake news' during election, experts say" by Craig Timberg (November 24th 2016)

[19] Ibid.

[20] https://twitter.com/danpfeiffer/status/802205196516368384?lang=en

Why all this concern about fake news, and why immediately after the election? As you will see in this book, the Liberal Establishment was creating a smokescreen to implement dramatic new censorship policies for social media and the Internet as a whole. They concluded that if they could control the information people see and hear on social media, they could possibly prevent the kind of upset that occurred when Hillary lost the election from happening again.

As Jim Morrison, singer of the 60s rock band *The Doors,* proclaimed, "Whoever controls the media, controls the mind,"[21] and with mainstream media losing its power in recent years from countless new websites, blogs, YouTube channels and Facebook pages functioning as news outlets — the monopoly that major media companies had on the control of information for decades was collapsing. Today, anyone with a Facebook page can post an article, a picture, or a video, and in a matter of minutes it can be seen by just as many people as something broadcast on the national news by a major television network.

The media oligarchy could no longer control what information the public was consistently fed, or what information was purposefully ignored. Many people started to see this new 'fake news' scare as a veiled attempt at censorship and a bold move to try and take back control of the distribution of media, which is why I wrote this book.

*The New York Post* ran an article titled, "The War on 'Fake News' Is All About Censoring Real News," which said, "Scrambling for an explanation for Donald Trump's victory, many in the media and on the left have settled on

---

[21] Brainy Quote - "Jim Morrison Quotes"

the idea that his supporters were consumers of 'fake news' — gullible rubes living in an alternate reality made Trump president,"[22] and noted that this new 'fake news' scare itself was fake news, and there was a growing backlash from conservatives who saw this witch hunt for what it was.

Just a few weeks later *The New York Times* admitted, "'Fake news' as shorthand will almost surely be returned upon the media tenfold,"[23] as conservatives began to throw the term back in the face of the mainstream media. One outlet published an article cautioning against the growing fake news panic titled, "Stop Calling Everything 'Fake News'" and pointed out, "Two months ago, almost no one was talking about fake news. A Google Trends search for the term shows that it barely registered before October. Now you can hardly turn on the real news without hearing it."[24] The backlash was getting so bad that even President-Elect Donald Trump, in a now-famous outburst, called CNN "fake news" at his first press conference of 2017.[25] Some people in the audience could be heard applauding him and "You are fake news" became an instant meme.

Like never before, the mainstream media kept making mountains out of molehills and using their platforms to influence public opinion by framing everything Donald

---

[22] New York Post "The war on 'fake news' is all about censoring real news" by Karol Markowicz (December 4th 2016)

[23] New York Times "Fixation on Fake News Overshadows Waning Trust in Real Reporting" by John Herrman (November 18th 2016)

[24] Slate "Stop Calling Everything 'Fake News'" by Will Oremus (December 6th 2016)

[25] USA Today "Trump to CNN: 'You are fake news'" by Donovan Slack (January 11th 2017)

Trump did and said in a negative light. Their constant criticism and nitpicking was soon difficult to distinguish from satire or parody because much of it was so absurd, but unfortunately millions of Americans couldn't help but get swept up in their manufactured controversies. Anti-Trump hatred would soon grow to extremes few could have imagined as the constant disinformation was whipping people into a frenzy.

Conservatives fought back and started fact checking the liberal media like hawks, and every time CNN or another major 'news' organization would report a false or absurdly biased story, Trump supporters would shout from the rooftops about it and use each instance to mock the diminishing credibility of mainstream media.

Liberals pushed back even harder and began labeling conservative websites, YouTube channels, and social media personalities not just as "fake news," but as "extremists" and "racists" who post "hate speech." Facebook began implementing "fact checkers" and issuing warnings when people would post links to certain stories or websites, as well as outright banning links to some or labeling them "spam" when someone tried to share them. The major social media platforms also implemented stricter terms of service and vowed to crack down on people posting "hateful content," which in reality is often just mild criticism of certain liberal policies or ideologies.

YouTube began demonetizing (removing advertisements from) videos covering certain topics they deemed "not advertiser-friendly," thus preventing 'YouTubers' like myself from making money off them, which for many people is a part-time or full-time job and how we pay our bills. This was just the beginning of a censorship tsunami that was heading our way. Liberals would begin going after the advertisers on conservative websites and TV shows to pressure them to pull their sponsorships.[26] Google began scrutinizing websites and YouTube channels which use their Ad Sense system to generate revenue. Anti-feminist videos, videos criticizing radical LGBT activists, or ones calling to stop illegal immigration or the massive influx of Muslim refugees were now being stripped of advertisers in droves.[27]

YouTube wasn't just for posting funny cat videos or online tutorials anymore. It had become a powerful platform for distributing news and commentary. The 'YouTube stars' weren't just entertainers, beauty vloggers and gamers anymore, but news commentators and anti-social justice warrior activists.

Many found that social media platforms weren't just useful for communicating with friends and family, but the technology could also easily be used as a massive publishing outlet allowing literally anyone to be able to have their content seen and heard by just as many people as a major newspaper or television network, and with little or no cost at all. The news and tech conglomerates figured if they could remove the financial incentives for this rapidly growing industry of alternative media platforms and personalities, they could dramatically discourage people from putting out content and commentary, and thus reduce the growing number of conservative voices online whose audience kept growing by the day as more people abandoned mainstream media

[26] Daily Caller "Media Matters Targets Hannity Advertisers" by Peter Hasson (May 25th 2017)

[27] Advertising Age "As YouTube Tinkers With Ad Formula, Its Stars See Their Videos Lose Money" by Garett Sloane (March 30th 2017)

and were turning to new independent outlets and online personalities for their news and commentary.

In this book we'll look not just at the recent phenomena of fake news and how trying to weaponize the term dramatically backfired on liberals, but we'll also look at the power and influence of the media in general. Media today now means more than just television, newspapers, and radio. It includes social media. Facebook, Twitter, Instagram, YouTube and Snapchat, which have become major media companies that host and distribute content in quantities previously unimagined.

We'll look at how these companies manipulate and censor the content that users post, how the trending lists function to restrict certain stories from going viral and artificially aid others to do just the opposite. We'll look at how powerful multibillion dollar networks can influence the public conversation through their agenda-setting power, and at the same time sweep important stories and issues under the rug through lying by omission. You'll see the real power mainstream media has to shape our culture, our fears, and our tastes; and how it keeps most people mesmerized by an endless stream of meaningless and mindless entertainment.

Because media has changed so dramatically with the creation of the Internet, smartphones, and social media; people don't just get their news from TV, radio, and newspapers anymore as you know. There are now countless blogs, YouTube channels, Twitter accounts, and Facebook pages dedicated to posting news and analysis — many of which rival or eclipse the reach of traditional media outlets. The distribution of content posted on these platforms has complex implications regarding how it spreads online, what role these companies have in distributing (and suppressing) user generated content, and how information flowing through these platforms influences their audience.

We'll also look at the role Google has as a search engine in filtering out certain information or websites and prioritizing others, as well as Wikipedia's role as an 'encyclopedia' that so many rely upon as a source of knowledge, and how it too is another cog in an Orwellian machine of censorship and media manipulation.

You may be surprised to hear the evidence and admissions that the CIA actually created a powerful program in the 1970s to place CIA agents and assets in high-level positions within major news organizations so they could kill stories and perpetuate government propaganda by facilitating its publication at the media outlets they controlled. It may sound like the plot of a communist conspiracy or a science fiction film, but you'll see it's a very real covert operation that happened right here in the United States of America.

Now, let's enter the fascinating maze of media manipulation and get a closer look at the forces behind what can only be called an information war. This is a war of facts vs. fiction, of perception vs. reality, of average well-meaning and hard working people vs. shady multibillion dollar international corporations that want to control what you see, hear, and think. This is *The True Story of Fake News*.

# Real Fake News

Grocery store tabloids have been a standard feature at the checkout stands for decades, and I'm not just talking about the clearly fake and satirical papers about finding "Bat Boy" or the "Redneck Vampire." Usually these rags cover celebrity gossip and just fabricate claims about cheating and breakups, but tabloids like *The National Enquirer* cover politics as well, and despite breaking a few legitimate stories like Senator John Edwards' affair and love child, they're usually just fake news that nobody ever takes seriously.

But with the development of the Internet, we've seen some shady websites pop up which are designed to look like actual news sites or have names sounding like a newspaper from a major city, and they post fake news stories in hopes of having them go viral trying to bring traffic to their site so they can earn some ad revenue or get some laughs from the joy of pranking people. These fake stories trick a small number of people, but most are smart enough not to fall for a "breaking" story coming from a "news" outlet they've never heard of. While people may succumb to their clickbait titles out of curiosity, most people can spot that the website is bogus or is just a satire site.

Many of the supposed "fake news" articles that went viral during the 2016 election weren't really 'fakes' but were just satire that some people thought were real after only reading the headline or the first few sentences of the stories. Before "the Russians" got blamed for fake news

15

being shared on social media, it was teenagers in Macedonia, a country in Southeastern Europe once part of communist Yugoslavia.[28] Mainstream media began writing stores about the "Macedonian teenagers" who were allegedly making thousands of dollars a month from writing fake news about Hillary Clinton in the run up to the election.[29] Macedonia was said to have been the home of various pro-Trump websites which were allegedly "cashing in" on writing fake news about things like Hillary Clinton's "imminent criminal indictment."[30]

While a small group of friends with a misguided entrepreneurial spirit in Macedonia may have registered a bunch of domain names, wrote some fake news stories that got shared on Facebook and made them some money from Google Ad Sense, no credible expert claimed that this amounted to anything more than one of a million Internet scams run by people trying to make a quick buck.

A few fake news websites the media focused on after the election were *National Report.net* and *The Denver Guardian,* both run by the same guy who calls himself Jestin Coler, who found a niche on the Internet by writing fake news stories which relied on people sharing them through social media.[31] Some of his articles include: "RFID Chip Now Being Issued in Hanna, Wyoming As

---

[28] NBC News "Fake News: How a Partying Macedonian Teen Earns Thousands Publishing Lies" by Alexander Smith and Vladimir Banic (December 9th 2016)

[29] Fox News "Here's a List of Everyone & Everything Hillary Has Blamed for Her Loss" (June 1st 2017)

[30] Wired "Inside the Macedonian Fake-News Complex" by Samantha Subramanian (February 15th 2017J)

[31] NPR "We Tracked Down A Fake-News Creator In The Suburbs. Here's What We Learned" by Laura Sydell (November 23rd 2016)

Part of New Obamacare Plan," "Trump to Nominate Chris Christie to Supreme Food Court," "Man Shouts 'Allahu Akbar' Before Blowing Up Friend's Inbox," and "Atlanta Falcons Win Popular Vote, Still Lose Super Bowl." Most of them are clearly just jokes, and not 'fake news' in the true sense of the word, but a few of them were, like the one titled, "FBI Agent Suspected In Hillary Email Leaks Found Dead In Apparent Murder-Suicide," which was posted a few days before the election.[32]

When *CBS's 60 Minutes* aired a segment on their investigation into fake news, one of the examples they used was from a site called *NTMY News* which had the headline, "After Colonoscopy Reveals Brain Tumor, Donald Trump Drops from Race." It's obviously a joke about Trump having his head up his ass — get it? How could CBS possibly consider this 'fake news?' *This* was their evidence that social media had a fake news problem?

Another example they showed was from Celebtricity.com, which published a story titled, "Donald Trump Caught Snorting Cocaine by Hotel Staff," which was an absurd article with no author's name mentioned, and not even a date it was published. After about three seconds of reading the article pretty much everyone would have known that it was satire, not fake news. It began, "The Internet is buzzing today after white supremacist presidential candidate Donald Trump was caught by hotel staff snorting cocaine." It continued, "Maria Gonzalez, an employee at the Folks INN & Suites

---

[32] The Denver Post "There is no such thing as the Denver Guardian, despite that Facebook post you saw" by Eric Lubbers (November 5th 2016)

Hotel in Phoenix, brought room service to his room witnessed it all."[33]

It then attributes an absolutely insane quote to her, that you can't help but laugh at, which says, "When I walked in I saw 3 naked prostitutes and maybe $100,000 in hundred dollars bills and a mountain of white powder on the table, I thought there was a dog on the floor asleep but it was his hair piece, he was bald and sweating like crazy. I asked him where to put the food and he asked me 'did I wanna take a hit' (snort some coke). I told him no, but I'll take some of that money, [and] he called me a free loader, told me to get the fuck out his room and go back to my country."[34]   The article was poorly written with awful grammar and was a complete joke, but *60 Minutes* used it as another example of 'fake news.'

Just because people click on a sensational headline from a fake news story, doesn't mean they actually believe it! While people posting links to these stories on Facebook may have generated traffic from curious readers who clicked on them, few people doing so were actually duped by them, and most just got a good laugh. As you will see, studies were conducted into fake news about the election, and yes some of it fooled people and went viral, but it actually had no effect on how people voted.[35]

What's far more sinister than some random fake news site or even trying to spoof a real one like the ABCNews.com.co or the CNN.com.de sites, are major mainstream media outlets that millions of people trust,

[33] Celebtricity.com "Donald Trump Caught Snorting Cocaine by Hotel Staff"

[34] Ibid.

[35] Columbia Journalism Review "Is Fake News a Fake Problem?" by Jacob L. Nelson (January 31, 2017)

actually reporting fake news, because their stories get spread far and wide across social media since they come from brand name 'news sites' like CNN or *The Washington Post.*

Former London mayor Ken Livingstone once stated, "The world is run by monsters and you have to deal with them. Some of them run countries, some of them run banks, some of them run news corporations."[36] And as you will see, those are often the real monsters we need to be concerned about.

Because the liberal media perpetuated the myth that Hillary Clinton would surely become the next president, they received a devastating blow to their credibility on election night. *The Hill* ran a headline reading, "The biggest loser in 2016? The mainstream media and journalism," and in the article stated, "There are many losers in the wake of Donald Trump's victory. They include Hollywood, pollsters, the Bush family and the GOP's donor class, and neocons. But the biggest losers are the mainstream media (MSM) and journalism itself."[37]

*The New York Times* had a headline asking "Can The Media Recover from This Election?"[38] *Fortune* magazine asked, "How Much Will Cable News' Record Ratings Drop Post-Election?"[39] Then a survey conducted by CBS and *Vanity Fair* magazine found that Americans now saw

---

[36] New Statesman "Preview: Ken Livingstone: 'The world is run by monsters'" by Alice Gribbin (February 8th 2012)

[37] The Hill "The biggest loser in 2016? The mainstream media and journalism" by Patrick Maines (November 15th 2016)

[38] New York Times "Can the Media Recover from This Election?" by Jim Rutenberg and James Poniewozik (November 8th 2016

[39] Fortune "How Much Will Cable News' Record Ratings Drop Post-Election?" by Tom Huddleston Jr. (November 12th 2016)

mainstream media as the most unethical business, more so than the pharmaceutical companies, and the banking industry.[40] Another survey from Monmouth University in New Jersey found that 6 out of 10 Americans believe that the mainstream media regularly reports fake news.[41]

Why weren't half of the hosts and contributors fired from CNN, MSNBC, ABC, CBS, and NBC after the election? How could these networks keep such incompetent and out of touch people on the payroll after everything they had been reporting for so long was so wrong? What's more disturbing is instead of 'cleaning up their act' after their embarrassing election coverage, the networks started getting more extreme and more biased by the day.

The anti-Trump mania exploded on cable news, the Big Three broadcast networks, late night comedy shows, and even on tech and sports websites like CNET, Gizmodo, and Deadspin when the stories had nothing to do with tech or sports at all. The liberal media was now in an existential crisis and had to try to explain to their viewers how their reporting had been so inaccurate. Instead of admitting their failures, they immediately started inventing excuses — first placing blame on 'racist white people,' and then on fake news spreading 'lies' about Hillary Clinton, and then they finally settled on one grandiose unifying conspiracy theory — that the Russians were behind it all.

---

[40] The Washington Times "'Watch out for the lying media'; Press ranked more unethical than drug, banking, tech industries" by Jennifer Harper (December 1st 2016)

[41] Politico "Poll: 6 in 10 Americans think traditional news outlets report fake news" by Kelsey Sutton (March 29th 2017)

One of the first things mainstream media began doing was labeling rising conservative social media stars as white nationalists or white supremacists. *The Hollywood Reporter*, *The Guardian*, *Wired* magazine, and even celebrity blogger Perez Hilton all mentioned me by name, trying to tie me to David Duke, Richard Spencer, and the white nationalist movement, even though I never said I was a supporter of the Alt-Right, and to the contrary have stated on numerous occasions that I'm not.

*The Guardian's* headline read, "Former Ku Klux Klan Leader and US Alt-Right Hail Election Result."[42] The article claimed, "Members of America's alt-right reacted with glee to the news of Trump's victory. The provocative conservative movement, largely active online, has been closely associated with Trump's campaign." It then quoted tweets from Alex Jones, Michael Savage, David Duke, and me! I immediately sent them a cease and desist and threatened to sue them for defamation so they removed me from the article and added a note on the bottom stating, "This article was amended on 16 November 2016 to remove a quoted individual who was mistakenly included."[43]

Another outlet also issued a retraction after I threatened legal action, saying, "An earlier version of this story incorrectly referred to Mark Dice as an 'alt-right' commentator. He is not and news.com.au sincerely apologizes for this error."[44]

---

[42] The Guardian "Former Ku Klux Klan leader and US alt-right hail election result" by Esther Addley (November 9th 2016)

[43] Ibid.

[44] News.com.Au "Netflix 'Dear White People' trailer sparks backlash" by Frank Chung (February 9th 2017)

The Establishment media were so furious that a whole group of social media savvy conservatives like myself were amassing huge followings that they tried to take us down using one of the oldest tricks in the liberal playbook — smearing us as racists.

One independent journalist decided to sue a reporter at Fusion, a social justice warrior cable channel, after she was accused of making a "white supremacist" hand sign, which was in reality just the "okay" hand sign which President Trump regularly uses.[45] *The Independent* in London also ran a story making the same absurd claim about the woman's 'okay' gesture being a "white supremacist hand sign."[46] The 'hand sign' story was laughed at online by Trump supporters who couldn't believe how crazy it was, and some commented that it signaled the "death of journalism."

## Washington Post's Story on Fake News was Fake News

After first blaming teenagers in Macedonia for the 'fake news' problem, and then 'racist' alt-right Trump supporters on the Internet for spreading 'hate' about Hillary, then came the Russian conspiracy theories about "collusion" and the Kremlin being behind all the fake news in order to supposedly help Donald Trump. It's important to point out that *The Washington Post* first tried to link Russia to fake news articles that had circulated

---

[45] The Hill "Pro-Trump journalist sues Fusion reporter for defamation" by Max Greenwood (June 1st 2017)

[46] The Independent "Two members of alt-right accused of making white supremacist hand signs in White House after receiving press passes" by Emily Shugerman (April 30th 2017)

online. Their "evidence" for this was a new group of "experts" called PropOrNot (Propaganda or Not) who nobody had ever heard of before, and whose "members" were anonymous.[47]

*The Washington Post* didn't even mention what these "expert's" credentials were, they just claimed this unknown "group" were the "experts" who "discovered" a Russian propaganda campaign was being amplified by a list of websites and YouTube channels they had compiled. This story, with the headline "Russian propaganda effort helped spread 'fake news' during election, experts say" dumped gallons of gasoline on a small little fire, which then exploded into the "fake news" phenomena.

Other news outlets quickly denounced *The Post's* story and their newfound supposed "experts" PropOrNot as McCarthyism.[48] Even *Rolling Stone*, which had previously hyped up concerns about fake news, called their story "shameful and disgusting."[49]

After the backlash kept growing, *The Washington Post* issued a retraction and posted an editor's note on the original story, reading: "*The Washington Post* on Nov. 24 published a story on the work of four sets of researchers who have examined what they say are Russian propaganda efforts to undermine American democracy and interests. One of them was PropOrNot, a group that insists on public anonymity, which issued a report

---

[47] The Intercept "Washington Post Disgracefully Promotes a McCarthyite Blacklist From a New, Hidden, and Very Shady Group" by Ben Norton and Glenn Greenwald (November 26th 2016)

[48] The Nation " 'The Washington Post' Promotes a McCarthyite Blacklist" by James Carden (December 28th 2016)

[49] Rolling Stone "The 'Washington Post' 'Blacklist' Story Is Shameful and Disgusting" by Matt Taibbi (November 28th 2016)

identifying more than 200 websites that, in its view, wittingly or unwittingly published or echoed Russian propaganda. A number of those sites have objected to being included on PropOrNot's list, and some of the sites, as well as others not on the list, have publicly challenged the group's methodology and conclusions. *The Post,* which did not name any of the sites, does not itself vouch for the validity of PropOrNot's findings regarding any individual media outlet, nor did the article purport to do so. Since publication of *The Post's* story, PropOrNot has removed some sites from its list."[50]

One site listed as a publisher of 'Russian propaganda' was Naked Capitalism, a finance and economic blog started in 2006, which threatened to sue *The Washington Post* for defamation if they didn't issue a retraction and an apology. Their lawyer sent a letter to the paper, which said in part, "You did not provide even a single example of 'fake news' allegedly distributed or promoted by Naked Capitalism or indeed any of the 200 sites on the PropOrNot blacklist. You provided no discussion or assessment of the credentials or backgrounds of these so-called 'researchers' (Clint Watts, Andrew Weisburd, and J.M. Berger and the 'team' at PropOrNot), and no discussion or analysis of the methodology, protocol or algorithms such 'researchers' may or may not have followed."[51]

*The Washington Post's* article even listed my friend Gary Franchi's YouTube channel, The Next News

---

[50] Washington Post "Russian propaganda effort helped spread 'fake news' during election, experts say" by Craig Timberg (November 24th 2016)

[51] The Daily Caller "Website Labeled 'Fake News' Threatens To Sue WaPo For Defamation" by Rachel Stoltzfoos (December 12th 2016)

Network, as one of the outlets "spreading Russian propaganda." It turns out someone from PropOrNot sent an email to *The New Yorker* hoping to have them report on their allegations before *The Washington Post* did. Adrian Chen at *The New Yorker* would later write, "Reporting on Internet phenomena, one learns to be wary of anonymous collectives freely offering the fruits of their research. I told PropOrNot that I was probably too busy to write a story, but I asked to see the report. In reply, PropOrNot asked me to put the group in touch with 'folks at the NY Times, WaPo, WSJ, and anyone else who you think would be interested.' Deep in the middle of another project, I never followed up."[52]

He said PropOrNot's report on which sites were "Russian Propaganda" was "a mess." Chen later interviewed Eliot Higgens, a researcher who has investigated Russian fake news stories for years, who told him, "To be honest, it looks like a pretty amateur attempt. I think it should have never been an article on any news site of any note."[53] Chen went on to say that, "To PropOrNot, simply exhibiting a pattern of beliefs outside the political mainstream is enough to risk being labeled a Russian propagandist."

*The Intercept*, an online outlet run by Glenn Greenwald who broke the story about Edward Snowden a few years earlier, slammed PropOrNot, saying, "the individuals behind this newly created group are publicly branding journalists and news outlets as tools of Russian propaganda — even calling on the FBI to investigate them for espionage — while cowardly hiding their own

---

[52] The New Yorker "The Propaganda About Russian Propaganda" by Adrian Chen (December 1st 2016)

[53] Ibid.

identities. The group promoted by the Post thus embodies the toxic essence of Joseph McCarthy, but without the courage to attach individual names to the blacklist."[54]

## Studies of Fake News Effects on Election

With this sudden concern about fake news 'affecting our election,' studies were conducted which actually proved fake news didn't swing the election or have any measurable effect on how people voted. New York University and Stanford reported that only eight percent of people were actually duped by fake news.[55] Of those eight percent who supposedly believed some fake news articles were real, it's highly unlikely those stories actually swayed their opinions at all about a candidate, and instead only reflected what they already believed. Columbia Journal Review conducted a study and found, "The fake news audience is real, but it's also really small."[56]

They also pointed out that, "the fake news audience does not exist in a filter bubble. Visitors to fake news sites visited real news sites just as often as visitors to real news sites visited other real news sites. In fact, sometimes fake news audiences visited real news sites

---

[54] The Intercept "Washington Post Disgracefully Promotes a McCarthyite Blacklist From a New, Hidden, and Very Shady Group" by Glenn Greenwald and Ben Norton (November 26th 2016)

[55] The Washington Post "Real research suggests we should stop freaking out over fake news" by Christopher Ingraham (January 24th 2017

[56] Columbia Journalism Review "Is Fake News a Fake Problem?" by Jacob L. Nelson (January 31, 2017)

*more* often."[57] They even asked, "Is fake news a fake problem?" and concluded their report saying that their findings, "call into question the scope of the fake news problem."[58]

Most voters got their news from TV and actual news websites, not from random stories posted on unknown websites. "Our data suggest that social media were not the most important source of election news and even the most widely circulated news stories were seen by only a small fraction of Americans," the researchers said.[59]

Even Facebook CEO Mark Zuckerberg admitted, "To think it influenced the election in any way is a pretty crazy idea."[60] He surprisingly confirmed what rational people understood — that Hillary supporters underestimated the amount of support for Donald Trump. "I do think there is a certain profound lack of empathy in asserting that the only reason someone could have voted the way they did is they saw some fake news. If you believe that, then I don't think you have internalized the message the Trump supporters are trying to send in this election," Zuckerberg said.[61]

Facebook's chief operating officer Sheryl Sandberg agreed. When she was asked if 'fake news' played a big role in the election, she answered, "Well, there have been

---

[57] Ibid.

[58] Ibid.

[59] Daily Mail "Fake news did NOT sway the election: Study shows only a 'small fraction' of voters saw bogus pro-Trump stories" by Jennifer Smith (February 2nd 2017)

[60] USA Today "Mark Zuckerberg: Facebook fake news didn't sway election" by Jessica Guynn (November 10th 2016)

[61] Ibid.

claims that it swayed the election, and we don't think it swayed the election, but we take those claims seriously."[62]

Even MSNBC's Joe Scarborough, a RINO Republican who hates Donald Trump, admitted, "When you look at this 'fake news,' and you see what happened up at Harvard and you hear everybody writing articles saying millennials cost Hillary Clinton the election, and dogs with three legs cost Hillary Clinton the election, and comets passing in the night — Hillary Clinton cost Hillary Clinton the election. Hillary Clinton's campaign staff cost Hillary Clinton the election."[63]

He continued, "Listen, if you care about Democrats digging out of the hole that they have put themselves in now, you've got to ask yourself — what have Democrats done to so offend Americans that they only have 11 governorships, they've lost control of the Senate, they've lost control of the House, they lost 900 legislative seats over the past six years." He concluded, "It wasn't fake news. It was something much, much bigger."[64]

His cohost Mika Brzezinski responded, "Ugh, I don't think people are ready to hear that, Joe," and of course, they weren't. Liberals were sinking deeper into a depression, unable to handle the reality that Donald Trump beat Hillary Clinton on election night 2016, and would soon be sworn in as our next president.

---

[62] Real Clear Politics "Facebook Executive Sheryl Sandberg: 'Fake News' Didn't Sway the Election" by Tim Haines (December 8th 2016)

[63] Yahoo "Joe Scarborough Doesn't Think Fake News Cost Hillary Clinton the Election" by Brian Flood (December 9th 2016)

[64] Ibid.

# The Media Circus

While there is a significant portion of people who strive to stay informed on current events, aware of our history, and who regularly read multiple news sources or listen to talk radio to get a complete understanding of the pressing issues of our time; unfortunately we are up against a well-funded, ruthless, and massive media machine which, like an alien parasite in a science fiction film, is dead set on taking over the minds of as many people as possible.

As you most likely know because you chose to pick up and read this book, much of the general public have been so dumbed down that they're entertained by almost anything that allows them to turn off their brain and mindlessly sit and stare at the magical moving pictures on their TV, tablet, or smartphone. Millions binge daily on what is the equivalent of junk food for the mind.

The fact that Maury Povich has done virtually the same show conducting DNA tests to find out who the father is of some trailer trash tramp's baby five days a week for 20 years shows the low level of standards the average TV viewer has. You'd think shows like Maury Povich and Jerry Springer would be a novelty for a season or two, but they have both been on the air for over 20 years!

We have become a society filled with mindless mass media-consuming morons who can't distinguish between fantasy and reality anymore. Famed media analyst Neil Postman explains in his historic work *Amusing Ourselves*

*To Death* that a drastic shift took place when Americans began getting their news from television instead of from newspapers, magazines and books. He noted, "under the governance of the printing press, discourse in America was different from what it is now — generally coherent, serious and rational...[but] under the governance of television, it has become shriveled and absurd."[65] Part of the reason for this is that the very nature of the television business is to get people to watch by any means necessary.

Postman points out that, "we are urged by newscasters to 'join them tomorrow.' What for? One would think that several minutes of murder and mayhem would suffice as material for a month of sleepless nights. We accept the newscaster's invitation because we know that the 'news' is not to be taken seriously, that it is all in fun, so to say. Everything about a news show tells us this — the good looks and amiability of the cast, their pleasant banter, the exciting music that opens and closes the show, the vivid film footage, the attractive commercials — all these and more suggest that what we have just seen is no cause for weeping."[66]

Even most supposed "hard news" networks today are primarily just entertainment outlets pretending to report on actual news. This becomes obvious every time a celebrity dies or an NFL player gets involved in a scandal since it's always the lead story on the evening news at all the major networks. When pop star Justin Bieber was arrested for a DUI, MSNBC interrupted a live interview with a congresswoman who was talking about the

---

[65] Postman, Neil - *Amusing Ourselves To Death* page 16

[66] Postman, Neil - *Amusing Ourselves To Death* page 87

National Security Agency illegally spying on Americans to cover the "breaking news" about Bieber's arrest.[67] This is far from an isolated incident, and is instead, sadly the norm. The same media frenzy occurred when Paris Hilton was arrested for a DUI. CNN and other news networks aired live footage being shot from helicopters which followed her car down the freeway as she drove to the courthouse.[68]

The "news" is now mainly infotainment — entertainment made to look like information. The Learning Channel (now called TLC) went from airing educational programming in the 1980s and 90s to now just showing trashy reality shows like *Here Comes Honey Boo Boo* and *19 Kids and Counting*. The History Channel, which once consisted solely of documentaries about — well — *history*, slowly changed into a personality driven "reality show" network as well.[69]

But television is more than just infotainment. It's not really hyperbole to say that television to a large extent controls the world. Television introduces new words, dances, styles of dress, behaviors, attitudes, and cultural norms which are instantly absorbed and mimicked by millions. For example, shows like *Will and Grace* and *Modern Family* have been heralded by the gay community for shifting cultural attitudes towards gay

---

[67] Independent "Justin Bieber arrested: MSNBC interrupts congresswoman during NSA interview for important Bieber news" by Christopher Hooton (January 24th 2014)

[68] ABC News "Hilton Headed Back to Jail for Full Sentence" by Monica Nista (June 8th 2007)

[69] Forbes "High Ratings Aside, Where's the History on History?" by Brad Lockwood (October 17th 2011)

people.[70] And in the 1980s *The Cosby Show* and *Diff'rent Strokes* changed the way millions of Americans viewed black people and interracial families.[71]

In the 1990s *Seinfeld* brought a few different terms into the lexicon such as, "Yada yada yada," "re-gifting," and "shrinkage;" ESPN announcer Stuart Scott's famous "boo-yah" is used by countless people as a celebratory cheer; and when Donald Trump's *Apprentice* first hit the airwaves everyone began telling others "you're fired!" The list goes on and on. The effects of television on our culture is immeasurable and since television is a tool, it can be used for either good or bad, and the more powerful a tool (or weapon) is — the greater potential for abuse, and the more devastating the effects can be if placed in the wrong hands.

A classic example of how easily large numbers of people can be manipulated by the power of the media is when Orson Welles broadcast *War of the Worlds* on his *Mystery Theater* radio show in 1938, causing many who were listening to panic, thinking it was a news broadcast about an actual alien invasion.[72] The incident is a common case study in mass media classes at universities used to demonstrate the amazing power of this seemingly magical medium. While many may think society has evolved from such ignorance in the information age, assuming people would no longer be tricked into

---

[70] NPR "How TV Brought Gay People Into Our Homes" (May 12, 2012)

[71] Los Angeles Times "'The Cosby Show' Was Profound, Influential-- and Indispensable" Los Angeles Times by Bobby Crawford (May 11th 1992)

[72] Time Magazine "Orson Wells' War of the Worlds" (October 30th 2008 by Gilbert Cruz

believing that a science fiction show was a news broadcast, the fact is, many people are just as gullible, if not more so today.

After the Discovery Channel aired a fictional show in 2012 titled *Mermaids: The Body Found* which appeared to be a "documentary" about scientists discovering a mermaid body, social media exploded with tweets and posts about how "mermaids are real" from people who thought one was actually discovered.[73] Despite a disclaimer at the beginning of the show saying it was fiction, and the cheesy 'scientists' clearly being actors along with poor quality computer generated graphics of the "mermaid," countless people actually believed that a mermaid body had been found.[74]

Other supposed "documentaries" about wildlife on Animal Planet and the Discovery Channel have also been faked or staged scenes using animals in zoos which are presented as if they've been captured on video in the wild.[75]

Some may argue that these shows are just entertainment, but the deception on supposed 'news' networks is even worse. Often the same stories are featured on the Big Three nightly news broadcasts (NBC, CBS and ABC) when they have no major importance to the country or any national significance. If a certain incident occurred or story broke that would obviously be

---

[73] Today "Were you fooled by Animal Planet's mermaid special?" by Gael Fashingbauer Cooper (May 30th 2012)

[74] Daily Mail "How HOAX Mermaid 'mockumentary' gave Animal Planet its biggest audience EVER" by Rachel Quigley (May 30th 2013)

[75] RedOrbit "Animal Planet filmmaker: Wildlife documentaries are often fabricated sensationalism" by John Hopton (March 13th 2015)

the talk of the town, then we would expect the different networks to all lead with the same story or cover it in some fashion, but the Big Three networks regularly cover the exact same stories which aren't of national significance or interest at all. This always happens when the stories serve to reinforce or promote whatever agenda they are trying to push at the time. Out of the thousands of possible (and important) stories they could each cover every night, the pattern of the Big Three networks working in concert with each other is just too obvious to deny.

Mainstream media talking heads are just actors and actresses reading teleprompter scripts drafted by teams of writers, editors, and lawyers. Not only do the hosts and anchors have little to no control over what they say on air, but they also have little say in how they look. There are always clauses in their contracts which dictate what they wear and how they do their hair and makeup.

After Megyn Kelly was given her own show on Fox News in primetime (*The Kelly File*), she underwent a series of dramatic hairstyle changed as producers were playing with her look trying to find one that audiences liked best. At one point it appears they even made her wear hair extensions to give her the appearance of having long flowing hair, only to quickly abandon the look for a short style.[76] During one of the presidential debates in 2016, her abnormally long fake eyelashes caught the

---

[76] Daily Mail "Notice anything different? Megyn Kelly reveals the 'personal surprise' she had been teasing is a new short hairdo... and Twitter erupts" (October 23rd 2015)

attention of viewers who widely ridiculed her online, causing the topic to trend on Twitter.[77]

One reason the media circus has spiraled out of control in recent years is the constant pressure to get people's attention. With countless media outlets and social media accounts competing for clicks and retweets, most 'journalists' put being first ahead of being accurate. Carl Bernstein, one of the reporters who broke the Watergate scandal which brought down Richard Nixon, remarked, "The greatest felony in the news business today is to be behind, or to miss a big story. So speed and quantity substitute for thoroughness and quality, for accuracy and context."[78]

Prime Minister of Australia Malcolm Turnbull echoed these sentiments when he said, "It's not a 24-hour news cycle, it's a 60-second news cycle now, it's instantaneous. It has never been easier to get away with telling lies."[79]

In competing with millions of other voices all screaming for our attention, many news outlets repeatedly try to one-up each other with more and more sensational clickbait claims, hoping to get noticed. And in their desperation for attention they have all but destroyed their journalistic integrity. Back in 1985, long before reality TV and Facebook or Instagram — media analyst Neil Postman ominously warned, "When a population becomes distracted by trivia, when cultural life is redefined as a perpetual round of entertainments, when

---

[77] Daily Mail "Megyn Kelly mocked by debate viewers for her 'comically large' fake eyelashes" by Erica Dempesta (March 4th 2016)

[78] Carl Bernstein in Forbes Book of Quotations: 10,000 Thoughts on the Business of Life edited by Ted Goodman (2007)

[79] BrainyQuote.com "Malcolm Turnbull Quotes"

serious public conversation becomes a form of baby talk, when, in short, a people become an audience and their public business a vaudeville act, then a nation finds itself at risk; [and] culture-death is a clear possibility."[80]

The millions who regularly get caught up in the latest "Internet challenge" or idiotic social media fad show that this 'cultural death' is more of an inevitability than a possibility, and that is it's not only here, but it is rapidly spreading every day.

For these reasons and many more, it is critically important that we choose to resist the temptation of getting swept away in the sea of meaningless entertainment that's at our fingertips, and instead create and maintain a regular habit of staying educated and informed. While perhaps occasionally snacking on this pop culture, we must avoid, at all costs, consuming it as our main course, or we will face the same fate as if we ate a steady diet of junk food — and we will not just be watching the media circus, but we will become a part of it ourselves.

---

[80] Postman, Neil — *Amusing Ourselves to Death* pages 155-156

# The Power of Propaganda

The media and the mechanisms for distributing information today are tools, and like most tools, if placed in the wrong hands they can be used as weapons. One of these weapons is propaganda, so we should take a close look at just how powerful it can be, and how hard it is at times to detect with an untrained eye.

In 1928 a man named Edward Bernays, who is considered the "father of public relations," published a book revealing his ingenious methods for shaping public opinion using the available media at the time (newspapers, magazines, black & white films, and radio). Television was just something that was being experimented with, and wouldn't become a major medium until over 20 years later, in the 1950s.[81]

Bernays was the nephew of Sigmund Freud, the famous psychologist, which may explain how he himself became such an expert in psychology. His knowledge of how to influence large numbers of people using the media was so far ahead of his time that still today, almost 100 years later, Bernays' methods are used as the standard operating procedure for advertisers, activists, and governments.

---

[81] Diggs-Brown, Barbara - *Strategic Public Relations: Audience Focused Practice* (Wadsworth 2011) page 48

The American Tobacco Company (manufacturer of the Lucky Strike brand) hired him in 1929 to help promote cigarettes, and as a result of his marketing campaign he is largely credited with making smoking seem "cool." What he did was hire a group of beautiful women to light up cigarettes while they were marching in New York City's Easter Sunday Parade since women smoking at the time was taboo. He then sent out a press release claiming they lit up "Torches of Freedom" to support women's rights. *The New York Times* published an article the next day with the headline, "Group of Girls Puff at Cigarettes as a Gesture of Freedom."[82] He had created a self-fulfilling prophecy by duping newspapers into portraying women smoking as part of the growing women's rights movement, when in reality it was just a marketing ploy by a tobacco company.

Bernays is also the man responsible for the tradition of men buying women diamonds as a symbol of love and marriage. As you know, at least in the United States of America, the tradition of proposing marriage to a woman "must" be done with a diamond ring, and every Christmas, Valentine's Day, and Mother's Day we are bombarded by advertisements about buying diamonds for the women in our lives. This cultural norm, however, was artificially created by Edward Bernays after the De Beers diamond company (in reality a monopoly) hired him to promote diamonds as the standard symbol of love.

Before Bernays scheme was launched, engagement and wedding rings were just a gold band, but using his techniques of social conditioning he was able to brainwash men and women into believing that a large

---

[82] New York Times "Group of Girls Puff at Cigarettes as a Gesture of Freedom" (April 1, 1929)

diamond ring was needed in order to propose marriage or to show a woman that a man loves her.[83]

When we look into Bernays' methods it becomes stunningly clear just how powerful they are, and how candid he was about this power in his book. He wrote, "Those who manipulate the unseen mechanism of society constitute an invisible government which is the true ruling power of our country. We are governed, our minds are molded, our tastes formed, our ideas suggested, largely by men we have never heard of...in almost every act of our lives whether in the sphere of politics or business in our social conduct or our ethical thinking, we are dominated by the relatively small number of persons who understand the mental processes and social patterns of the masses. It is they who pull the wires that control the public mind, who harness old social forces and contrive new ways to bind and guide the world."[84]

He also admitted, "Whatever of social importance is done today, whether in politics, finance, manufacture, agriculture, charity, education, or other fields, must be done with the help of propaganda. Propaganda is the executive arm of the invisible government."[85] This "invisible government," he says, "tends to be concentrated in the hands of the few because of the expense of manipulating the social machinery which controls the opinions and habits of the masses."[86]

---

[83] The Atlantic "How an Ad Campaign Invented the Diamond Engagement Ring" by Uri Friedman (February 13th 2015)

[84] Bernays, Edward – *Propaganda* pages 37-38

[85] Bernays, Edward – *Propaganda* pages 47-48

[86] Bernays, Edward – *Propaganda* page 63

The expensive "machinery" he was referring to are the printing presses and film studios, as well as the large costs associated with producing and distributing newspapers and radio broadcasts at the time which was so expensive that only a handful of companies could afford to be in these businesses. It wasn't until fairly recently with the creation of computers, the Internet, smartphones, and social media that this monopoly has changed; although the multi-billion dollar mainstream media conglomerates still have enormous influence and control over the creation of content and its distribution, and are constantly trying to adapt to hold on to what was once an iron clad grip on the industry.

As Ben Bagdikian, the former dean of the University of California, Berkeley Graduate School of Journalism points out in *The New Media Monopoly*, "The possibilities for mutual promotion among all their various media is the basic reason the Big Five [now six: Comcast, News Corporation, Time Warner, Disney, Viacom, and CBS] have become major owners of all kinds of media. For example, actors and actresses in a conglomerate's wholly owned movie studio can appear on the same company's television and cable networks, photographs of the newly minted celebrities can dominate the covers of the firm's wholly owned magazines, and those celebrities can be interviewed on the firm's wholly owned radio and television talk shows. The conglomerate can commission an author from its wholly owned book publishing firm to write a biography or purported autobiography of the new stars, which in turn is promoted on the firm's other media."[87]

---

[87] Bagdikian, Ben - *The New Media Monopoly* page 8

Bagdikian points out that these multi-platform conglomerates, "have power that media in past history did not, power created by new technology and the near uniformity of their political goals"[88] and that, "Technically, the dominant media firms are an oligopoly, the rule of a few in which one of those few, acting alone, can alter market conditions."[89] He continues, "The major media socialize every generation of Americans. Whether the viewers and listeners are conscious of it or not, they are being 'educated' in role models, in social behavior, in their early assumptions about the world into which they will venture, and in what to assume about their unseen millions of fellow citizens."[90]

George Orwell warned of this same propaganda power in his classic novel *Nineteen Eighty-Four* when he said, "All the beliefs, habits, tastes, emotions, mental attitudes that characterize our time are really designed to sustain the mystique of the Party and prevent the true nature of present-day society from being perceived."[91]

The editors of a college textbook titled *Questioning The Media,* which I still have from my days as a student earning my bachelor's degree in communication, point out that the major media conglomerates, "serve to define what is of political concern, of economic importance, of cultural interest to us. In short, we live in what is often

---

[88] Bagdikian, Ben - *The New Media Monopoly* page 11

[89] Bagdikian, Ben - *The New Media Monopoly* page 5

[90] Bagdikian, Ben - *The New Media Monopoly* page 261

[91] Orwell, George – *Nineteen Eighty-Four* page 187

described as a media culture."[92] Even though this book is over 20 years old, it still rings true to this day.

## The 1960 Presidential Debate

Television is such a powerful form of media that it is credited with being the reason John F. Kennedy became president. When he was running against Richard Nixon in 1960, television had just become a household medium and for the first time in history the presidential debates were televised. Before this they had been aired on the radio, but now Americans could *see* the debates, and that changed everything.

Marking the 50th anniversary of this historic event, *Time* magazine said, "It's now common knowledge that without the nation's first televised debate — fifty years ago Sunday — Kennedy would never have been president."[93] Why, you wonder? Well, people who listened to the debate on the radio (which many did because not everyone had a television back then) thought that Nixon won, but the people who saw it on TV had a completely different conclusion. The reason was that because of the hot lights on the stage, which were needed to properly light the candidates, and because Nixon refused to put on makeup to take the shine off his face, which today everyone on TV knows is a standard practice — he looked pale, sweaty and shiny; while Kennedy had a tan from campaigning outdoors in the days leading up to the debate, and took the advice of producers and wore

---

[92] Questioning the Media: A Critical Introduction (Sage Publishing 1995) page xvi

[93] Time "How the Nixon-Kennedy Debate Changed the World" by Kayla Webley (September 23rd 2010)

makeup, so he looked to be "radiating health" and confidence to the viewers watching on TV, whereas Nixon looked kind of sickly and weak.[94]

# War

Over 2500 years ago the Chinese military strategist and philosopher Sun Tzu wrote *The Art of War,* which isn't just a manual of strategies for physical battle, but also psychological operations as well. He formulated tactics to both intimidate the enemy, and to encourage people to support a conflict. Since then, war propaganda has advanced in step with technology, and now instead of a group's leader giving an impassioned speech to their citizens in the town square about the 'need' to go to war, now they do it through newspapers, radio and television.

William Randolph Hurst and Joseph Pulitzer were partially, if not largely, responsible for the Spanish-American War in 1898 because their newspapers sensationalized and misreported an incident after a U.S. ship, the USS Maine, blew up in Havana harbor in Cuba.[95] The explosion was just an accident, but America's two most popular papers at the time, *The New York Journal* (owned by Hearst) and *New York World* (owned by Pulitzer) whipped the American people into a frenzy by publicizing misinformation about the explosion

---

[94] CNN "The day politics and TV changed forever" by Greg Botelho (March 14th 2016)

[95] Spencer, David R. - *The Yellow Journalism: The Press and America's Emergence as a World Power.* Northwestern University Press 2007

and blamed the Spanish for allegedly bombing the ship.[96] Both Hearst and Pulitzer used their papers to call for war, and historians often use their sensational stories about the incident as examples of yellow journalism and propaganda, but unfortunately this would become just one of many examples of disinformation being used to convince Americans to support going to war.

Both liberal and conservative mainstream media in America endlessly repeated the fear mongering false claims of the Bush administration about the (nonexistent) weapons of mass destruction Saddam Hussein supposedly had, and hyped up the looming War in Iraq as if it were an exciting plot in a Hollywood thriller. [97] A few years after the war started many people began doubting the reasons for it, and people's skepticism fueled a closer look at why we were really there.

One of the key "reasons" for going into Iraq was that Saddam Hussein was supposedly somehow involved in the 9/11 attacks, which we now know is completely false.[98] That, and he had allegedly acquired, or was manufacturing, weapons of mass destruction — WMDs. The documents that purported to show that Saddam had attempted to purchase yellowcake uranium, which is used to build nuclear weapons turned out to be forged.[99] If the documents were real, it would have been proof that Iraq

---

[96] PBS "Crucible of Empire - The Spanish American War: Yellow Journalism"

[97] New York Times "Pentagon Weighs Use of Deception in a Broad Arena" by Thom Shanker and Eric Schmitt (December 13th 2004)

[98] CNN "Cheney: No link between Saddam Hussein, 9/11" (June 1st 2009)

[99] CNN "Fake Iraq documents 'embarrassing' for U.S." by David Ensor (March 14th 2003)

had been in violation of United Nations sanctions, but for at least a year after the Bush Administration knew they were fake, they kept using them to build support for their invasion.[100]   Unfortunately, every mainstream television network including liberal MSNBC seemed to support the looming war.   It wasn't just the forged documents that led us to war — they were just one part of an international propaganda campaign trying to make it happen.

The CIA's British counterpart, MI6, was found to have planted propaganda pieces in the media in the UK and other parts of the world claiming Iraq had weapons of mass destruction in order to drum up support for the war in what was dubbed Operation Mass Appeal.[101]   Former UN arms inspector Scott Ritter said, "Mass Appeal served as a focal point for passing MI6 intelligence on Iraq to the media, both in the UK and around the world.   The goal was to help shape public opinion about Iraq and the threat posed by WMDs."[102]

*The Sunday Times* of London later published a story titled "How MI6 Sold the Iraq War," and said, "The Secret Intelligence Service has run an operation to gain public support for sanctions and the use of military force in Iraq.   The government yesterday confirmed that MI6 had organized Operation Mass Appeal, a campaign to

---

[100] Time "Bush and Iraq: Follow the Yellow Cake Road" (July 9th 2003)

[101] BBC "MI6 ran 'dubious' Iraq campaign" (November 21st 2003)

[102] Ritter, Scott - *Iraq Confidential: The Untold Story of the Intelligence Conspiracy to Undermine the UN and Overthrow Saddam Hussein* (2005)

plant stories in the media about Saddam Hussein's weapons of mass destruction."[103]

At the onset of the Iraq War in 2003, the Department of Defense paid Iraqi newspapers to publish stories supporting the U.S. invasion which were written by Americans but appeared as if they were from Iraqis.[104] A year before the 9/11 attacks it was also discovered that soldiers from the U.S. Army's Psychological Operations Group had been working undercover at CNN and NPR (National Public Radio).[105] Once this was reported in the European press they were fired.[106]

Phil Donahue was fired by MSNBC in February 2003, less than a month before the invasion of Iraq, which he was very much against. The network claimed they canceled his show because of low ratings, but it was actually the highest rated show on MSNBC at the time.[107] A leaked internal memo said he was a "difficult public face for NBC in a time of war,"[108] thus confirming he was fired for opposing the planned invasion of Iraq.

Years later he would reveal, "This was not an assistant program director who decided to separate me from

---

[103] The Sunday Times "Revealed: how MI6 sold the Iraq war" by Nicholas Rufford (December 28th 2003)

[104] Los Angeles Times "U.S. Military Covertly Pays to Run Stories in Iraqi Press." by Borzou Daragahi and Mark Mazzetti (November 30th 2005)

[105] The Guardian "CNN let army staff into newsroom" by Julian Borger (April 11th 2000)

[106] NPR "Army Media Intern Flap" (April 10th 2000)

[107] New York Times "MSNBC Cancels the Phil Donahue Talk Show" by Bill Carter (February 26th 2013)

[108] TruthDig "The Day that TV News Died" by Chris Hedges (March 24th 2013)

MSNBC. They were terrified of the antiwar voice. And that is not an overstatement. Antiwar voices were not popular. And if you're General Electric, you certainly don't want an antiwar voice on a cable channel that you own; Donald Rumsfeld is your biggest customer."[109] [General Electric was the co-owner of MSNBC at the time, and GE has been a major manufacturer of military products].[110]

Several years after the invasion, public opinion on the War in Iraq dramatically changed as the reasons for getting involved in it kept falling apart, but people have short memories and as the years passed, after George W. Bush's presidency ended and was replaced with Obama, the anger about the deceptions that lead to the war quietly faded. Well over four thousand U.S. soldiers have been killed in Iraq alone, not to mention the countless who have been injured, with many missing limbs and permanently disabled, all with nobody in the government or the media held accountable for the lies which caused it all.

## Late Night Talk Shows

Propaganda isn't just something that's used by the news industry — it's used in comedy as well. Less than two months into Donald Trump's presidency, Jimmy Fallon was reportedly under pressure to make his show

---

[109] Democracy Now "Phil Donahue on His 2003 Firing from MSNBC, When Liberal Network Couldn't Tolerate Antiwar Voices" (March 21st 2013)

[110] The Guardian "Arms sales: Who are the world's 100 top arms producers?" (March 2nd 2012)

"more political" because "he's too weak on Trump."[111] He also apologized for having Donald Trump on his show shortly before the election and regretted 'humanizing' him after viewers (and the media) were outraged that Fallon was "too nice" to him.[112]

Fallon, while making regular use of Trump as a punchline, tends to shy away from politics and focuses his humor on other things like skits and games with celebrities, but since network executives felt the anti-Trump theme is what viewers want, or perhaps, that's what they themselves wanted in order to use the show as their own political weapon, Fallon was forced to turn up the heat on President Trump. Some even speculated that *The Tonight Show* was shut out of the Emmys in 2017 because Jimmy Fallon wasn't attacking Trump enough.[113]

After NBC fired Jay Leno as *The Tonight Show* host and replaced him with Jimmy Fallon in 2014, rumors were rampant in the industry that Leno was forced out because he was going too hard on President Obama. He was number one in the ratings for 20 years and still number one when he was forced out, so many people wondered why NBC would get rid of him since he was still on top.[114] Leno was the first late night comedian to take the gloves off and really start bashing President Obama. For years, most comedians treated him with kid

[111] Page Six "Fallon forced to change 'Tonight Show' amid Colbert ratings wins" by Carlos Greer (March 7th 2017)

[112] New York Times "Jimmy Fallon Was on Top of the World. Then Came Trump." by Dave Itzkoff (May 17th 2017)

[113] Los Angeles Times "It'll be hard to ignore Trump-era politics in these Emmy races" by Glenn Whipp (June 15th 2017)

[114] The Hollywood Reporter "Jay Leno on His No. 1 Talk Show and His Biggest 'Tonight Show' Blunder" (January 29, 2014)

gloves and very few of their jokes really took him to task, but after the "hope and change" wore off and was replaced by regret and despair for many Americans, Jay Leno started bashing Obama like nobody else in the business.[115]

Right after Leno's final episode, Johnny Carson's head writer Raymond Miller wrote an Op-Ed saying that most late night hosts protected Obama, and that Leno broke the mold by taking Obama to task, while "Leno's competitors haven't exactly hammered President Barack Obama, hardly a smidgen."[116] Sure, they joked about him, but it was all light-hearted humor, and nothing like the way comedians had treated previous presidents. A lot of people feel NBC got rid of Leno because he was helping turn too many people away from Barack Obama. It's interesting that immediately after Jimmy Fallon replaced Jay Leno as *The Tonight Show* host, one of his first guests was Michelle Obama who came on to promote Obamacare.[117]

Unlike Jimmy Fallon, Stephen Colbert, who took over *The Late Show* from David Letterman in 2015, made Trump-bashing a staple of his show to the point where it is an obsession.[118] President Trump is his number one enemy, and after the election he made no secret of the fact that he uses his show, not just to get laughs at Trump's

---

[115] Mediaite "Jay Leno Does Not Hold Back On The Obama Jokes… While Obama Waits Backstage" by Matt Wilstein (August 7th 2013)

[116] Breitbart "Johnny Carson's Head Writer: Late Night Comics Protest Obama (February 14th 2014)

[117] The Wrap "Michelle Obama to Guest on Debut Week of 'Tonight Show Starring Jimmy Fallon' by Tony Maglio (January 24, 2014)

[118] BillMoyers.com "What's the Matter with Stephen Colbert?" by Todd Glitlin (November 14th 2016)

expense, but to paint him in as negative a light as possible.[119] Many nights his entire monologue is about Donald Trump, and it serves as more of a nightly anti-Trump editorial than stand-up comedy. The liberal media regularly boasts of Colbert's anti-Trump rants, writing stories about them in order to bring them to the attention of those who don't watch his show.[120]

Colbert's constant pushing of the liberal agenda resulted in *The New York Post* running a story with the headline, "Colbert's 'Late Show' has become propaganda for Democrats."[121] And that's not even a secret at this point. In fact, one of the emails Wikileaks released of Hillary's campaign manager John Podesta shows that a Clinton insider was able to get Colbert to do two different segments to promote the Clinton Foundation.[122] *The Hollywood Reporter* conducted a survey and found that many conservatives quit watching his show because of the blatant liberal bias, and that he was most popular amongst Democrats and atheists.[123]

Jimmy Kimmel also uses his show as part of the anti-Trump entertainment complex, but not with the level of distain and hatred of Colbert. Kimmel also uses his show to regularly promote liberal political agendas. After his

---

[119] Los Angeles Times "Stephen Colbert under attack by conservatives for joke about Trump and Putin" by Kurtis Lee (May 4th 2017)

[120] Variety "Trump Will Soon Be Target of More Late-Night Jokes Than Any Other President" by Ted Johnson (May 4th 2017)

[121] New York Post "Colbert's 'Late Show' has become propaganda for Democrats" by Kyle Smith (November 21st 2015)

[122] https://wikileaks.org/podesta-emails/emailid/46703#efmABaACc

[123] Hollywood Reporter "The Great Late-Night Poll: Where the Hosts Stand Now" by Matthew Belloni (November 19th 2015)

newborn son was found to have a heart defect and had emergency surgery, Kimmel gave a tearful monologue telling his viewers what happened, thanking the doctors and the nurses, but then turned his emotional story into an anti-Trump rant, blasting the President for his plan to fix Obamacare.[124]    The next day *New York Magazine* said Kimmel might have "struck the final blow against the GOP health-care plan."[125]

Other late night hosts like Samantha Bee on TBS, Trevor Noah on Comedy Central, Seth Meyers on NBC, John Oliver on HBO, and Chelsea Handler on Netflix, all use their platforms to constantly push the liberal agenda and attack conservatives.  There is really no debating that they're doing this, and I only mention this to encourage you to not watch them or give them one more follower on social media.  But if you still have any doubt that comedy can be a vehicle for political propaganda, just keep reading.

In an interview with CNN in 2008, Chevy Chase openly admitted that he used his position on *Saturday Night Live* back in the 1970s for propaganda purposes. One of his skits was playing then-President Ford, who was facing off against Jimmy Carter in the 1976 election, and Chase admitted, "I just went after him.    And I certainly, obviously my leanings were Democratic and I wanted Carter in and I wanted [Ford] out, and I figured look, we're reaching millions of people every weekend, why not do it."

---

[124] NBC News "Jimmy Kimmel Reveals Newborn Son Survived Heart Surgery" by Alexander Smith (May 2nd 2017)

[125] New York Magazine "Jimmy Kimmel Might Have Struck the Final Blow Against the GOP Health-Care Plan" by Margaret Hartmann (May 2nd 2017)

Alina Cho, the CNN reporter interviewing him, responds, "Wait a minute, you mean to tell me in the back of your mind you were thinking, 'Hey I want Carter?'"

Chase responds: "Oh, yeah."

Cho: "And I'm going to make him [Ford] look bad?"

Chase continues, "Oh yeah. What do you think they're doing now, you think they're just doing this [mocking Sarah Palin] because Sarah's funny?," talking about *SNL* skewering her when she was John McCain's running mate that year. He continued, "I think that the show is very much more Democratic and liberal-oriented, [and] that they are obviously more for Barack Obama."[126] Many people actually credit Tina Fey's depiction of Sarah Palin on *Saturday Night Live* with being largely responsible for people seeing her in a negative light.[127]

Since John Oliver uses his HBO show *Last Week Tonight* as more of a political soapbox than a place for comedy, some people are actually crediting him with influencing U.S. legislation, court rulings, and American culture. The media has actually dubbed it, 'The John Oliver Effect.' *Time* magazine actually ran a story titled, "How the 'John Oliver Effect' is Having a Real-Life Impact," and detailed some of his political activism and its real world consequences.[128] *Fortune* magazine says the comedian's impact is no joke and that his show "could

---

126 CNN "Chevy Chase: I Wanted Carter to Win" (November 3rd 2008)

127 Boston Globe "How Tina Fey destroyed Sarah Palin" by Kevin Lewis (March 3rd 2012)

128 Time "How the 'John Oliver Effect' Is Having a Real-Life Impact" by Victor Luckerson (January 20th 2015)

very well be the envy of most newsrooms around the country."[129]

## Agenda-Setting

The mainstream media often steers the public conversation by giving constant coverage to certain stories which reinforce the ideologies they are trying to promote. They'll often choose an isolated incident that's making news in the local community where it happened, and while it has no real national significance, the major networks will 'coincidentally' determine it should be one of the top stories in the country and then sensationalize it so the incident then becomes a widely talked about topic.

These stories often include rare police brutality incidents involving a white police officer and a black suspect. But when it's a white officer and a white victim, or a black officer and a white victim, the incidents remain local stories and don't get national attention. Similarly, if a celebrity happens to call a gay or transgender person a derogatory name, then the big networks all have panels of pundits complain about it for hours, days, or even weeks on end to emphasize how 'hateful' and 'dangerous' such language is.

When these mountains out of molehills are turned into the top stories on the evening news of the Big Three broadcast networks (ABC, NBC, CBS) it doesn't take a professional media analyst to see a pattern and realize there is coordination among these companies behind the scenes to decide which topics will be the "top stories." It's statistically impossible that the Big Three would

---

[129] Fortune "The John Oliver Effect: Why the British comedian's impact is no joke" by Beth Kowitt (September 29th 2015)

regularly choose the same little-known local stories from the newswires to all report on nationally. Many events of the day warrant being the top stories on all networks, but most do not and shouldn't make it any further than their local news channels, yet they regularly get the national spotlight, and always when they fit the current agenda of the time.

The technical term for what they're doing is called agenda-setting. They magnify selected stories and topics through their constant coverage and endless panel discussions about every little detail. Talking for hours on end about the stories creates a self-fulfilling prophecy by building certain instances into major issues, and by treating them as if they *are* major issues when they are not, and getting people to talk and think about them so much, they then *become* major issues.

As television became part of everyone's lives, a study was conducted during the 1968 presidential election called the Chapel Hill Study, which showed the strong correlation between what people thought were the most important election issues and what the national news media repeatedly reported were the most important issues.[130] It basically showed that instead of just reporting on the news, the networks were actually influencing what people thought *was* news. Since then, hundreds of studies into the agenda-setting power of the mainstream media have been conducted which consistently show the immense power the industry has to shape public opinion

---

[130] Public Opinion Quarterly "The Agenda-Setting Function of Mass Media" by Max McCombs and Donald Shaw (1972)

and not only influence what people think about, but *how* they think about it.[131]

Aside from agenda-setting, the major networks also frame topics in a certain light trying to influence how they are perceived. Through their carefully selected panelists and pointed questions, they can easily paint a person or issue in a positive light or a negative one.

For example, during the height of the Black Lives Matter protests in 2016, the liberal media always portrayed the protests (and riots) as a civil rights movement on par with Martin Luther King's of the 1950s and 60s, consisting of people who were fighting against an 'epidemic' of white police officers shooting 'innocent' black men. In reality, the vast majority of black men shot and killed by police are armed and dangerous thugs with criminal histories, but those facts are ignored and the incidents are always framed as another 'innocent' black man who has been 'murdered' by police because 'they're all racists.'

The media likes to take rare and isolated instances of officer involved shootings and magnify them to give the appearance that there is a nation-wide epidemic of 'racist' police officers who are gunning down innocent young black men, thus adding fuel to the fire of black power groups and further straining race relations in America. People like Travyon Martin and Michael Brown are turned into celebrities from the nonstop coverage. Their names even trend on Twitter on their birthdays and the

---

131 Journalism Studies "A Look at Agenda-Setting: Past, Present, and Future" by Max McCombs and Donald Shaw (2005)

anniversaries of their deaths.[132] Leftist organizations had signs and T-shirts printed with their faces on them which people wore to protests and they are revered as if they're Martin Luther King or Tupac Shakur.

CNN and MSNBC love to give airtime to any Republican who expresses sympathy for a liberal cause. Congressmen who are completely unknown outside of their own small districts are held up as examples of a "growing trend" of "resistance" against conservatives when they speak out against members of their own party, when in reality, most of the time they're just an eccentric member of the House of Representatives with no national influence at all.

## Normalizing Insanity

Radio talk show host Michael Savage released a book in 2006 titled *Liberalism is a Mental Disorder*, and it's unclear if he coined the phrase or if he just used it for the title of his book because it was being used regularly by conservatives.  But whoever came up with it, it's more than just a joke, it is an empirical fact, and unfortunately that mental disorder is getting progressively worse as those affected by it are embracing and promoting behavior and policies so bizarre, it seems like their agenda is a plot out of a science fiction horror film. What's worse is the mainstream media is trying to normalize insanity, and at the same time demonize anyone who doesn't accept it.

---

[132] Bustle "On Michael Brown's 20th Birthday, Activists Are Marking The Moment Everything Changed" by Madhuri Sathish (May 20th 2016)

One of these agendas is trying to destroy any distinction between men and women, and implement a new "genderless society." Transgender activists like Riley J. Dennis and Zinnia Jones are promoting the idea that 'some women have penises' and 'men can menstruate.'[133] *The Charlotte Observer* published an editorial saying that women and girls need to get used to sharing bathrooms and locker rooms with people who have "different genitalia" than them and concluded that, "Yes, the thought of male genitalia in girls' locker rooms — and vice versa — might be distressing to some. But the battle for equality has always been in part about overcoming discomfort — with blacks sharing facilities, with gays sharing marriage — then realizing that it was not nearly so awful as some people imagined."[134]

Transgenderism is now being celebrated as if it's cool and special. At the 2015 Golden Globe Awards, Amazon.com's original series *Transparent* was given two awards, one for best TV series, and another for best actor. In the show, Jeffrey Tambor plays a retired college professor who, in his late 50s, decided he wanted to live as a woman. Critics hailed the show saying it was "making history."[135] That same year ESPN gave Caitlyn Jenner the "courage" award at the ESPYs, an award show that's supposed to be about sports.[136]

---

[133] The Blaze "Transgender 'feminist' lays down the law: 'Some women have penises'" by Dave Urbanski (March 23rd 2017)

[134] Charlotte Observer "Taking the fear out of bathrooms" by The Observer Editorial Board (May 13th 2016)

[135] Variety "Amazon, 'Transparent' Make History at Golden Globes" by Jenelle Riley (January 11th 2015)

[136] Los Angeles Times "Is Caitlyn Jenner the wrong honoree for ESPYs' courage award?" by Greg Braxton (July 15th 2015)

The December 2016 edition of *National Geographic* put a transgender 9-year-old 'girl' on the cover, who is actually a biological male.[137] And various Hollywood celebrities appear to be raising their kids transgender or are defying the social norms of boys and girls. Charlize Theron has been photographed with her son wearing dresses and other girl clothes on numerous occasions.[138] Brad Pitt and Angelina Jolie have been dressing their daughter Shiloh in boy's clothes, making many wonder if they're raising her as a boy.[139] And Will Smith's teenage son Jaden regularly wears women's clothes to 'challenge' gender norms.[140]

It's not just people who want to switch genders who are being held up as heroes — they are only one part of what's being called the "gender revolution." The state of New York now recognizes 31 different genders, *thirty-one!* Not just male and female, but a whole list, including gender fluid (meaning sometimes male and sometimes female), androgynous and gender-nonconforming (which means neither male nor female), and a whole bunch more like 'pangender,' 'two spirit,' and 'gender gifted,' whatever the Hell those are.[141]

---

[137] NewsBusters "'Science' Magazine? National Geographic Celebrates 9-Year-Old Trans 'Girl' on the Cover" by Melissa Mullins (December 21st 2016)

[138] BET "Is Charlize Theron's 5 Year-Old Son Transitioning Into a Female?" (January 20th 2017)

[139] OK Magazine "Shiloh Jolie-Pitt 'Only Wears Boys' Clothes' After Questioning Gender Identity To Brad & Angelina " (August 4th 2016)

[140] Entertainment Tonight "Jaden Smith Opens Up About Wearing Skirts: 'I Don't See Man Clothes and Woman Clothes'" by Alex Ungerman (March 14th 2016)

[141] Daily Caller "New York City Lets You Choose From 31 Different Gender Identities" by Peter Hasson (May 24th 2016)

Instead of referring to these people as 'he' or 'she,' there are now new pronouns including 'ze,' 'xe,' 've,' 'tey,' 'hir' that they demand to be called. Not only are these legally recognized genders in New York (and probably California soon as well), but if employers or landlords don't call these people by their "preferred pronouns" they can be fined for discrimination! The city of New York warns, "refusal to use a transgender employee's preferred name, pronoun, or title may constitute unlawful gender-based harassment."[142] Civil penalties up to $250,000 may be issued for "violations" of willfully "mispronouning" someone.[143]

California governor Jerry Brown signed a similar bill into law in October 2017, which made it a crime for healthcare workers to "willfully and repeatedly" decline to use a patient's "preferred name or pronouns."[144] Violations can result in a $1000 fine or up to a year in jail.[145] How much longer until similar laws are put in place for teachers, business owners, or everyone?

In 2014 Facebook increased the gender options from just male and female to include 58 (yes *fifty-eight*) different choices, and then felt they didn't include enough so they changed the entry field from the list of fifty-eight options to a blank box so users can just make up their

---

[142] The Washington Post "You can be fined for not calling people 'ze' or 'hir,' if that's the pronoun they demand that you use" by Eugene Volokh (May 17, 2016)

[143] New York City Gender Identity/Gender Expression: Legal Enforcement Guidance (June 28th 2016)

[144] Fox News "New California law allows jail time for using wrong gender pronoun, sponsor denies that would happen" by Brooke Singman (October 9th 2017)

[145] Ibid.

own.[146]  The cover of *Time* magazine in March 2017 featured an "agender" person (someone who claims to be neither male, nor female, even though this person is a biological female with a uterus and two x chromosomes). The caption read "Beyond 'He' or 'She.' How a new generation is redefining the meaning of gender."[147] This insanity isn't just being promoted on some little-known fetish website, this is *Time* magazine.

Of course gay and bisexual people are hailed as heroes today, and every time an actor or musician "comes out" it's major news as the media celebrates their sexuality as if it's some kind of special achievement. Fortune 500 companies are increasingly including gay themes in their commercials for products like Campbell Soup, Coca-Cola, Starbucks, General Mills, Tylenol, and many others, hoping to normalize the behavior by repeatedly exposing people to it.[148]

Even Disney has been introducing gay characters in their shows beginning in 2014 with *Good Luck Charlie*, which was the Disney Channel's most popular show at the time.[149] Soon after that, the Disney-Owned ABC Family Channel (now called Freeform) included a same-sex kiss

---

[146] BC News "Here's a List of 58 Gender Options for Facebook Users" by Russell Goldman (February 13th 2014)

[147] Time "Behind the TIME Cover Story: Beyond 'He' or 'She'" by Katy Steinmetz (March 15th 2017)

[148] Huffington Post "Gay-Themed Ads Are Becoming More Mainstream" by Leanne Italie (March 6th 2013)

[149] Entertainment Weekly "Disney Channel Introduces Its First Lesbian Couple on *Good Luck Charlie*" by Alyssa Toomey (January 28th 2017)

between two thirteen-year-old boys on *The Fosters*.[150] The show's creator and executive producer Peter Paige (who is a homosexual) bragged that it was the youngest gay kiss on television in U.S. history.[151] Disney's live-action version of *Beauty and Beast* (2017) also included a gay couple.[152] And there is increasing pressure by liberals to have Disney cartoons star gay characters.[153]

Not even *Star Wars* is safe from the gay agenda. At the end of 2015 when *Star Wars: The Force Awakens* was released it brought the film franchise back into the spotlight, and Mark Hamill, who plays Luke Skywalker, decided to come out and say that Luke might be gay.[154] The producer JJ Abrams said he would like to include a gay character in a future episode.[155] Of course, all of this is reported in the mainstream media as if it's a good thing as newscasters celebrate such "achievements."

The liberal media industrial complex wants to make Sodom and Gomorrah seem like it was populated with Puritans. If you're not going to be bisexual or a gender bender then they at least want you to be a sexual deviant.

---

[150] Breitbart "ABC Family's 'The Fosters' Airs Youngest-Ever Gay Kiss Between Two 13-Year-Old Boys" by Kipp Jones (March 4th 2015)

[151] https://twitter.com/ThePeterPaige/status/572573175336181761

[152] Los Angeles Times "New 'Beauty and the Beast' to feature Disney's first 'exclusively gay moment' in film" by Libby Hill (March 1st 2017)

[153] Time "*Frozen* Fans Lobby Disney to Give Elsa a Girlfriend in Sequel" by Eliana Dockterman (May 3rd 2016)

[154] Time "Mark Hamill Says Luke Skywalker Could Be Gay" by Charlotte Alter (March 4th 2016)

[155] Independent "JJ Abrams says gay characters will appear in Star Wars" by Jack Shepherd (February 28th 2016)

Foul-mouthed skanks are always promoted as role models for young girls to emulate. Beyoncé, Kim Kardashian, Katy Perry and Lady Gaga all promote rampant sexual promiscuity, materialism, and reckless lifestyles, and are unfortunately idolized by millions of impressionable teenage girls. Holding onto one's virginity and having committed and monogamous relationships are frowned upon and seen as old-fashioned and boring.

Recently the media has even been glorifying "Eyes Wide Shut" sex parties that are now regularly held at a growing number of sex clubs across the country where strangers wearing Venetian masks gather to have sex with each other.[156] While sex before marriage went from being taboo to now the social norm (as is having sex partners numbering in the dozens) — in the not-so-distant future we may likely see the taboo of sex clubs, swinging, and orgies broken as well, and such activities may actually be considered just as normal as one night stands by future generations.[157]

None of these cultural shifts would be taking place without the media constantly exposing people to such behaviors because through psychological desensitization, as people are repeatedly exposed to something, no matter how offensive, they gradually begin to accept it as a normal part of life — that's the power of propaganda.

---

[156] New York Post "A night of erotic freedom' at NYC's most exclusive sex party" by Heather Hauswirth and Jane Ridley (April 5th 2017)

[157] Huffington Post "One Night Stands: 8 Reasons To Have Them" by Jill Di Donato (August 28th 2012)

# Lying by Omission

Aside from making mountains out of molehills to promote certain agendas, the mainstream media regularly lies by omission, purposefully ignoring important stories they don't want people to know about. So, while at the same time they're having endless panel discussions and rehashing the same story every night for a week or sometimes months, absent from that airtime are important topics that should actually be discussed at length and reported on in detail with the network's resources to ensure a large number of people hear about them; but covering those stories would be counterproductive to their agenda.

Pulitzer Prize winning writer Nicholas Kristof made a profound statement that illustrates the power and the danger of ignoring important stories when he was talking about the War in Darfur, Africa, where an estimated 300,000 people died from ongoing fighting between different tribes in the Sudan. "The news media's silence," he said, "particularly television news, is reprehensible. If we knew as much about Darfur as we do about Michael Jackson, we might be able to stop these things from continuing."[158]

---

[158] Guernica "Nicholas Kristof: The Crisis of Our Times" Interview with Nicholas Kristof (June 28th 2008)

*The New York Times* lied to millions of Americans for over a year by withholding all stories about the NSA's mass-surveillance of Americans after the editor-in-chief had a meeting at the White House where the Bush administration asked him to keep quiet about it.[159] *The New York Times* couldn't stop their own reporter James Risen from releasing his book, *State of War: The Secret History of the CIA and the Bush Administration*, which contained detailed revelations of the domestic spying operation, and because *The Times* didn't want to be scooped by their own reporter's book, they reluctantly published a story on the massive illegal eavesdropping program being conducted by the NSA and even admitted they sat on it for a year.[160]

The decades of blackouts regarding the Bilderberg Group's annual meeting and the weird activities that go on inside the Bohemian Grove every summer can only be explained by an overt effort to keep these topics out of the national news in the United States.[161] Certainly they're newsworthy and interesting topics that you would expect to be making headlines and included in the nightly news on the big television networks, but it's as if they don't exist.[162]

When every June, one hundred or so of the world's most powerful people gather in a fancy hotel surrounded by armed guards for three days to discuss geopolitics and

---

[159] Washington Post "At the Times, a Scoop Deferred" by Paul Farhi (December 17th 2005)

[160] The New York Times "Bush Lets U.S. Spy on Callers Without Courts" by James Risen and Eric Lichtblau (December 16th 2005)

[161] Tucker, Jim - Jim Tucker's Bilderberg Diary (2005)

[162] See my previous book *The Bohemian Grove: Facts & Fiction* (2015)

the global economy, certainly it's something significant that should be reported on. But only in recent years with word of the Bilderberg Group spreading through social media have some national outlets begun to mention it, with usually nothing more than a fifteen second segment or one lonely news article online that's buried at the bottom of the page.[163]

A British newspaper tycoon named Lord Northcliffe, who founded *The Daily Mail* and *Daily Mirror*, is often credited with having said, "News is what somebody somewhere wants to suppress; all the rest is advertising."[164]

## Censoring Leftist Violence

During the 2016 presidential campaign when peaceful Trump supporters kept being assaulted as they were leaving Trump rallies or targeted on the street for wearing their red "Make America Great Again" hats, most incidents were only briefly covered in local papers or by online conservative outlets.[165] These politically motivated attacks weren't just rare or isolated incidences, they were part of a disturbing pattern that was ignored by the liberal media, despite videos and photos of the attacks going viral online.[166]

---

[163] See my book *The Bilderberg Group: Facts & Fiction* (2015)

[164] BrainyQuote.com "Lord Northcliffe Quotes"

[165] Town Hall "Disgusting: Anti-Trump Protesters Smash Police Car, Bloody Trump Supporter" by Guy Benson (April 29th 2016)

[166] Breitbart "10 Violent Actions Against Trump Supporters" by John Hayward (November 17th 2016)

The mainstream media is also always reluctant to call politically motivated riots what they are when leftists instigate them, and instead usually just call them 'protests' when they're perpetrated by Black Lives Matter supporters, college students trying to prevent conservative speakers from holding their events, and even in the case of leftist anarchists rioting after Trump's inauguration.

In Ferguson, Missouri, the birthplace of Black Lives Matter, Michael Brown's stepfather urged an angry crowd to "burn this bitch down" after a grand jury decided not to indict officer Darren Wilson for shooting and killing Brown, the 6-foot-4, three hundred pound thug who attacked him after being confronted shortly after robbing a convenience store.[167] As I'm sure you recall, the lawless thugs rioted and looted liquor stores, broke into hair salons to steal weaves which are popular in the black community, and set local businesses on fire.[168] CNN host Jason Carroll admitted that the network chose to censor footage of people rioting in Ferguson, because it didn't fit with how they were trying to frame their coverage.[169]

Anti-police hatred boiled over in July 2016 when a black supremacist opened fire on police officers in Dallas, Texas during a Black Lives Matter march, killing five officers and wounding nine others. The perpetrator was a 25-year-old black man who was incited to violence from

---

[167] New York Post "Brown family lawyer blasts stepdad's 'burn this b—h down' rant" by Chris Perez (December 3rd 2014)

[168] USA Today "Ferguson burning after grand jury announcement" by Yamiche Alcindor, Greg Toppo, Gary Strauss and John Bacon (November 24th 2014)

[169] Gateway Pundit "CNN Admits Censoring #Ferguson Reports; Media Ignores Armed Attacks on Reporters" by Kristinn Taylor (November 26th 2014)

the mainstream media continuing to paint police as racists who regularly kill African Americans and get away with it. This horrible tragedy was in the news for just a few days, and then it was quickly forgotten. Many people started comparing the Black Lives Matter movement to "the black KKK" and began labeling them a hate group, but the liberal media continued to frame them as if they were a modern day civil rights group, despite regular violence at their events, chanting about killing cops when they marched, and now a Black Lives Matter-inspired terrorist attack on police officers.

When Milo Yiannopoulos was scheduled to speak at U.C. Berkeley, leftists wearing black ski masks began rioting, smashing windows in school buildings and setting things on fire, which led to Milo's speech being canceled for safety reasons. One commentator on CNN actually said he thought that Breitbart News and Milo secretly organized the riots themselves as a false flag in order to get him more publicity.[170] He just couldn't bring himself to admit that liberals were regularly using violence to silence and intimidate conservatives.

When we began seeing the rise of Antifa, which are leftist anarchists who wear all black (including ski masks) and see themselves as "freedom fighters" who embrace violence and assault Trump supporters and anyone who supports Conservatism (or as they call them "Nazis"), the liberal media compared them to American patriots who stormed the beaches of Normandy on D-Day.[171] Many in the liberal media framed conservative ideas as 'violent'

---

[170] Newsweek "Robert Reich: Who Sent the Thugs to Berkeley?" by Robert Reich (February 4th 2017)

[171] Daily Caller "Major Figures Work To Mainstream Violent Antifa Protesters" by Alex Pfeiffer (August 16th 2017)

and claimed that Antifa's violence was 'ethical' because they aimed to stop 'hate speech.'[172] Antifa literally look like ISIS terrorists and should be declared a terrorist organization, but for months the mainstream media kept ignoring them and the only place you would even hear of Antifa was on social media by people who were posting videos and photos of their increasingly violent acts.[173]

## Ignoring Illegal Immigrant Crimes

While the majority of illegal immigrants who snuck into the United States did so to seek a better life for themselves and their families, unfortunately an extraordinarily high number of them have ties to Latin American gangs or bring the lawless mentality of their own countries to ours. The fact is, each year illegal aliens commit countless serious crimes — from human trafficking, to violent assaults, rape and murder; and most of these crimes are only reported on the local news in a 15 or 30 second segment.

Department of Justice statistics reveal that one out of every four federal prison inmates are actually foreign-born.[174] But a source within Immigration and Customs Enforcement (ICE) revealed that before the Trump

---

[172] NBC News "Antifa Violence Is Ethical? This Author Explains Why" by Benjy Sarlin (August 26th 2017)

[173] Berkeleyside "Police arrest Eric Clanton after bike lock assaults during Berkeley protests" by Emilie Raguso (May 24th 2017)

[174] The Hill "DOJ releases data on incarceration rates of illegal immigrants" by Lydia Wheeler (May 2nd 2017)

administration the federal government did not keep statistics on illegal immigrant crime.[175]

To make things worse, in 2015 President Obama's Justice Department released 20,000 convicted criminal illegal aliens back onto the streets of the United States, instead of deporting them.[176] These weren't just undocumented immigrants, but people who were charged *and convicted* of serious crimes, including 12,307 for drunk driving, 1,728 for assault, 216 for kidnapping, and over 200 for homicide or manslaughter, according to U.S. Immigration and Customs Enforcement (ICE).[177] Such an egregious miscarriage of justice should have led to congressional hearings and indictments of government officials for putting American citizens' lives at risk, but their release received little attention so hardly anyone even knows about it.

The House Committee on Oversight and Government Reform Chairman Jason Chaffetz said, "These are not just numbers. These are individuals in this country illegally who were arrested, prosecuted and convicted. But instead of removing these criminals, ICE put them back on American streets."[178] How could this not create a national outrage? How could this not be the top story in the country for weeks? 200 convicted killers, who aren't

---

[175] Fox News "Elusive crime wave data shows frightening toll of illegal immigrant criminals" by Malia Zimmerman (September 16th 2015)

[176] CBS News "DHS freed nearly 20,000 convicted criminal immigrants in 2015" (May 11th 2016)

[177] Washington Times "20,000 illegals with criminal convictions released into U.S. communities in 2015" by Stephan Dinan (April 27th 2016)

[178] Ibid.

even citizens of our country, were set free from prison and allowed to walk among us again!  We regularly hear the media warning about "climate change" or saying we need more "equality" or "diversity," but why isn't the fact that hundreds of convicted killers have been released back onto our streets a major story, especially when they're here illegally?

The media doesn't just systematically ignore the crimes of illegal aliens, they also ignore the massive burden they put on the criminal justice system, the healthcare system, and our public schools.  The city of Los Angeles, for example, paid over 1.3 billion dollars in welfare to illegal aliens between 2015 and 2016 alone.[179] There are also concerns that non-citizens may be voting in elections.[180]  An investigation in Ohio found 385 non-US citizens registered to vote, and 82 of those people actually did vote.[181]

Thankfully, the Trump administration is finally taking the dangers of illegal aliens seriously, but the mainstream media continues to ignore the serious and costly problems of our broken immigration system and actually demonize anyone who wants to enforce laws that have been on the books for decades.

---

[179] Fox News "LA made $1.3B in illegal immigrant welfare payouts in just 2 years" by Tori Richards (August 3rd 2017)

[180] Washington Times "Study supports Trump: 5.7 million noncitizens may have cast illegal votes" by Rowan Scarborough (June 19th 2017)

[181] NBC4i WCMH-TV Columbus "Ohio investigation found 385 non-US citizens registered to vote, 82 cast illegal ballots" (February 27th 2017)

## Anti-White Racism

While giving nonstop coverage to incidents of alleged racism committed by random white people, police officers, or businesses, the major news networks do their best to never report on racist black people who commit hate crimes against whites. They want people to believe that racism is a one-way street and that only white people can be racist, when in fact many in the black community harbor hatred for whites and frequently commit hate crimes against them.[182]

For example when a Nation of Islam member gunned down three white people in Fresno, California because he hated whites, the story barely made a blip on the mainstream media's radar.[183]    At San Francisco State University, a black student was caught on video assaulting a white student simply because he had dreadlocks. The black person was upset that a white person had a 'black hairstyle' and claimed it was "cultural appropriation."[184] Mainstream media ignored the story, but if a white student attacked a black student because they didn't like their hair, it would have been the story of the week all across the country.

In New York City, a black man was arrested for trying to shove a random white person onto the tracks of the

---

[182] Breitbart "Anti-White Racism: The Hate That Dares Not Speak Its Name" by David Horowitz (April 26th 2016)

[183] Daily Caller "AP Changes Fresno Shooter's Words From 'Allahu Akbar,' Removes Islam Reference" by Peter Hasson (April 18th 2017)

[184] The College Fix "Black student who attacked white student for his dreadlocks is under investigation" by Mark Schierbecker (March 29th 2016)

subway train because he "hated white people."[185] A group of black thugs were caught on video beating up a white man at an intersection in Chicago yelling, "You voted Trump," and then stole his car.[186]  In Kansas City, Missouri, a group of black teens asked a random white man waiting at a bus stop who he voted for, assuming he was a Trump supporter because he was white, and then proceeded to start punching him.[187]  These are not just rare isolated incidents of violence, but are part of a disturbing pattern of racist hate crimes against white people.[188]

After a black man shot up a white church in Tennessee during their Sunday service to get 'revenge' for white supremacist Dylann Roof's massacre at a black church two years earlier in South Carolina, it was barely mentioned in the media.  *Newsweek* actually said that racist 'alt-right conspiracy theories' claimed the attack was under-reported because the shooter was black and targeted white people.[189]  *The New York Times* buried the story on page 14 and didn't even mention the shooter's

---

[185] New York Daily News "Queens man cuffed for trying to push straphanger onto Harlem subway tracks; yelled, 'I hate white people'" by Graham Rayman (November 23rd 2016)

[186] CBS Chicago "Group Yelling 'You Voted Trump' Beats Man In Intersection, Steals Car" (November 10th 2016)

[187] Fox4KC "Man attacked at Plaza bus stop says teens asked him political question before throwing punches" by Katie Banks (November 29th 2016)

[188] FBI 2015 Hate Crime Statistics (18.7% were victims of anti-white bias) https://ucr.fbi.gov/hate-crime/2015/topic-pages/victims_final

[189] Newsweek "Tennessee Church Shooting Is a 'Reverse Dylann Roof' Story, 'Alt-Right' Claims" by Michael Edison Hayden (September 28th 2017)

motive.[190]   Most Americans are completely unaware of the incident, but painfully remember the months of coverage after the Confederate flag-loving Dylann Roof opened fire inside an African American church, which sparked the beginning of the Confederate flag being banned and even *Dukes of Hazzard* reruns being pulled from TV because the Duke boys' car, the General Lee, has the flag painted on it.[191]

In late 2013 a disturbing trend surfaced when random and unsuspecting white people were being sucker-punched in the face by black kids hoping to knock them out.[192]   It was dubbed the "knockout game" or "polar bear hunting" (polar bear being a slang term for white people), and the victims were of all ages, including senior citizens, chosen at random, when they were just walking down sidewalks of city streets, simply because they were white. Some of the incidents were captured on video by nearby security cameras, and some of the perpetrators' friends videotaped the attacks themselves and posted the footage on social media or World Star Hip Hop, a website that caters to black fight videos.[193]

Most of these attacks were only reported on the local news where they occurred, and they usually left the racial elements out of their stories.  It wasn't until word of these

---

[190] New York Times "Shooting at a Church Near Nashville Leaves One Dead and Seven Wounded" by Christina Caron (September 24th 2017)

[191] ABC News "TV Land Pulls 'Dukes of Hazzard' Reruns" by Luchina Fisher (July 1st 2015)

[192] Frontpage Magazine "Media Blackout of the 'Knockout Game'" by David Paulin (November 21st 2013)

[193] ABC 7 "New Jersey police investigating disturbing 'knockout game' punch posted on Facebook" (February 5th 2016)

incidents began spreading through social media that the 'knockout game' phenomenon, and its anti-white racist patterns became clear.[194]

A black serial killer in Kansas City murdered five random white men, four of them on biking and hiking trails over the course of a few months between 2016 and 2017, by walking up to them and shooting them in the back of the head.[195] There was no motive for the attacks other than he wanted to "kill all white people," as he had admitted to police while in custody during a previous incident involving harassment charges. Have you heard about this story? Probably not.

After four black thugs were arrested in Chicago for torturing a mentally handicapped white man while broadcasting it on Facebook Live, the disturbing video went viral on social media and then mainstream media reluctantly covered the incident briefly, once, and then never made any mention of it again.[196]

If it had been white perpetrators torturing a black man while broadcasting it on Facebook, it would have stayed in the news cycle for weeks, perhaps months. The networks would have devoted prime time specials to their "exclusive" interview with the victim, and he would have become the left's poster boy and rallying cry against racism and hatred perpetrated from white people. We would have heard his name as often as Trayvon Martin or

---

[194] Breitbart "CBS, NBC, ABC, CNN, MSNBC Primetime Ignore 'Knockout Game'" by William Bigelow (November 21st 2013)

[195] USA Today "'Kill all white people,' suspected serial killer said in 2014" by William Cummings (August 31st 2017)

[196] Daily Caller "Clay Travis On Chicago Attack: Media Doesn't Want To Cover Racism From Blacks" by David Hookstead (January 5th 2017)

Michael Brown, but instead this incident, and the victim, was immediately forgotten.

Shepard Smith, a liberal host at Fox News, cut off a reporter mid-sentence when he was reporting on this crime after he brought up the fact that many were concerned that the Black Lives Matter movement were fanning the flames of anti-white racism and might have helped create an environment which incited the perpetrators.[197] "Wait, wait, wait, Matt, Matt, Matt, Matt, Matt, Matt, Matt, Matt, Matt, Matt, Matt, Matt. The police chief made clear what this was...let's leave the politics of this alone," Smith interjected.[198]

Shepard Smith also cut off Louisiana governor Bobby Jindal while he was live on the air commenting on a black perpetrator who ambushed three police officers in Baton Rouge, Louisiana, killing them for Black Lives Matter.[199] Jindal was saying, "It is time for folks across party lines, across ideological lines, to condemn this violence, to condemn this insanity, we've got to come together, we've got to say that all lives matter. It doesn't matter what color you are, black, white, brown, red, it doesn't matter, all lives matter. We've got to protect and value our police."[200]

Smith interrupts him, saying, "Governor you know that that phrase you just used is one that's seen by many

[197] YouTube "Shepard Smith Cuts Off Reporter For Saying the Truth About Black Lives Matter" (Clip posted January 5th 2017)

[198] Ibid.

[199] Reuters "Black Lives Matter leaders sued over Baton Rouge police shooting" (July 7th 2017)

[200] Breitbart "Fox News' Shepard Smith Scolds Bobby Jindal, Says 'All Lives Matter' is 'Derogatory'" by Warner Todd Huston (July 17th 2016)

as derogatory, right? (referring to 'All Lives Matter') I just wonder why it is that you used that phrase when there's a certain segment of the population that believes it's a real dig on 'em?"

Jindal responded, "Well, Shepard, it's not meant to be. The point is we've got to move beyond race. Look, these police officers, these are the men and women that run towards danger, not away from it, so that we can be safe. It is time for us to be unified as, as a country. We've got to look beyond race. I think that's one of the dumbest ways for us to divide people. It's one of the dumbest ways to for us to classify people, or categorize people. We shouldn't be divided, we do need to be united. These are police officers — they don't care whether you're black or white, they will run towards danger to protect you. That's what they swear, that's their duty, that's what they do first. These are heroes."[201]

While most major media cover-up anti-white racism, others regularly try to paint all white people as being racist. *The New York Daily News* hired Shaun King in 2015 as their "senior justice writer," a man who for all intents and purposes looks white, but identifies as black and has dedicated his life to exposing the "evils" of white police officers and "white privilege" in America. His columns primarily consist of him putting out slanted stories filled with half-truths and innuendo about how white people are constantly causing countless problems for black people in America today. He even called the Boy Scouts Jamboree a "white supremacist rally."[202]

---

[201] Gateway Pundit "Video: Shepard Smith Attacks, Lectures Bobby Jindal for Saying 'All Lives Matter'" by Kristinn Taylor (July 17th 2016)

[202] https://twitter.com/ShaunKing/status/889657321852465153

# Censoring "Radical Islamic Terrorism"

Because of Barack Obama's Muslim roots and his desire to craft the narrative of his legacy to give the impression that he was the president who 'helped bring peace' to the world, he did everything he could to downplay the dangers of radical Islam, and of course the liberal media had his back and followed his lead.[203] For example, the attack at Fort Hood, Texas in 2009 by a Muslim U.S. Army major who shot and killed 13 people and injured more than 30 others was labeled "workplace violence" despite the fact that the gunman had been exchanging emails with al-Qaeda leader Anwar Al-Awlaki.[204]

Networks also largely ignored the fact that one of the biggest mass shootings in American history at the Pulse nightclub in Orlando, Florida in 2016 was carried out by a radical Islamic terrorist who told a 911 operator he was doing it for the Islamic State.[205] The gunman killed 49 people for ISIS, but the Big Three TV news networks just referred to the shooter as a "lone gunman," ignoring his true motivation for the attack which wasn't just a hatred

---

[203] Washington Times "Obama's scrub of Muslim terms under question; common links in attacks" by Rowan Scarborough (April 25th 2013)

[204] Washington Times "Pentagon will not label Fort Hood shootings as terrorist attack" by Susan Crabtree (October 22nd 2012)

[205] Sunday Express "Omar Mateen swore allegiance to ISIS in 911 call before worst mass shooting in US history" by Vickie Oliphant (June 13th 2016)

of gays, but was actually fueled by his extremist Islamic beliefs.[206]

When the FBI released transcripts of his call to 911 they redacted all references he made to Islam, ISIS, and Allah.[207] Only after outrage from members of Congress over the censorship did the FBI release the actual transcript.[208] Speaker Paul Ryan denounced the FBI's cover-up saying, "We know the shooter was a radical Islamist extremist inspired by ISIS. We also know he intentionally targeted the LGBT community. The administration should release the full, unredacted transcript so the public is clear-eyed about who did this, and why."[209]

A former senior intelligence official also revealed that President Obama repeatedly ignored warnings in 2011 and 2012 about the growing threat of what would become ISIS in order to perpetuate his re-election narrative that he was helping bring an end to the War on Terrorism.[210] He even infamously called ISIS the "JV Team" (Junior Varsity) downplaying the danger they pose, which he said

---

[206] The Guardian "Omar Mateen described himself as 'Islamic soldier' in 911 calls to police" by Spencer Ackerman (June 20th 2016)

[207] USA Today "FBI, DOJ issue new transcript of Orlando 911 call amid outrage" by Kevin Johnson and Mary Bowerman (June 20th 2016)

[208] The Hill "Feds reverse course, release full Orlando shooter transcript" by Julian Hattem (June 20th 2016)

[209] NBC News "FBI Releases Full Transcript of 911 Calls from Orlando Massacre" by Corky Siemaszko (June 20th 2016)

[210] The Hill "Ex-spy head: Obama ignored ISIS intelligence to fit reelection 'narrative'" by Julian Hattem (December 1st 2015)

was "contained."[211]   Obama wanted his legacy to be that of the president who ended the wars in the Middle East, so he not only kept downplaying radical Islamic terrorist activity in the United States and around the world, but kicked the can down the road so he could pass the problem off onto the next administration.[212]

When President Trump said that there are terrorist attacks that happen but people don't know about them because the media won't report them, he obviously meant they won't report on them for more than a 15 second blurb or that they might cover the story one time and then forget all about it.  However, the media pretended to take him literally,[213] when obviously he meant that several instances were *under-reported* and that relatively few people sensed the devastation and danger due to such little coverage.

When radical Islamic terror attacks occur in Europe and the United States and are only briefly covered before the media reverts back to their constant complaining about Trump, most people quickly forget about them or may not even hear about them at all.

## George Orwell's Memory Hole

In George Orwell's classic novel *Nineteen Eighty-Four* he coined a variety of phrases which describe different aspects of life under the totalitarian "Big

---

211 CNN "Obama: ISIS not growing, but not 'decapitated'" (November 13th 2015)

212 National Review "Obama Trades Real Security for Spin to Secure His Legacy" by Matthew Continetti (August 29th 2015)

213 CBS News "Trump claims media is covering up terror attacks, citing no evidence" by Rebecca Shabad (February 6th 2017)

Brother" regime. One such term, a *memory hole,* refers to quietly deleting or altering news stories in order to make it seem as if they were never changed, or never even existed in the first place.

One scene in *Nineteen Eighty-Four* depicts the lead character Winston Smith editing newspaper articles that had already been published (which was part of his job at the "Ministry of Truth") to change what they said, and then new ones were printed to replace the originals, which were all confiscated and destroyed, leaving no evidence of what they actually said. The information was said to have disappeared down a "memory hole" because as the main antagonist O'Brien later reveals to Winston, 'he who controls the past controls the future, and he who controls the present controls the past.'

Any information the government (called the Party in the book) didn't want people to have access to anymore disappeared into a memory hole, and with no physical evidence of an original newspaper which had later been altered, there was no possible way for someone to verify whether or not a certain story was actually true. The truth was what the government (the Party) said it was.

Unfortunately, memory holes aren't just something from Orwell's imagination, they actually exist in our modern media age where it is much easier to delete something or change it once it's been posted online since actual newspapers are being replaced by digital versions on tablets and smartphones. Unless retrieved from Google cache, or someone taking a screenshot, then an original version of something posted on a news website and later altered is almost impossible to discover. We see these alterations all the time on articles from mainstream outlets when part of a story is changed or deleted, and oftentimes the entire headline rewritten.[214]

Some outlets may add a small note on the bottom of an article saying something to the effect that it had been changed to 'fix a mistake,' but usually doesn't mention what that mistake was. Sometimes a misleading and inflammatory headline will send shockwaves across social media, and once word of the story has gone viral, the headline will be quietly changed, or parts of the story altered or removed in attempts to avoid a defamation lawsuit, but the damage is often done with the false allegations continuing to spread and taking on a life of their own.[215]

The same things happen when news agencies or celebrities tweet out something completely false (or criminal, when celebrities help incite violence to support their causes). Oftentimes someone will take a screenshot to preserve evidence and post it after the tweet has been deleted, but unless they have the URL of the original tweet which can be retrieved from the archive, a screenshot's authenticity is called into question. Was it actually a screenshot, or did someone fake the screenshot using Photoshop or one of the fake tweet generating websites?

An MSNBC terrorism analyst once appeared to encourage ISIS to bomb Trump Tower in Turkey in a tweet that was later deleted.[216] Actor Patton Oswald once

---

[214] Daily Caller "CNN Changes Headline After Antifa Complains" by Phillip Stucky (August 20th 2017)

[215] Breitbart "TIME Editor Defends Reporter of False Martin Luther King Bust Story" by Jerome Hudson (January 24th 2017)

[216] Washington Times "MSNBC terrorism analyst nominates Trump property for 'ISIS suicide bombing'" by Jessica Chasmar (April 19th 2017)

tweeted encouragement for terrorists to bomb one of Trump's properties and later deleted it.[217]   *New York Times* columnist Ross Douthat actually tweeted his hopes for a Trump assassination,[218] as did London *Guardian* reporter Monisha Rajesh,[219] with both later deleting the tweets after the backlash.   Oftentimes once someone deletes such inciting tweets they and their fans insinuate that screenshots are fake, casting doubt on whether or not they had actually posted such statements at all.   It's as if the truth has vanished down a memory hole.

An eerie 'memory hole' situation occurred in 2010 when an episode of Jesse Ventura's *Conspiracy Theory* television show was remotely deleted from people's DVRs after they had recorded it.   The show ran for three seasons on TruTV and followed Jesse Ventura around the country investigating various conspiracy theories, and one of those episodes was about 'FEMA camps,' the secretive detention centers that have been set up in major cities across America in order to detain large numbers of people in the event of massive civil unrest which may be sparked from any number of reasons.

After the *Police State* episode first aired, it was scheduled to be replayed the following week as a lead-in for the new episode, but it didn't air.   All the information about the episode was also deleted from TruTV's website, and even more strange, the people who had recorded it on

[217] New York Daily News "Patton Oswalt backtracks from tweet suggesting terrorists should attack Trump properties" by Ethan Sacks (November 28th 2016)

[218] New York Post "New York Times columnist tweets joke about killing Trump" by David K. Li (February 25th 2016)

[219] Mediaite "Journalist Deletes Account After Tweeting 'Time For a Presidential Assassination'" by Alex Griswold (November 10th 2016)

their DVRs found the episode had been deleted from there as well.[220] The show's producers later revealed that the government put pressure on the network to pull the episode from airing again, and also had cable companies remotely delete copies from people's DVRs at home since they are linked directly to the cable providers.[221]

And so, just like the cable companies remotely change the clocks on customer's boxes every fall and spring to adjust them for Daylight Savings Time, they also deleted an episode of Jesse Ventura's *Conspiracy Theory*. It couldn't get more ironic! A government conspiracy behind censoring a TV show about conspiracies! In all seriousness this instance illustrates the vulnerabilities of using streaming technology over the old fashioned VHS or DVD recorders because once something was recorded on those systems, the only way for a media company to get rid of it would be to physically come to your house and take it, but now they can just make things disappear down a memory hole from miles away with just the push of a button.

---

[220] Infowars.com "Confirmed: Ventura's Conspiracy Theory Episodes Disappearing from DVRs" (January 5, 2011) by Kurt Nimmo

[221] Infowars.com "Police State episode of hit Ventura show covering FEMA camps pulled from air" (December 3, 2010)

*Author's Note: Please take a moment to rate and review this book on Amazon.com or wherever you purchased it from to let others know what you think. This also helps to offset the trolls who keep giving my books fake one-star reviews when they haven't even read them. Almost all of the one-star reviews on my books are from NON-verified purchases which is a clear indication they are fraudulent, hence me adding this note. These fraudulent ratings and reviews could also be part of a larger campaign trying to stop my message from spreading by attempting to tarnish my research through fake and defamatory reviews, so I really need your help to combat this as soon as possible. Thank you!*

# Fake Hate Crimes

While it's undeniable that hate crimes unfortunately happen and are committed by members of all races against one another, the mainstream media frames the issue as if white people are always the perpetrators, and that black people or other minorities like Muslims or gays are always the victims. There is another interesting phenomenon involving hate crimes that is usually ignored, and that is the practice of people faking them.

The mainstream media has repeatedly hyped-up hate crime hoaxes started by fraudsters and mentally disturbed individuals who know what kind of sensational bait the media is looking for to push their leftist agenda.[222] Oftentimes these perpetrators are soon exposed as frauds after investigators discover their stories are fabricated, with many of them ultimately confessing, but by that time the damage has already been done. Their fake stories have spread across social media and gotten picked up by news outlets across the country and social justice warriors have added the incidents to their mental list of reasons to believe that white people or Christians are all out to get them.

The 'hate crimes' getting debunked barely garner any media attention at all, while the initial sensational claims spread across the country and galvanize the social groups with the same identity as the phony victims who use the

---

[222] New York Post "Pay-up time for Brawley: '87 rape-hoaxer finally shells out for slander" by Michael Gartland (August 4th 2013)

fake stories to prop up their beliefs that 'their people' are being systematically targeted and attacked.

Immediately after the 2016 presidential election, we saw a series of hate crime hoaxes that were designed to paint Donald Trump and his supporters in a false light, hoping to dupe people into believing that they were all dangerous right-wing extremists on a rampage against minorities. Just two days after the election a Muslim woman in Louisiana falsely claimed that two Trump supporters yelled racial slurs at her, attacked her, and then stole her hijab. She later admitted to police that she made up the whole story.[223]

In Indiana, a man spray-painted a swastika and "Heil Trump" on the side of a church, even though he hated Donald Trump, and after he was caught admitted that he wanted to "mobilize a movement" against him.[224] A small African American church in Mississippi was burned down and had "Vote Trump" spray-painted on the side, causing initial reports to claim it was done by white supremacist Donald Trump supporters. Soon after, however, a black man was arrested for the crime and police said he painted the 'Trump' message on the building to throw off investigators about his true motive which was some personal grievance he had with the church.[225]

In Philadelphia a black man was caught spray painting racist, anti-black and pro-Trump graffiti on cars and

---

[223] 4WWL "Lafayette woman faces criminal charges after falsely claiming Trump supporters robbed her" by Amanda McElfresh (November 11th 2016)

[224] RTV6 ABC "Church organist who reported vandalism was actually the one who did it" by Katie Cox (May 3rd 2017)

[225] New York Post "Black church member charged in 'Vote Trump' arson" Associated Press (December 21st 2016)

businesses after he tried to make it look like a white supremacist had done it.[226]  In Charlotte, North Carolina a small local market owned by an Indian had a rock thrown through its window and the front door set on fire.  A note was left at the scene which praised President Trump and said, "We need to get rid of Muslims, Indians and all immigrants," and was signed, "White America."   A surveillance camera caught the perpetrator on video and he was identified and arrested a few days later.  He was black.[227]

Others posted on social media about non-existent 'crimes' right after the 2016 election that were made up, claiming they or someone they knew were 'victims' of Trump supporters who were randomly attacking Muslims or blacks. [228]  The saturation of fake 'white supremacist incidents' spread through social media has caused paranoia and panic in many minorities.  Lab equipment covered by white plastic tarps at one college was confused for a KKK meeting by a paranoid student who contacted the dean to complain about it after she spotted the 'KKK hoods' through a window when walking by.[229] At another university some students got scared and "no longer felt safe on campus" after seeing that other students wrote "Trump 2016" in chalk on some sidewalks

---

[226] Philly.com "S. Jersey man arrested in 'Pro-Trump', racist post-election vandalism in South Philly" by Julie Shaw (December 1st 2016)

[227] Fox News "What is fueling fake hate crimes across the U.S.?" by Doug McKelway (April 20th 2017)

[228] Philly Voice "Police: No official report of ugly racial incident at Delaware gas station" by Brian Hickey (November 10th 2016)

[229] Washington Times "College student reports seeing KKK hood in classroom, actually saw lab equipment cover" by Ken Shepherd (January 25th 2017)

and stairs.[230]    The Millennial generation has been so brainwashed that they believe when a white person wears dreadlocks or dresses up as Bruce Lee for Halloween that it's "cultural appropriation" and hence 'racist' and 'offensive.'[231]

Members of the LGBT community have been caught hoaxing hate crimes on a regular basis in order to gain sympathy for their cause or to defame their neighbors who they're having a squabble with. A lesbian waitress in New Jersey collected thousands of dollars in donations after she claimed a couple wrote on their receipt that they stiffed her out of a tip because she was gay.[232] Her story immediately unraveled and she was fired from the restaurant for lying and had to refund the donations.[233] A lesbian couple in Colorado were charged with criminal mischief and filing a false police report after they spray painted "Kill the Gay" on their own garage door and said they suspected their neighbors had done it.[234]    Another gay couple spray painted "Queer" on their own house, and

---

[230] Washington Post "Someone wrote 'Trump 2016' on Emory's campus in chalk. Some students said they no longer feel safe." by Susan Svrluga (March 24th 2016)

[231] MTV News "Decoded" "12 Racist Halloween Costumes for Kids" by Franchesca Ramsey (October 21st 2015)

[232] New York Post "Lesbian waitress in 'anti-gay' receipt flap fired" by Kate Briquelet (December 7th 2013)

[233] ABC News "Waitress in Anti-Gay Tipping Scandal No Longer at Restaurant" by Liz Fields and Gillian Mohney (December 8th 2013)

[234] ABC News "Lesbian Couple Charged With Staging Hate Crime" by Alyssa Newcomb via Good Morning America (May 19th 2012)

then burned it down to collect the insurance money while also blaming their neighbor.[235]

One lesbian in St. Louis even carved anti-gay slurs into her own skin and then said she was attacked by some 'homophobic' bigots.[236] At Connecticut State University a lesbian wrote some anti-gay notes and slid them under her dorm room door which then resulted in students holding a "solidarity rally" to show that they're "not intimidated by hate." A surveillance camera caught the lesbian on video planting the notes herself, and she was charged with filing a false police report.[237] With the rise of social justice warriors plaguing American universities in recent years, such incidents seem to now be commonplace. Laird Wilcox, author of *Crying Wolf: Hate Crime Hoaxes in America*, estimates that 80% of alleged hate crimes on college campuses are hoaxes or just harmless pranks.[238]

A gay man in Montana who claimed he was beaten up outside of a club because of his sexuality was charged with filing a false police report after surveillance footage showed he actually hurt himself attempting a backflip on the sidewalk outside, and nobody had attacked him at

---

[235] New York Daily News "Tennessee lesbian couple faked hate crime and destroyed own home with arson for insurance claim, jury rules" by Nicole Hensley (August 5th 2015)

[236] CBS St. Louis "Cops: Lesbian Fakes Attack In Which She Carved Anti-Gay Slurs Into Skin" (August 22nd 2012)

[237] Hartford Courant "CCSU Police Say Student Faked Anti-Gay Notes" by David Owens and Hilda Munoz (July 2nd 2012)

[238] Fox News "What is fueling fake hate crimes across the U.S.?" by Doug McKelway (April 20th 2017)

all.[239]  A gay YouTuber who made videos promoting "gay rights" was also arrested for faking a hate crime against himself for publicity.[240]  Someone even claimed that a baker at Whole Foods wrote "fag" in frosting on a cake he ordered and then sued the store, but once again surveillance footage showed the truth and proved that when he left with the cake there was no such thing on it, and he too admitted he wrote "fag" on the cake himself after he bought it.[241]  There are so many more of these LGBT hoaxes that they could fill an entire book.

Of course the same kinds of hate crime hoaxes are perpetuated by other minorities like black people and Jews who are looking to smear a neighbor they don't like or trying to "raise awareness" about racism.[242]  A black student at Kean University in New Jersey was arrested for tweeting death threats to her fellow students who were attending an anti-racist rally on campus after she was caught using a fake twitter account trying to make the threats appear as if they were coming from a white person.[243]

After a wave of threats to Jewish Community Centers across the United States raised concerns that neo-Nazism

---

[239] Missoulian "Gay man pleads guilty to false report of attack in downtown Missoula" by Gwen Florio (August 8th 2012)

[240] Variety "YouTube Star Faked His Own Assault, Police Say" by Maane Khatchatourian (June 29th 2016)

[241] NBC News "Texas Pastor Apologizes, Drops Whole Foods Suit for Fake 'Anti-Gay' Cake" by Alex Johnson (May 16th 2016)

[242] FakeHateCrimes.org keeps a current database of hate crime hoaxes with links to local news reports for each instance.

[243] NBC New York "Activist Charged With Making Twitter Threats to Black Students, Staff at Kean University" (December 1st 2015)

was on the rise, a Jew was arrested for making them.[244] Other Jews have been caught painting swastikas on their own homes in order to fake hate crimes.[245] Swastikas have even been spray painted on synagogues by Jews for the same reason.[246] These kinds of hoaxes seem as if they're a plot out of a cheesy 1980s TV crime drama, but they have been thoroughly documented by police for years. One has to wonder how many more hate crime hoaxes don't get exposed because of undiscovered evidence which would prove they too are fake.

The 'victimhood is virtue' mindset of liberals has created an Oppression Olympics of sorts, where people find value in being a member of a group that is supposedly under attack or marginalized due to their race, sexual orientation, or gender identity. Organizations like the Southern Poverty Law Center and the Anti-Defamation League are often seen as money making schemes that exaggerate the kinds of 'threats' they claim to monitor in order to justify their ongoing fundraising efforts. One ADL operative named James Rosenberg was actually caught posing as a right-wing extremist who worked as an agent provocateur, attending white supremacist rallies in order to presumably rile up the attendees to make them look violent.[247]

---

[244] New York Times "Jewish Center Bomb Threat Suspect Is Arrested in Israel" by Isabel Kershner, Adam Goldman, Alan Blinder, and Richard Perez-Pena (March 23rd 2017)

[245] Syracuse.com "Jewish man arrested after spray painting swastikas on his own home in Upstate NY" by Ben Axelson (March 21st 2017)

[246] The Times of Israel "Jewish suspects arrested over swastika graffiti on synagogues" by Stuart Winer and Judah Ara Gross (June 11th 2017)

[247] Jeffrey Kaplan, Heléne Lööw, *The Cultic Milieu: Oppositional Subcultures in an Age of Globalization* ISBN 0-7591-0204-X

The Southern Poverty Law Center is the organization that routinely labels conservatives "racists," "sexists," "homophobic," "bigots," "anti-government," and claims they're members of "hate groups." Radical Islamic groups are never included on their "hate watch" articles, only 'anti-Muslim' ones, and 'right-wing extremists.'[248] They also ignore and have even censored reports of anti-white racism and hate crimes against white people.[249]

Many see the SPLC as just a way for its founder, Morris Dees, to make easy money through tax-exempt donations. He pays himself a six-figure salary from the organization which helped him build a luxury 200-acre estate, complete with tennis courts, a swimming pool and horse stables.[250] The president of another civil rights organization, the Southern Center for Human Rights, has called Morris Dees "a con man and a fraud" who "has taken advantage of naive, well-meaning people — some of moderate or low incomes — who believe his pitches and give to his $175-million operation."[251]

Well, that is a $175 million operation back in 2007. Since then, the Southern Poverty Law Center's wealth has skyrocketed. In 2015 alone they raised more than $50 million dollars and their IRS filing shows they have

[248] https://www.splcenter.org/fighting-hate/intelligence-report/2017/active-hate-groups-2016

[249] New York Post "Report buried Trump-related 'hate crimes' against white kids" by Paul Sperry (December 5th 2016)

[250] Harpers Magazine "The Church of Morris Dees: How the Southern Poverty Law Center Profits from Intolerance" by Ken Silverstein (November 2000 Issue)

[251] Harper's Magazine "The Southern Poverty Law Center's Business Model by Ken Silverstein (November 2nd 2007)

accumulated more than $328 million dollars in assets.[252] They have even transferred millions of dollars to offshore accounts in the Cayman Islands.[253]

It's ironic that an organization with the word 'poverty' in their name is stashing millions of dollars in offshore accounts, which may be why the SPLC's hometown newspaper, *The Montgomery Advertiser*, even said they exaggerate the threats of hate groups in order to rake in millions of dollars in donations.[254]

---

[252] Washington Times "SPLC transferring millions to offshore tax havens: Report" by Valerie Richardson (September 1st 2017)

[253] Ibid.

[254] The New York Times "Conversations/Morris Dees: A Son of Alabama Takes On Americans Who Live to Hate" by Kevin Sack (May 12th 1996)

# Operation Mockingbird

No discussion about fake news would be complete without a thorough examination of the CIA's Operation Mockingbird, which at first may sound like a conspiracy theory or the plot of a Hollywood thriller, but it is a very real and well-documented program that was exposed during a 1975 Congressional hearing called the Church Committee.[255] In the early 1970s there were widespread allegations that the CIA was involved in a variety of corrupt activities, including spying on American citizens, and even assassinating foreign leaders. The Church Committee was set up to investigate these reports and one of the surprising things they uncovered was that the CIA had been covertly spending millions of dollars a year to pay key figures at major news outlets to work as government propagandists and gatekeepers.[256]

The scope of Operation Mockingbird is staggering. Thomas Braden who helped lead the program, admitted, "If the director of the CIA wanted to extend a 'present,' say, to someone...suppose he just thought, this man can use fifty thousand dollars ($250,000 adjusted for inflation today), he's working well and doing a good job — he

---

[255] Formally called the Select Committee to Study Government Operations With Respect to Intelligence Activities

[256] Final Report of the Select Committee to Study Government Operations With Respect to Intelligence Activities. April 1976.

could hand it to him and never have to account to anybody... There was simply no limit to the money it could spend and no limit to the people it could hire and no limit to the activities it could decide were necessary."[257]

Such reporters could be considered to be members of the Deep State, using their position of influence to serve intelligence agencies rather than their news agency or their readers. These were people who would also be given classified information to leak to the public, a practice that still goes on today which we saw in the case of transcripts of President Trump's phone calls and those of his advisors being given to the press after they were intercepted, which is obviously a serious felony. [258]

During the initial investigation into Operation Mockingbird, a congressman asked William Colby, who was then the head of the CIA, "Do you have any people paid by the CIA who are working for television networks?" Colby responded, "This, I think, gets into the kind of details, Mr. Chairman, that I'd like to get into in executive session."[259] Executive session, meaning a closed session with only a handful of senators who were authorized to have access to classified information.

Despite the CIA's attempts to contain the details and scope of the program, a lot of information was revealed, but many investigators believe that the full extent of Operation Mockingbird was never made public, and insist that the Church Committee's hearings were just a "limited hangout," meaning despite *some* damaging revelations,

[257] Thomas Braden, interview included in the Granada Television program, *World in Action: The Rise and Fall of the CIA* (1975)

[258] Fox News "Trump transcript leak likely a federal crime, former prosecutors say" (August 3rd 2017)

[259] Church Committee Hearings (1975) testimony by William Colby

the true nature and scope of the program remained classified. Former Special Assistant to the Deputy Director of the CIA, Victor Marchetti, said that limited hangouts are used by the CIA, "When their veil of secrecy is shredded and they can no longer rely on a phony cover story to misinform the public," so "they resort to admitting — sometimes even volunteering — some of the truth while still managing to withhold the key and damaging facts in the case. The public, however, is usually so intrigued by the new information that it never thinks to pursue the matter further."[260]

Frank Wisner, who led the Office of Strategic Services which would later become the CIA, called Operation Mockingbird the "Mighty Wurlitzer" after the Wurlitzer jukebox because he and his operatives could get the media to "play any tune" they wanted.[261] The Church Committee also uncovered assassination plots, a frozen poison dart gun built by the CIA for such operations, poison pen letters, and other shocking activities which was actually their primary objective. Discovering the CIA's media manipulation was an unexpected side effect.

## Covert Relationships With the United States Media

The Church Committee's final report on the investigation admits, "the Central Intelligence Agency has used the U.S. media for both the collection of intelligence

---

[260] 720 F. 2d 631 - Hunt v. Liberty Lobby DC

[261] Wilford, Hugh - *The Mighty Wurlitzer: How the CIA Played America*. Harvard University Press (May 2009)

and for cover,"[262] and that, "The CIA maintained covert relationships with about 50 American journalists or employees of U.S. media organizations. They are part of a network of several hundred foreign individuals around the world who provide intelligence for the CIA and at times attempt to influence opinion through the use of covert propaganda. These individuals provide the CIA with direct access to a large number of foreign newspapers and periodicals, scores of press services and news agencies, radio and television stations, commercial book publishers, and other foreign media outlets."[263] Notice they stressed 'foreign' outlets, which was just a diversion. The program was very much a domestic operation as well.

Shortly after Operation Mockingbird was exposed George Bush senior, then director of the CIA, issued a statement saying that, "The CIA will not enter into any paid or contractual relationship with any full-time or part-time news correspondent accredited by any United States news service, newspaper, periodical, radio or television network or station [anymore]."[264]

The CIA also claimed, "As soon as feasible, the Agency will bring existing relationships with individuals in these groups into conformity with this new policy. CIA recognizes that members of these groups (U.S. media and religious personnel) may wish to provide information to the CIA on matters of foreign intelligence of interest to

---

[262] Church Report page 191

[263] Church Report page 192

[264] Ibid.

the U.S. Government. The CIA will continue to welcome information volunteered by such individuals."[265]

The Church Committee report noted that, "Of the approximately 50 U.S. journalists or personnel of U.S. media organizations who were employed by the CIA or maintained some other covert relationship with the CIA at the time of the announcement, fewer than one-half will be terminated under the new CIA guidelines."[266]

It goes on to say, "About half of the some 50 CIA relationships with the U.S. media were paid relationships, ranging from salaried operatives working under journalistic cover, to U.S. journalists serving as 'independent contractors' for the CIA and being paid regularly for their services, to those who receive only occasional gifts and reimbursements from the CIA...More than a dozen United States news organizations and commercial publishing houses formerly provided cover for CIA agents abroad. A few of these organizations were unaware that they provided this cover."[267]

The report also admits, "While the CIA did not provide the names of its media agents or the names of the media organizations with which they are connected, the Committee reviewed summaries of their relationships and work with the CIA."[268]

During the Church Hearings, the CIA claimed they never tried to engage in any "clandestine use of staff employees of U.S. publications which have a substantial

---

[265] Church Report page 197

[266] Church Report page 195

[267] Ibid.

[268] Ibid.

impact or influence on public opinion,"[269] but this is an obvious lie and the report whitewashed such actions as "fallout" which they described as unintended and incidental 'side effects' of their propaganda, which they admitted was spread through the U.S. media, not just the foreign press.

They said this "fallout" in the United States was, "inevitable and consequently permissible" and that "there is no way to shield the American public from such 'fallout.'"[270] As a former senior official of the Agency said in his testimony, "If you plant an article in some paper overseas, and it is a hard-hitting article, or a revelation, there is no way of guaranteeing that it is not going to be picked up and published by the Associated Press in this country."[271]

The report also admitted, "The domestic fallout of covert propaganda comes from many sources; books intended primarily for an English-speaking foreign audience, press placements that are picked up by international wire services, press services controlled by the CIA, and direct funding of foreign institutions that attempt to propagandize the United States public and Congress."[272]

Even if they aren't officially paying reporters anymore (which is most likely a complete lie), the fact is that they openly invited reporters and executives to work with the CIA "voluntarily," and the report admits that this relationship would be of a great benefit to the careers of

---

[269] Church Report page 197

[270] Church Report page 198

[271] Ibid.

[272] Ibid.

journalists who take them up on that offer.[273] The report also admitted that CIA propaganda "contaminating" U.S. media ('fall-out' as they called it), "occurs in virtually any instance of propaganda use," and that "it is truly impossible to insulate the United States from propaganda fallout."[274]

It goes on to say, "The fallout problem is probably most serious when the U.S. public is dependent on the 'polluted' media channel for its information on a particular subject...Another situation in which the effects of 'fallout' in the United States may be significant is that in which specialized audiences in the United States — area study specialists, for example — may unknowingly rely heavily on materials produced by, or subsidized by, the CIA."[275]

They even admitted that, "the propaganda effort had an impact on the American public and congressional opinion."[276] One example was the CIA paying $170,000 to create pro-Vietnam War propaganda magazines in the 1970s which were then distributed to American readers including the offices of all United States Congressmen and Senators."[277] The CIA funded magazine (which wasn't named) even sponsored American Congressmen to travel to Vietnam. The Church report admits that, "Through this institution the CIA engaged in propagandizing the American public, including its

---

[273] Church Report page 199

[274] Church Report page 200

[275] Ibid.

[276] Ibid.

[277] Ibid.

Congress, on the controversial issue of U.S. involvement in Vietnam."[278]

The report even noted, "The CIA recognizes that it risks seriously misleading U.S. policymakers,"[279] and that their propaganda, "might influence the thinking of senior U.S. officials or affect U.S. intelligence estimates," and "No mechanism exists to protect the U.S. public and the Congress from fallout from black propaganda or any other propaganda."[280]

The CIA also secretly ran various newspapers in foreign countries to take their propaganda to a whole new level and provide cover for CIA operatives. One paper was *The Daily American* in Rome which was used by the Agency to help influence Italy's electorate.[281] Operation Mockingbird also funded the publishing of various books, although they refused to mention which ones.

Former CBS president Sig Mickelson was later asked if he thought despite these revelations the CIA was still covertly working with reporters, and he answered, "Yeah, I would think probably, for a reporter it would probably continue today, but because of all the revelations of the period of the 1970s, it seems to me a reporter has to be a lot more circumspect when doing it now or he runs the risk of at least being looked at with considerable disfavor

---

278 Ibid.

279 Church Report page 200-201

280 Church Report page 201

281 New York Times "Worldwide Propaganda Network Built by the C.I.A." (December 26th 1977)

by the public. I think you've got to be much more careful about it."[282]

It's interesting to point out that CNN's Anderson Cooper interned for the CIA during the summer after his sophomore year of college, and again the following summer while he was attending Yale University, a hotbed of the CIA.[283]  Radar Online reported in 2006 that, "Anderson Cooper has long traded on his biography, carving a niche for himself as the most human of news anchors. But there's one aspect of his past that the silver-haired CNN star has never made public: the months he spent training for a career with the Central Intelligence Agency."[284]

Cooper then confirmed his connections with the CIA in a blog post on CNN's website and said he decided not to talk about it publicly until Radar contacted CNN telling them they were going to publish their story and were looking for a comment.[285]

## More Operation Mockingbird Revelations

Carl Bernstein, who worked for *The Washington Post* when he blew the lid off the Watergate scandal which led to the resignation of President Nixon in 1974, became an instant icon in the news business and gained a reputation for his continued investigations into government

---

[282] Sig Mickleson in a clip widely available on YouTube about the CIA and the news

[283] New York Times "Yale - a Great Nursery of Spooks" by Godfrey Hodgson (August 16th 1987)

[284] Radar "Anderson Cooper's CIA Secret" (September 6th 2006)

[285] CNN.com "My Summer Job…Nearly 20 Years Ago" by Anderson Cooper (September 6th 2006)

corruption and abuse of power. A few years after his Watergate bombshell he left *The Washington Post*, and for six months investigated the CIA's relationship with the press, leading to a cover story in *Rolling Stone*.[286]

While the Church Committee was reluctant to name names and news agencies, he certainly wasn't. He named some of the papers and reporters who had cooperated with Operation Mockingbird, including people at *The New York Times, Newsweek, Time, The New York Herald Tribune, The Associated Press,* and even his former employer, *The Washington Post;* although he did defend the paper saying that the publisher (Katherine Graham at the time) and the managing editors were unaware of the operation and claimed only "stringers" were involved. Was he protecting his former employer, or treating his investigation into them with kid gloves? While that is likely the case, it's also possible he was just in denial about their involvement, but his *Rolling Stone* story was still packed with information not mentioned at all during the Church Hearing.

Bernstein wrote, "Journalists provided a full range of clandestine services — from simple intelligence gathering to serving as go-betweens with spies in Communist countries. Reporters shared their notebooks with the CIA. Editors shared their staffs…CIA documents show journalists were engaged to perform tasks for the CIA with the consent of the managements of America's leading news organizations."[287]

He pointed out that part of the operation included using journalists to "aid in the recruitment and 'handling'

---

[286] Rolling Stone "The CIA and the Media" by Carl Bernstein (October 20, 1977)

[287] Ibid.

of foreign nationals who are channels of secret information reaching American intelligence."[288]    He continued, "Many journalists were used by the CIA to assist in this process and they had the reputation of being among the best in the business. The peculiar nature of the job of the foreign correspondent is ideal for such work: he is accorded unusual access by his host country, permitted to travel in areas often off-limits to other Americans, spends much of his time cultivating sources in governments, academic institutions, the military establishment and the scientific communities. He has the opportunity to form long-term personal relationships with sources and — perhaps more than any other category of American operative — is in a position to make correct judgments about the susceptibility and availability of foreign nationals for recruitment as spies."[289]

He goes on, "The tasks they performed sometimes consisted of little more than serving as 'eyes and ears' for the CIA; reporting on what they had seen or overheard in an Eastern European factory...On other occasions, their assignments were more complex: planting subtly concocted pieces of misinformation; hosting parties or receptions designed to bring together American agents and foreign spies; serving up 'black' propaganda to leading foreign journalists at lunch or dinner; providing their hotel rooms or bureau offices as 'drops' for highly sensitive information moving to and from foreign agents; conveying instructions and dollars to CIA controlled members of foreign governments."[290]

---

[288] Ibid.

[289] Ibid.

[290] Ibid.

Bernstein even explained how unsuspecting journalists were recruited for the program. "Often the CIA's relationship with a journalist might begin informally with a lunch, a drink, a casual exchange of information. An Agency official might then offer a favor — for example, a trip to a country difficult to reach; in return, he would seek nothing more than the opportunity to debrief the reporter afterward. A few more lunches, a few more favors, and only then might there be a mention of a formal arrangement — 'That came later,' said a CIA official, 'after you had the journalist on a string.'"[291]

Could this explain how *The Washington Post* and *The New York Times* keep getting classified information leaked to them in order to damage the Trump administration? Are they willing servants of the Deep State trying to bring down the president by any means necessary? Senator Chuck Schumer once gave an ominous warning to President Trump when he said that the intelligence agencies have "six ways from Sunday to get back at you," if they don't like what he's doing.[292]

Bernstein quotes one CIA official as admitting, "In return for our giving them information, we'd ask them to do things that fit their roles as journalists but that they wouldn't have thought of unless we put it in their minds."[293] This was all informal and unofficial. The "formal recruitment" of reporters, Bernstein says, only occurred after they had been vetted with background

291 Ibid.

292 Washington Examiner "Schumer warns Trump: Intel officials 'have six ways from Sunday at getting back at you'" by Daniel Chaitin (January 3rd 2017)

293 Rolling Stone "The CIA and the Media" by Carl Bernstein (October 20, 1977)

checks to ensure they could be trusted as "agents of the government." Journalists being considered had to sign non disclosure agreements before the offer was even made, and Bernstein quotes an unnamed former assistant to the CIA Director as saying, "The secrecy agreement was the sort of ritual that got you into the tabernacle." David Atlee Phillips, a former CIA chief operations officer himself, admitted that more than 200 journalists had signed non disclosure agreements with the CIA, which Bernstein described as making up a "good old boy" network that "constituted something of an establishment elite in the media, politics and academia," who wrote "propaganda for CIA proprietary publications."[294]

Once uncovered during by the Church Committee the CIA tried to paint Operation Mockingbird as something that only functioned to influence foreign press, but Carl Bernstein admits, "The CIA's use of the American news media has been much more extensive than Agency officials have acknowledged publicly or in closed sessions with members of Congress." He goes so far as to say, "The use of journalists has been among the most productive means of intelligence–gathering employed by the CIA."

CIA director William Colby admitted during the Church Hearing that "people in management" were involved, not just reporters, and that they helped the CIA with the program. And while Colby wouldn't name names, Carl Bernstein pointed to William Paley, who was President of CBS; Henry Luce, the founder of *Time* magazine; and Arthur Hays Sulzberger, the publisher of *The New York Times*, who actually admitted the CIA had him sign a non disclosure agreement.

---

[294] Ibid.

At least ten employees at *The New York Times* were working as CIA assets or were actual CIA agents who the paper was providing a cover for, often in their foreign bureau. The CIA even had a training program in the 1950s which taught agents how to pretend to be journalists and were sometimes "placed in major news organizations with help from management."

It wasn't just newspapers of course, the Big Three television networks (NBC, CBS, and ABC) were involved as well. CBS provided "journalistic cover" for CIA employees and allowed their newsrooms to be monitored by the CIA. Bernstein says that in the 1950s and 60s CBS officials even met for an annual dinner with the CIA.

Sig Mickelson later admitted that when he became president of CBS News, "I was told by Paley [President of CBS] that there was an ongoing relationship with the CIA...He introduced me to two agents who he said would keep in touch. We all discussed the Goodrich situation [one of the undercover agents] and film arrangements. I assumed this was a normal relationship at the time. This was at the height of the Cold War and I assumed the communications media were cooperating—though the Goodrich matter was compromising."[295]

High-level CIA officials worked with "top management" of the news agencies to give agents working undercover as journalists assignments in foreign countries, according to Bernstein, and the CIA had, "some of the best-known correspondents in the business" as operatives using TV networks for "journalistic cover." He also noted that a reporter is the perfect cover for a CIA operative because it's a reporter's job to ask questions, investigate things, and travel around the world to do so.

---

[295] Ibid.

Colby admitted that the agency had "some three dozen" American reporters, editors, or executives, "on the CIA payroll," including five who worked for "general-circulation news organizations."[296] William Bader, who supervised the Senate committee's investigation, admitted that there were CIA officers at management levels in major media companies.[297] Malcolm Muir, *Newsweek's* former editor said, "Whenever I heard something that I thought might be of interest to Allen Dulles, I'd call him up.... At one point he appointed one of his CIA men to keep in regular contact with our reporters."

## The Church Hearing Was a Cover-Up

During the Church Hearings, then-CIA director William Colby tried to claim they weren't doing any of this anymore and downplayed the program saying it didn't work as well as they had hoped, but he was just whitewashing its effectiveness and many have said that even the Church Hearing itself was part of the cover-up.

For example, they didn't even question any of the journalists or executives who were working for the CIA. Why wouldn't they want to get major media executives and reporters on the witness stand to testify under oath about what they were doing? This should have been a key part of the investigation, but it wasn't. Why? Because they didn't want to dig that deep. They didn't want the extent of the program, and who was involved, to be known. The committee was compromised and limited

[296] Ibid.

[297] Ibid.

their investigation to prevent the magnitude of what was happening from being made public.

Carl Bernstein wrote that the CIA "were able to convince key members of the committee that full inquiry or even limited public disclosure of the dimensions of the activities would do irreparable damage to the nation's intelligence-gathering apparatus, as well as to the reputations of hundreds of individuals."[298]

At the time of the Senate investigation George Bush senior was the director of the CIA and pressured members of the committee, and successfully persuaded them to essentially whitewash the investigation. The CIA refused to turn over documents about which journalists were working for them, and only gave the Committee rewritten summaries of documents, all of which had the names of journalists and media executives removed. Most of the documents they did turn over were about foreign journalists on foreign soil, giving the false impression that such thing wasn't happening in America.

Speaking of the Church Committee's final report, Senator Gary Hart said, "It hardly reflects what we found. There was a prolonged and elaborate negotiation [with the CIA] over what would be said."[299] In other words, it was a whitewash — just another limited hangout with *some* damning information, but as usual, the full truth would remain hidden. Most people are completely unaware of the Church Committee today, and if they were told about Operation Mockingbird, would just think it's a conspiracy theory, but as one unnamed Senator quoted in Carl Bernstein's *Rolling Stone* story says, "From the CIA point

---

[298] Ibid.

[299] Ibid.

of view this was the highest, most sensitive covert program of all.... It was a much larger part of the operational system than has been indicated."

# White House Correspondents' Dinner

The same reporters who are supposed to function as watchdogs over the White House are wined and dined every spring at the luxurious red carpet White House Press Correspondents' Dinner where they rub elbows and share some laughs with the very people they're supposed to be holding accountable for their actions. The name of the event implies that it would consist of reporters and media executives, but each year A-list Hollywood celebrities are among the most popular guests. Why would movie stars and sitcom actors be key fixtures at a dinner that's supposed to be for serious journalists covering the White House?

The event includes a professional comedian who cracks jokes about the current administration and the media's coverage of them, and also involves a scripted stand up routine by the current president who makes jabs at the press, and himself, as those in attendance appear to laugh at the fact that most politicians are liars and fail to deliver on the promises they made during their campaigns.

In 2004, just one year after the War in Iraq started, George W. Bush made some tasteless jokes about not finding the weapons of mass destruction that he and his

administration had falsely claimed were there. While at
the podium, a slide show of photos were put up on screen
showing him bending over and looking under his desk in
the oval office to which he then commented, "Those
weapons of mass destruction have got to be here
somewhere," earning him laughter and applause from the
audience. "Nope, no weapons over there." Another photo
was put up on the screen of him strangely looking at
another part of his office as he said, "Maybe under
here."[300] The audience loved it, laughing and applauding
which is so bizarre because he was literally joking about
the lies that led us to war. What happened to journalists
being watchdogs and keeping those in power in check?

Senator John Kerry, who ran against Bush in the 2004
election, commented, "If George Bush thinks his
deceptive rationale for going to war is a laughing matter,
then he's even more out of touch than we thought.
Unfortunately for the president, this is not a joke. 585
American soldiers have been killed in Iraq in the last year,
3,354 have been wounded and there's no end in sight.
George Bush sold us on going to war with Iraq based on
the threat of weapons of mass destruction. But we still
haven't found them, and now he thinks that's funny?"[301]

At the 2010 dinner Barack Obama joked about killing
people with drones which had become a controversial
new topic since the technology was now being used to kill
people with the remote control aircraft.[302] While much of

[300] USA Today "Bush's joke about WMD draws criticism" (March 26th 2004)

[301] The Guardian "Bush jokes about search for WMD, but it's no laughing matter for critics" by David Teather (March 26th 2004)

[302] The Atlantic "Obama Finds Predator Drones Hilarious" by Max Fisher (May 3rd 2010)

the audience laughed, others who are not part of the elite White House press corps didn't think it was so funny. Alex Pareene at Salon wrote, "It's funny, because Predator drone strikes in Pakistan have killed literally hundreds of completely innocent civilians, and now the president is evincing a casual disregard for those lives he is responsible for ending by making a lighthearted joke."[303]

After the 2007 dinner, *New York Times* columnist Frank Rich claimed that the paper would stop attending the event, saying it is, "a crystallization of the press's failures in the post-9/11 era," and that it "illustrates how easily a propaganda-driven White House can enlist the Washington news media in its shows."[304]

*The New York Times* Washington bureau chief Dean Baquet later confirmed they would stop going, saying, "We came to the conclusion that it had evolved into a very odd, celebrity-driven event that made it look like the press and government all shuck their adversarial roles for one night of the year, sing together (literally, by the way) and have a grand old time cracking jokes. It just feels like it sends the wrong signal to our readers and viewers, like we are all in it together and it is all a game. It feels uncomfortable."[305]

While working for *Rolling Stone* magazine, Michael Hastings revealed that many journalists write "puff

---

[303] Salon "Obama threatens Jonas Brothers with drone strikes" by Alex Pareene (May 3rd 2010)

[304] New York Times "All the President's Press" by Frank Rich (April 29th 2007)

[305] Observer "The Situation and the Story: Press Corps Parties While White House Makes History" by Foster Kamer and Kat Stoeffel (May 4th 2011)

pieces" in order to cozy up with government officials hoping to gain or maintain access to them.[306] A column in *The Guardian* denouncing the White House Correspondents Dinner stated that "Journalism's job is to speak truth to power — not refill its glass and laugh at its jokes," and highlighted that in their view, "The celebrities sitting at almost every table of the Washington Hilton gave the distinct impression that both journalism and politics are now wholly beholden to the whims of the entertainment-industrial complex."[307]

In 2013 *New York Times Magazine's* Chief National Correspondent Mark Leibovich said that journalists in Washington D.C. have become a "celebrity class."[308] When asked why his paper doesn't have reporters attend the dinner, he said, "There's a level of self-congratulation and self-celebration and so forth that can be very, you know, somewhat at odds with the mood of the country and how people view the media. It did not feel like the right message to be sending to our readers to really be, you know, in such a chummy in sort of festive setting with the people we're covering."[309]

BuzzFeed, the clickbait bottom feeders of the Internet, whose articles mostly consist of a few lines of text accompanied by animated Gifs, were granted press

---

[306] Reliable Sources "Rolling Stone Reporter Michael Hastings: Reporters Write Puff Pieces for Access" by Susie Madras (June 28th 2010)

[307] The Guardian "The White House correspondents' dinner: an unseemly schmoozefest" by Atossa Araxia Abrahamian (May 2nd 2011)

[308] Mediaite "NY Times Reporter Savages WH Correspondents Dinner: D.C. Journalists 'More Of A Celebrity Class'" by Noah Rothman (April 27th 2013)

[309] Ibid.

credentials and a table at the White House Correspondents' Dinner, to give you an idea of how low the standards are for who they consider to be 'journalists.' The Huffington Post is also a member of the White House Press Corps and are granted access to the presidential daily briefings where they are allowed to ask the president or his press secretary direct questions.

It certainly is odd that the people who are supposed to function as watchdogs and keep administrations accountable are wining and dining with them. The inside jokes and the overall atmosphere of the dinner reeks of elitism and hypocrisy and is just one more example of the collusion between the top mainstream media outlets and the people they're supposed to hold accountable.

University of Texas Radio-Television and Film professor América Rodriguez points out, "The ownership of the national media system is centralized in very few hands. These owners, and the journalists they employ, in turn have close personal and professional relationships with the political elites of their respective nations. The interaction of these two factors — ownership concentration and the tight web of relations within the political elite — has created national news production processes intent on safeguarding privilege and status."[310]

The government is actually the most frequent source of news, so a cozy relationship between politicians and journalists further tarnishes the credibility of their reporting. One study showed 46% of stories from *The Washington Post* and *The New York Times* originated from the government.[311] Another primary source of 'news' is

---

[310] Questioning the Media "Control Mechanism of National News Making" by América Rodriquez page 145

[311] Sigal, Leon V. - *Reporters and Officials* (Lexington Books, 1973)

from what's been dubbed 'churnalism,' which is when news outlets use press releases sent by government agencies or corporations as the basis for stories and often report the information contained in them virtually verbatim.[312] The term refers to journalists quickly "churning out" stories from the information they mostly just take from press releases or news wires, often without even fact checking it or doing any original research.

Part of the churnalism problem comes from the constant pressure to continuously keep posting new content in our never-ending 24-7 news cycle. This leaves reporters little time to do original research or fact-check, because there is an urgency to "be first" to post a story in hopes of having it go viral so it drives a bunch of traffic to their website. A study by British journalist Nick Davies found that 80% of the stories in British newspapers were just rewritten wire copy and press releases.[313]

## White House Press Corps Shakeup

The tone of the White House Correspondents' Dinner dramatically changed when Donald Trump became president. As the first dinner of the Trump administration approached, *Vanity Fair* and *The New Yorker* announced that they would not be attending "in protest" because of the way Trump was treating the media.[314] Then sources

---

[312] The Guardian "Churnalism or news? How PRs have taken over the media" by Paul Lewis (February 23rd 2011)

[313] The Australian "Fearing the Rise of 'Churnalism'" by Sally Jackson (June 5th 2008)

[314] The New York Times "New Yorker and Vanity Fair Pull Out of Correspondents' Dinner Parties" by Michael M. Grynbaum and Katei Rogers (February 3rd 2017)

within CNN and MSNBC revealed that those networks were considering boycotting the 2017 dinner as well.[315]

Then President Trump trumped the media again, and announced that *he* wasn't going to go, breaking a long-held tradition of presidents attending, and instead held a rally to celebrate his first 100 days in office. "I'm treated very unfairly and very dishonestly by the press and I thought it was inappropriate to go this year. If I were treated even slightly fairly by the press I would have gone," Trump said. "I thought it would be very disingenuous if I went. I thought it would be actually, in a certain way, dishonest if I went."[316]

There were other changes regarding White House press correspondents now that Trump was in office. The Trump administration had considered moving the White House press briefing to another location so they could include more reporters since the briefing room is rather small. One location considered was the White House Conference Center, which is across the street from the White House, and another was the Old Executive Office Building which is right next door. The Establishment media cried about a 'lack of transparency,' even though this move would have expanded the number of reporters who had access to the president and the press secretary.

Then-Chief of Staff Reince Priebus said, "I know some of the folks in the press are uptight about this and I understand. The only thing that's been discussed is whether or not the initial press conferences are going to be in that small press room. For the people listening to this that don't know this, the press room that people see

---

[315] The Hill "CNN might not attend White House correspondents' dinner" by Joe Concha (February 24th 2017)

[316] Reuters - Interview with President Trump (April 27th 2017)

on TV is very, very tiny — 49 people fit in that press room."[317]

He continued, "We had like 500 or 600 folks at the press conference last week so we started thinking, 'if we can have more people involved [rather] than less people involved, that would be a good thing' — that's what this is about."[318] They decided not to move locations, but came up with a way to include more reporters by allowing them to call in on Skype, the video conferencing service from anywhere in the country.[319]

After the very first press briefing of the Trump administration the liberal media were complaining that the first outlets called on to ask questions weren't CNN, or *The Washington Post*, but instead the *New York Post*, and then the second question went to the Christian Broadcasting Network (CBN), and the third went to Univision, the Spanish-language network.

CNN's Jim Acosta even went on air and complained about the seating arrangement at one of the president's press conferences since he was placed in one of the back rows, saying it was the equivalent of being sent to Siberia.[320]

"If you're legacy media and have been trading on that access for decades, when the new guy comes in and gets your access, it's enraging," said Sean Davis, a co-founder

---

[317] ABC News "Trump Team May Move Press Briefing Room Out of White House: Reince Priebus" by Ali Dukakis (January 15th 2017)

[318] Ibid.

[319] Fox News "'Skype seats' provide awkward, but substantive exchanges at White House briefing" by Cody Derespine (February 1st 2017)

[320] Mediaite "'Retaliation'? Acosta, Blitzer Criticize White House for CNN's Distant Seating at Presser" by Josh Feldman (June 9th 2017)

of The Federalist. "This is legacy outlets acting like an entitled monopoly or a cartel when someone new comes in and does the job better than they do."[321]

The liberal media kept crying about Trump not calling on them enough during his press conferences. Politico complained, "President Donald Trump on Wednesday continued his streak of calling only on conservative-leaning outlets at his bilateral press conferences with foreign leaders," saying, "During his press conference with Israeli Prime Minister Benjamin Netanyahu Wednesday afternoon, Trump called on David Brody of the Christian Broadcasting Network and Katie Pavlich, the editor of TownHall.com."[322]

As I'm sure you recall, CNN's Jim Acosta was acting more like a protester than a reporter during one press conference, literally yelling at the president and interrupting him, causing Trump to point at him and declare, "You are fake news!" Maybe someone should tell CNN that the First Amendment's protection of the Freedom of the Press means that the government won't shut down media outlets by forcing them out of business, it doesn't guarantee that the president or his press secretary has to invite them to the White House or answer their questions.

---

[321] The Hill "Conservative media struggles with new prominence under Trump" by Jonathan Easley (March 27th 2017)

[322] Politico "At Netanyahu presser, Trump continues trend of calling on conservative outlets" by Hadas Gold (February 2nd 2015)

# Liberal Bias Confirmed

It seems only the liberal media denies that there is a liberal bias problem in the media, but decades of studies and polls (not to mention common sense) have proven an overwhelming bias in their coverage of just about everything. A Harvard study analyzing the media coverage of President Trump's first 100 days in office found that 80% of it was negative.[323] Of course that was obvious to anyone old enough to pay attention during the election, but it was surprising that Harvard, a very liberal university, would actually investigate the matter.

The study analyzed reports from *The New York Times*, *The Washington Post*, and *The Wall Street Journal;* as well as CNN, CBS, NBC, ABC, Fox News, and even the BBC, and found the average coverage was 80% negative. Also not surprising was that CNN's coverage was 93% negative. Fox News, on the other hand, was shown to be 52% negative and 48 percent positive, which fits in almost perfectly with their trademarked slogan "Fair & Balanced." Professor Thomas E. Peterson, who conducted the study, said, "The nation's watchdog has lost much of its bite and won't regain it until the public

---

[323] Washington Times "As first 100 days in office approaches, media coverage of Trump is 89% negative: Study" by Jennifer Harper (April 19th 2017)

perceives it as an impartial broker, applying the same reporting standards to both parties."[324]

This kind of slanted coverage is certainly nothing new. A famous study of liberal bias in the American media was conducted in 1986 and found that most journalists working for the major national news outlets were Democrats with liberal views on issues like gay rights, abortion, affirmative action, and welfare programs.[325] The study, later published in a book called *The Media Elite*, gathered its data by conducting surveys of journalists at the Big Three broadcast news networks (ABC, CBS, NBC), along with print outlets including *The New York Times, The Washington Post, The Wall Street Journal, Time,* and *Newsweek.*

It concluded that because liberals dominated most news organizations, their coverage reflected their political attitudes both consciously and unconsciously; even if they didn't think they were being biased because they unconsciously believed that their views were 'correct,' so in their minds they didn't see their coverage as biased at all.

A decade later in 1997, another major study of journalists was conducted by the American Society of Newspaper Editors and that found that 61% of reporters leaned Democrat, but only 15% leaned Republican.[326] 24% of those surveyed appeared to be independent.[327]

---

[324] Ibid.

[325] *The Media Elite* (1986) Robert Lichter, Stanley Rothman, and Linda Lichter

[326] "The Newspaper Journalists of the '90s" A Survey Report by the American Society of Newspaper Editors (April 1997).

[327] Ibid.

In 2002 a professor at Dartmouth College published his research on media bias in his book *Press Bias and Politics: How the Media Frame Controversial Issues,* which also showed that most mainstream media in America present liberal views in a more favorable light.[328] Another study in 2005 by researchers at UCLA found a "strong liberal bias" at most mainstream media outlets with the exception of Fox News and *The Washington Times.*[329]     A 2007 study at Harvard University also confirmed a liberal bias in television news.[330] They noted that as soon as the 2008 presidential campaign kicked off that, "Democrat Barack Obama, the junior Senator from Illinois, enjoyed by far the most positive treatment of the major candidates during the first five months of the year," and that, "the press overall has been more positive about Democratic candidates and more negative about Republicans."     They calculated that in the first five months of the year just 12% of the coverage of John McCain, the Republican frontrunner, was positive.

In 2008 a study looked into political donations made by employees at NBC, ABC, and CBS and found that over one million dollars was given to the Democrat Party from 1,160 different people at those networks.[331]     It also found that the Republican Party only received $142,863

[328] Kuypers, Jim A. - *Press Bias and Politics: How the Media Frame Controversial Issues* (2002)

[329] Tim Groseclose of UCLA and Jeff Milyo of the University of Missouri at Columbia

[330] Project for Excellence in Journalism "The Invisible Primary-Invisible No Longer" (October 29th 2007)

[331] The Daily Caller "Obama, Democrats got 88 percent of 2008 contributions by TV network execs, writers, reporters" by Tom Sileo (August 28, 2010) Report about study by Center for Responsive Politics

from just 193 employees.[332]   If you do the math, the Democrat Party got seven times as much money from people who worked at the Big Three networks, and six times as many employees donated to the Democrats vs. the Republicans.

After the study was published, NBC News surprisingly admitted, "Whether you sample your news feed from ABC or CBS (or, yes, even NBC and MSNBC), whether you prefer Fox News Channel or National Public Radio, *The Wall Street Journal* or *The New Yorker*, some of the journalists feeding you are also feeding cash to politicians, parties or political action committees."[333]

A 2016 poll of the White House Press Corps revealed that of the 72 members, there were zero registered Republicans.[334]   In 2017 the same poll found that there were only three.[335]

## Wikileaks Reveals Reporters Working with Hillary Clinton

After Hillary's campaign manager John Podesta got his emails hacked and they were published by Wikileaks, some of them showed various journalists actually coordinating with Hillary's campaign. *New York Times* writer and CNBC anchor John Harwood gave Hillary

---

[332] Ibid.

[333] NBCNews.com "Journalists dole out cash to politicians (quietly)" by Bill Dedman (June 6th 2007)

[334] Washington Free Beacon "Poll: Not a Single White House Reporter Is a Republican" by Lachlan Markay (April 29th 2016)

[335] Politico Magazine "What It's Really Like to Cover Trump" (May/ June 2017)

Clinton "veto" power over what not to include in an interview with her.[336] Politico's Glenn Thrush even called himself a "hack" and let John Podesta review parts of his story before it was published. "No worries. Because I have become a hack I will send you the whole section that pertains to you. Please don't share or tell anyone I did this," he said.[337]

Another reporter for *The New York Times* named Mark Leibovich also emailed the campaign parts of his interview with Hillary and asked if it was okay if he included them in his article.[338] In one of the emails the Clinton campaign named *New York Times* writer Maggie Haberman as someone who they said had "teed up stories" for them in the past and "never disappointed" them.[339]

Hacked emails from the DNC showed that CNN's Donna Brazil gave Hillary Clinton debate questions in advance.[340] She initially denied doing such thing, but

---

[336] New York Observer "No Consequences From Media Peers for Reporters Caught Colluding With Hillary" by Evan Gahr (October 24th 2016)

[337] Daily Caller "Journalists Exposed By WikiLeaks Will Now Cover Trump White House" by Peter Hasson (January 2nd 2017)

[338] Breitbart "Wikileaks: NY Times' Mark Leibovich Obeyed Request to Cut Palin Joke from Hillary Interview" by Dustin Stockton (October 11th 2016)

[339] The Intercept "EXCLUSIVE: New Email Leak Reveals Clinton Campaign's Cozy Press Relationship" by Glenn Greenwald and Lee Fang (October 9th 2016)

[340] Politico "Brazile under siege after giving Clinton debate question" by Hadas Gold (October 31st 2016)

later apologized, saying, "sending those emails was a mistake I will forever regret."[341]

The Wikileaks email dump also showed that Marjorie Pritchard of *The Boston Globe* coordinated with the Clinton campaign to determine when to publish an article for the maximum amount of positive exposure. "It would be good to get it in on Tuesday, when she is in New Hampshire," Pritchard wrote. "That would give her a big presence on Tuesday with the piece and on Wednesday with the news story. Please let me know."[342]

Another of the leaked emails from the DNC showed then-DNC Chair Debbie Wasserman Schultz emailed NBC's Chuck Todd telling him that the negative coverage of Hillary Clinton "must stop" and asked to schedule a phone call to discuss the matter with him. He replied, agreeing to schedule a call.[343]

The Clinton campaign didn't deny any of these emails were real, instead they just tried to deflect from the controversy by claiming 'the Russians' had hacked them in order to help Donald Trump.

When talking about Hillary Clinton, CNN's Chris Cuomo admitted on air that, "We could not help her any more than we have... she's got just a free ride so far with the media, we're the biggest ones promoting her campaign,"[344] and Wolf Blitzer was seen for a brief

---

[341] Washington Times "Donna Brazile admits leaking debate questions to Clinton camp: 'A mistake I will forever regret'" by Douglas Ernst (March 17th 2017)

[342] https://wikileaks.org/podesta-emails/emailid/4180

[343] Mediaite "Leaked Emails Show DNC Chair Told Chuck Todd Negative Coverage 'Must Stop'" by Sam Reisman (July 22nd 2016)

[344] Real Clear Politics "CNN's Chris Cuomo on Hillary: "We Couldn't Help Her Anymore Than We Have"" by Tim Hains (June 9th 2014)

moment dancing and drinking wine at the Democratic National Convention of 2016 after Hillary gave her big speech and was formally nominated as the Democrat Party's candidate.[345]

So we know that the overwhelming number of news networks and their employees are liberal, but why? One theory is that the media industry was started by privileged elitists due to the high costs associated with the equipment needed to manufacture and distribute media. Television studios, cameras, editing bays, satellite uplinks, and broadcasting antennas have traditionally been very expensive. Not to mention the costs of printing presses and the infrastructure needed to deliver hundreds of thousands of newspapers per day.

Political commentator Noam Chomsky points out, "those who occupy managerial positions in the media, or gain status within them as commentators, belong to the same privileged elites, and might be expected to share the perceptions, aspirations, and attitudes of their associates, reflecting their own class interests as well. Journalists entering the system are unlikely to make their way unless they conform to these ideological pressures, generally by internalizing the values; it is not easy to say one thing and believe another, and those who fail to conform will tend to be weeded out by familiar mechanisms."[346]

---

[345] The American Mirror "VIDEO: CNN Wolf Blitzer drinks wine, dances to celebrate Hillary's nomination" by Olaf Ekberg (July 29th 2016)

[346] Chomsky, Noam - *Necessary Illusions: Thought Control in Democratic Societies* (1989) Chapter 1: Democracy and the Media

# The Sun Valley Conference

Every time people talk about the mainstream media conglomerates secretly collaborating with each other, visions of smoke filled rooms and shadowy figures wearing expensive suits sitting around a table come to mind. While this may be an exaggerated expectation of a behind the scenes look at the issue, it isn't all that far from the truth.

Every July since 1983 a small group of media moguls, tech titans, investors, politicians, and intelligence agency insiders, all gather in the small town of Sun Valley, Idaho for a week of meetings to develop a consensus regarding policies for mainstream media, social media, and emerging communications technology. It is basically like the Bilderberg Group meeting for media, and since tech companies like Facebook, Twitter, Apple, and Google have become major players in the media industry, they all come together each year in Sun Valley trying to make sure no emerging platforms can threaten their power.

This is where industry leaders meet to buy up any small startups that have the potential to siphon off some of the market share from the dominant handful who are in control. It's also the place where they develop and agree upon new Orwellian terms of service, gate-keeping strategies, and censorship tactics for the major social media platforms to make sure certain voices and messages don't get too loud.

The conference is hosted by a mysterious investment bank headquartered on Fifth Avenue in New York City called Allen & Company which deliberately tries to avoid publicity, and for many years didn't even have a website. They were one of the underwriters for Google's initial public offering (IPO) in 2004 and did the same thing for Twitter when they went public in 2013. Allen & Company have a long history of brokering major media deals we all hear about, while keeping themselves largely out of the spotlight.

*Fortune* magazine once said, "To say the firm is unusual would be an understatement."[347] It's a privately held company so their financial records are not public like they would be if they were traded on the New York Stock Exchange like other major financial institutions. Who attends the Sun Valley Conference and what is discussed there is also confidential, but it is impossible for some of the high-profile attendees to stay under the radar.

"All the signs are well recognized," reports *The Idaho Mountain Express*, Sun Valley's local paper, which says it's obvious to the residents of the small town when the conference occurs: "The sudden parking of 50 sleek corporate jets at Friedman Memorial Airport in Hailey, the hiring of dozens of local escorts and baby-sitters for VIP families, the presence of celebrities such as TV's Oprah Winfrey, Disney's Michael Eisner and Microsoft's Bill Gates, and the recent post-9/11 heavy security with Allen-imported guards."[348]

---

[347] Fortune "Inside the Private World of Allen & Co. Putting a premium on personal ties, this family firm thrives in the land of the giants." by Carol J. Loomis and Patricia Neering (June 28, 2004)

[348] Idaho Mountain Express "Media moguls alight in valley - Allen & Co. opens 22nd annual conference" by Pat Murphy (July 2nd 2004)

This is the place where Comcast agreed to acquire NBC Universal in 2009 — the parent company of NBC Broadcasting, Universal Pictures, DreamWorks, Syfy, E!, USA Network, Bravo, The Weather Channel, Telemundo, and many more. It's also where the America Online and Time Warner merger was negotiated, creating AOL Time Warner;[349] where Microsoft's merger with NBC was settled, forming MSNBC the 24-hour cable news channel; where Instagram and WhatsApp were bought by Facebook; where Microsoft bought LinkedIn; and where BET (Black Entertainment Television) was sold to Viacom, making the channel's founder Robert Johnson the first black billionaire in America.[350]

Viacom (which also owns MTV, Nickelodeon, Spike, VH1, Comedy Central, Paramount Pictures, and many more media assets) is responsible for turning BET from what was supposed to be a network about African American issues, into a ghetto-culture channel that airs rap videos and TV shows encouraging the very worst aspects of the black community. Co-founder Sheila Johnson later admitted that she was ashamed of what happened to BET after she and her husband Robert sold it to Viacom at the Sun Valley Conference.[351]

This is the place where new and promising media and tech companies (which are often one in the same now) are bought up by major media conglomerates like Viacom, Time Warner, CBS, Disney, News Corporation, and

[349] Business Week "Where Vacationing Media Moguls Enjoy More Than Scenery" by Michael Dolgow (July 09, 2012)

[350] Forbes "The Wealthiest Black Americans" by Matthew Miller (May 6th 2009)

[351] The Daily Beast "Sheila Johnson Slams BET" by Lloyd Grove (April 29th 2010)

Comcast (also known as the Big Six media monopolies) which work together to buy any new emerging tech companies, social media platforms, news websites or apps which they feel could grow into threats to their oligarchy.

While the meeting receives little press coverage, *The New York Times* once admitted, "Yes, high-net-worth individuals, many of whom have their hands on the levers of the media and entertainment economy, gather in one place, and business is undoubtedly being conducted. But anything noteworthy takes place out of view. In fact, much is out of view."[352]

Facebook founder Mark Zuckerberg, Microsoft founder Bill Gates, Apple's CEO Tim Cook, the founders and CEOs of Google, YouTube, Yahoo, Twitter, Instagram, WhatsApp, and most of the top names in tech and social media startups, are all there.[353] While it may not seem all that strange to have an annual gathering of the top names in media and tech, what is strange is the fact the heads of U.S. intelligence agencies are also in attendance. When he was director of the CIA, George Tenet was the Sun Valley keynote speaker in 2003 and again in 2005.[354] And after he retired from the Agency, he still regularly attends.[355] When General David Petraeus

---

[352] New York Times "Business Casual" by David Carr (July 13th 2007)

[353] Variety "Sun Valley Conference Guest List Includes Chris Christie, Mark Zuckerberg" by Rachel Abrams (July 2nd 2013)

[354] Variety "Gang talks Turkey at Sun Valley" by Jill Goldsmith (July 10th 2005)

[355] Los Angeles Times "Allen & Co.'s Sun Valley conference to focus on foreign affairs" by Joe Flint (July 10th 2012)

was the director of the CIA, he too attended, as is customary for the head of the Agency each year.[356]

Why would the head of the CIA be meeting with the CEOs of all the top tech and media companies? In her book *The CIA in Hollywood*, media analyst Tricia Jenkins notes, "The purpose of the meeting is to discuss collective media strategy for the coming year."[357] This likely involves lobbying the tech giants to include back doors in their software to enable the U.S. intelligence agencies to spy on users, and to censor some information being distributed through the platforms which is deemed to have 'national security' implications, and so the government can covertly monitor (and manipulate) the data these megalithic corporations control.[358]

Considering the history of the CIA covertly influencing and censoring major news media through Operation Mockingbird (and their Entertainment Liaison Office overseeing the production of major blockbuster movies and television shows with the purpose of using them as covert containers for propaganda) combined with their mass-surveillance of American citizens; their involvement with the Sun Valley Conference should be of great concern to everyone.

---

[356] Ibid.

[357] Jenkins, Tricia - *The CIA in Hollywood* page 50

[358] The Wall Street Journal "U.S. Military Plugs Into Social Media for Intelligence Gathering" by Julian E. Barnes (August 6th 2014)

*Author's Note: Please take a moment to rate and review this book on Amazon.com or wherever you purchased it from to let others know what you think. This also helps to offset the trolls who keep giving my books fake one-star reviews when they haven't even read them. Almost all of the one-star reviews on my books are from NON-verified purchases which is a clear indication they are fraudulent, hence me adding this note. These fraudulent ratings and reviews could also be part of a larger campaign trying to stop my message from spreading by attempting to tarnish my research through fake and defamatory reviews, so I really need your help to combat this as soon as possible. Thank you!*

# The New Media

There was a time not long ago when posting comments on Internet forums or chat rooms was seen as something that only computer geeks or people living in their mothers' basements did, but beginning around 2005 with the creation of MySpace, this kind of activity started becoming mainstream and would soon virtually takeover most aspects of our lives. MySpace became a thing of the past as people moved over to Facebook, and then Instagram, Twitter, and Snapchat came on the scene. Today most people feel they need to have social media accounts, not just to communicate with their friends, but to share their views and opinions with the world hoping to get some 'likes' 'retweets' and new followers.

In 2005 YouTube gave anyone the equivalency of having their own cable TV channel for free, and would soon begin paying people for posting videos by putting advertisements on them. Soon many channels grew to sizes not only rivaling major television networks, but completely eclipsing them, and a new form of celebrity emerged known as YouTubers.[359]

Once these new social media/tech companies included trending lists and hashtags, countless people began feeding the monster constantly, hoping to get noticed for a witty joke or a controversial comment on what's going on. The trending boxes would start compiling lists of the most

---

[359] Entertainment Weekly "Five YouTubers bigger than Hollywood celebs — according to teens" by Jackson McHenry (August 6th 2014)

talked about topics, giving people an insight into what were supposedly the things being posted about the most.

Many people stopped going to websites directly which were often "bookmarked" in their browser as a sort of "favorites" list, and instead started following the accounts of people, businesses, television shows, etc., on social media. This made companies like Facebook and Twitter a "middleman" which now stands in between people and the websites they used to visit directly by typing in the URLs. Because of the simplicity of aggregating so many different websites, these social media companies have left people vulnerable to an array of censorship and manipulation by these powerful new middlemen. In the next few chapters we'll take a look specifically at Facebook and Twitter and see how they can, *and do,* manipulate and censor information for political reasons and to subtly shift the opinions of users; and we'll discuss the near limitless ramifications and dystopian possibilities this kind of manipulation has.

Most people don't consider the complexities and dangerous precedents that have been set by relying on a handful of mega corporations for the distribution of information, or the risks of allowing themselves to become vulnerable to their ambiguous and agenda-driven terms of service which dictate what is supposedly 'hate speech' or 'harassment.'

Studies show that the majority of people engage in self-censorship when posting online because they don't want their accounts to get shut down or have someone contact their employer about what they have said if it is deemed 'politically incorrect' which could put their job or entire career at risk.[360]

Tech companies are changing so rapidly that in just a few years Twitter went from a website where people posted tweets (brief 140 character-max statements), to a place to watch live football games and news. In 2016 Twitter signed a deal with the NFL to live stream games, and over 2 million people began watching that way.[361] Twitter is also developing a 24-hour live news network by partnering with Bloomberg News and signed deals with BuzzFeed for a morning show, The Verge, for a weekly tech show, and Cheddar for a daily financial show.[362]

Snapchat, which started out as an app for 'sexting' since the messages are 'deleted' after being viewed, has morphed into a multi-billion dollar media company as well, partnering with CNN, ESPN, BuzzFeed and dozens of other networks which produce original content for the app.[363] Snapchat is basically just like Facebook, Twitter, and Instagram, except the posts are automatically deleted after someone reads them once, or "expire" after a short period of time once they're posted. This is why on the campaign trail Hillary Clinton joked about having just opened an account, saying, "I love it. Those messages disappear all by themselves," referring to her trying to

---

[360] The Atlantic "71% of Facebook Users Engage in 'Self-Censorship'" by Alexis Madrigal (April 15th 2013)

[361] GeekWire "Twitter says live streaming of NFL games went 'incredibly well'; no word on deal for next season" by Taylor Soper (January 3rd 2017)

[362] Business Insider "Twitter's live streaming strategy takes form" by Kevin Gallagher (May 3rd 2017)

[363] CNBC "Media companies are starting to cash in on Snapchat" by Julia Boorstin (February 28th 2017)

wipe her illegal personal e-mail server clean before handing it over to the FBI during their investigation into her using it to send and receive classified material. Even Amazon.com, once only a bookstore, is now producing original television series and films through Amazon Studios. CEO Jeff Bezos is now attending the Golden Globes and the Oscars for producing films and television shows like *Manchester by the Sea, Transparent,* and *The Salesman.*[364] Netflix also evolved from just a streaming service to producing original content; YouTube is producing original shows now, and both Facebook and Apple have jumped into the content producing business as well.[365]

Because of this, a record number of people are canceling their cable subscriptions. There were 1.4 million fewer people subscribing to cable TV in the first quarter of 2017 compared to the previous year.[366] These people have been called "cord cutters," and with Netflix and Hulu offering On Demand streams of shows from major networks, and HBO now having their own app, more people are abandoning traditional cable TV.

Even with all these new technologies and methods people are using to get their information, those who control them aren't without their biases. *New York Observer* writer Liz Crokin decided to investigate Apple's liberal bias, so she set up an Apple News account on her iPhone and immediately noticed that her news feed was

---

[364] Reuters "Amazon, Netflix grab a share of Oscar glory" by Lisa Richwine (February 27th 2017)

[365] Los Angeles Times "Apple's original TV production to begin small: 'We are just starting out'" by Meg James (February 14th 2017)

[366] Time "A Record Number of People Just Cancelled Their Pay TV Subscriptions" by Brad Tuttle (August 31st 2016)

predominately liberal and anti-Trump. "Of all the channels listed in the Apple News politics section, only two of the 16 arguably lean right — the rest are reliably left-wing," she wrote.[367]

Of course, Apple CEO Tim Cook openly supported Hillary Clinton's campaign and held fundraisers for her, including a $50,000 a plate dinner, and is a big promoter of the liberal agenda.[368] More liberal bias can be seen on iTunes. For example, the pro-Trump podcast, *MAGAPod* was labeled with an "explicit" warning, simply because the show is pro-Trump. It was only after this bias began making headlines that iTunes removed the explicit warning from the podcast.[369]

Even Apple's App Store is problematic. They refused to publish a satirical Hillary Clinton e-mailgate game called *Capitol HillAwry* claiming it was "offensive" and "mean spirited," but had approved dozens of games targeting Donald Trump. One such game is called *Dump Trump*, which depicts him as a giant turd; and even *Punch Trump* and *Slap Trump* games where players assault Donald Trump for points were approved.[370] Breitbart published an article exposing this bias, and a few days later Apple decided to finally allow the Hillary Clinton

---

367 Observer "Tech Companies Apple, Twitter, Google and Instagram Collude to Defeat Trump" by Liz Crokin (August 12, 2016)

368 Fortune "Apple CEO Tim Cook is Hosting Fundraiser for Hillary Clinton" by Aaron Pressman (August 24th 2016)

369 Washington Examiner "Report: Apple branded Donald Trump podcast as 'explicit'" by Rudy Takala (August 12th 2016)

370 Breitbart "Apple App Store Rejects Satirical Clinton Game Deemed 'Offensive,' Despite Dozens Of Anti-Trump Games" by Charlie Nash (July 25th 2016)

game to be included in the App Store.[371] Apple (and Google) have rejected the Twitter alternative Gab app several times, claiming that people use it to post, "content that could be considered defamatory or mean-spirited."[372] The real reason is that Gab isn't following in line with Silicon Valley's social justice warrior agenda. Apple has also banned apps that use the image of Pepe the Frog, a cartoon character often used in pro-Trump memes.[373]

Instagram has been shown to selectively ban certain topics and accounts as well.[374] They have even deleted several of my posts claiming they were violations of their terms of service. One in which I called singer Lana Del Rey a "skank," and another which consisted of a meme showing a nice white family with the caption, "White People: The only race you can legally discriminate against." After singer Rihanna posted fully topless photos of herself, her Instagram account was temporarily shut down for violating their nudity policy, but because she's a celebrity, they reinstated it.[375] The company even apologized for taking it down. Rappers like 50 Cent, Soulja Boy, and others have posted death threats on their Instagram accounts and the company doesn't suspend

---

[371] Breitbart "Apple Caves to Breitbart News: Satirical Clinton App No Longer Considered 'Offensive'" by Charlie Nash (July 30th 2016)

[372] Inc. "Rejected Again by Apple, Gab Says It's a Victim of Anti-Trump Bias" by Salvador Rodriquez (January 23rd 2017)

[373] Vice News "Pepe Is Banned From the Apple App Store" by Jason Koebler and Louise Matsakis (June 9th 2017)

[374] Advertising Week "Instagram's Banned Hashtags Reveal Moderation Challenges" by Kimberlee Morrison (May 19th 2016)

[375] Daily Mail "Rihanna's Instagram account BACK UP after it was suspended for posting racy photo of her naked derriere" by Heidi Parker (May 5th 2014)

them.[376] But the account of a graffiti artist named Lushsux was banned after he posted photos of an anti-Hillary Clinton mural he painted which just consisted of her in a bikini.

"I don't want to sound like a conspiracy theorist with a tin foil hat, but the timing of the Hillary Clinton mural posting and the deletion that ensued can't just be a coincidence," he said.[377] The artist had previously posted photos depicting Donald Trump naked and Melania Trump topless, but those photos weren't censored by Instagram — only his anti-Hillary painting.

Facebook also regularly censors what people post and manipulates which of your friends' posts actually show up on your news feed.[378] If someone posts something that contains certain keywords that Facebook has determined they do not want to go viral for whatever reason, their algorithms filter it out and prevent the post from showing up.[379]

The social media giant openly admits they manipulate which posts are shown on our friends' news feeds, and even conduct experiments to determine how they can

---

[376] XXL "Wisconsin Man Files Police Report Against 50 Cent for Apparent Threat on Instagram" by Ted Simmons (November 23rd 2016)

[377] Daily Mail "Provocative street artist accuses Instagram of 'political censorship' for deleting his account after his murals of a half-naked Hillary Clinton and Melania Trump go viral" by Harry Pearl and Hannah Moore (September 5th 2016)

[378] The Guardian "When algorithms rule our news, should we be worried or relieved?" by Alex Hern (August 28th 2014)

[379] CNN "Facebook censorship under the microscope" by Sarah Ashley O'Brien (February 4th 2016)

affect people's moods and behavior.[380] Twitter, as you will see in a following chapter, also censors certain hashtags, tweets, and trending topics. The censorship is sometimes subtle, but once you know how it works, it becomes as clear as day.

Twitter founder and CEO Jack Dorsey, and most of Twitter's top executives, are liberals and have repeatedly ignored calls for violence by anti-Trump accounts and Black Lives Matter supporters despite clearly violating the site's terms of service (not to mention the law).[381] There is also increasing evidence that Twitter is limiting the reach of popular controversial conservative accounts.[382] The site has also awarded verified accounts (the often-coveted blue checkmark) to many liberal trolls like racist and anti-police Black Lives Matter activists as well as LGBT and gender bending advocates.[383]

YouTube, as we will discuss in detail in a later chapter, isn't just a place where people upload their own videos, but is a huge media giant with an agenda other than being a place where independent content creators can share their work. YouTube chooses which videos will show up on their home page, on the "trending" box, and in the "recommended" section, which result in a flood of new views; and the company admits that they suppress

---

[380] New York Times "Facebook Tinkers With Users' Emotions in News Feed Experiment, Stirring Outcry" by Vindu Goel (June 29th 2014)

[381] Breitbart "Twitter Takes No Action As Calls For Cop-Killing Sweep Platform" by Mike Ma (July 8th 2016)

[382] WND "Twitter accused of censoring conservatives" by Cheryl Chumley (April 29th 2015)

[383] Cowger Nation "Riley J. Dennis: His disturbing control over the Internet" by Hunter Avallone (March 17th 2017)

and censor videos which they deem to contain "controversial" messages.[384]

A video that few people had noticed with hardly any views can quickly go viral by a moderator adding it to the trending tab. YouTube has also been accused of censoring certain channels by preventing notifications from showing up when a new video is uploaded and keeping certain channels' videos from appearing in the trending section at all.

YouTube regularly includes little rainbow graphics to promote LGBT events and features LGBT pride videos,[385] and even once secretly flew dozens of little-known black YouTubers to their headquarters in California for private mentoring and seminars to help them grow their channels.[386]   Black Lives Matter 'leader' Deray McKesson was there to give the keynote address, and other speakers included Russell Simmons and comedian Wanda Sykes.   The event was dubbed "YouTube BLACK."

Barack Obama appeared on the national stage at the same time social media was rapidly integrating into people's lives, and having a Facebook page was becoming almost as standard as having a telephone. His inner circle of political operatives could see the communication landscape was changing, and they jumped on it

---

[384] Gizmodo "YouTube has a New Naughty Corner for Controversial Religious and Supremacist Videos" by Jennings Brown (August 1st 2017)

[385] Forbes "YouTube's #ProudToBe Campaign Struggles With Haters" by Shelby Carpenter (June 27th 2016)

[386] Fusion "Last year I accused YouTube of failing to promote black talent. Here's what happened next." by Akilah Hughes (April 7th 2016)

immediately. Obama was seen as the first "social media president" and was the first president to have a Facebook page and a Twitter account.[387] The White House would later get its own YouTube channel.[388]

Since people are no longer limited to getting their information from the major news networks, and as our society rapidly moved away from newspapers and magazines to online websites, blogs, and social media pages — not only did these new media monopolies begin manipulating the flow of information that users were posting and viewing, but cunning individuals within the government looked for opportunities to manipulate users of this new technology as well.

An executive in the Obama administration recommended that the government pay online trolls to flood the comment sections on websites and videos in attempts to discredit certain posts deemed "conspiracy theories" or "extremist." Cass Sunstein, who headed up the White House Office of Information and Regulatory Affairs for Obama, wrote that such a plan "will undermine the crippled epistemology of believers by planting doubts about the theories and stylized facts that circulate within such groups, thereby introducing beneficial cognitive diversity."[389]

A few years earlier a military intelligence officer and a defense analyst drew up a white paper discussing the growing popularity of blogs and independent news

387 Reuters "Obama gets his own account on Twitter: 'It's Barack. Really!'" by Roberta Rampton (May 18th 2015)

388 The Telegraph "President Barack Obama's weekly address posted on White House YouTube channel" (January 25th 2009)

389 Sunstein, Cass R.— "*Conspiracy Theories*" Harvard University - Harvard Law School (January 15, 2008) page 15

websites and explored, "the possibility of incorporating blogs and blogging into military information strategy, primarily as a tool for influence."[390] The paper, *Blogs and Military Information Strategy*, also floated the idea of hiring bloggers to attack people and promote certain causes.[391] It also suggested the government hack popular blogs and make subtle changes in articles, not to just spread propaganda, but to discredit the writers.

"Hacking the site and subtly changing the messages and data — merely a few words or phrases — may be sufficient to begin destroying the blogger's credibility with the audience," it says.[392]

These tactics were proposed before the social media era, which took the information age to a whole new level of user interactions through Internet comments as people began to rely on these apps and websites to communicate with their friends, family, and total strangers. It's now how most people interact with the outside world, slipping further away from actual interpersonal interactions and embracing parasocial relationships with YouTubers who are their virtual friends, playing hashtag games and spending hours on end scrolling through Instagram or Snapchat posts reading comments and posting replies in what amounts to a historic waste of time.

Social media is filled with fraud, posers, D-list celebrities with fake followers, and people who get paid to post about how much they supposedly like certain products in what's called "influence marketing." Kim

---

[390] *Blogs and Military Information Strategy* page 5 by James Kinniburgh and Dororthy Denning (2006)

[391] *Blogs and Military Information Strategy* page 20 by James Kinniburgh and Dororthy Denning (2006)

[392] Ibid.

Kardashian can get paid tens of thousands of dollars just to tweet something about a product or post a picture of something on Instagram.[393] The Federal Trade Commission has started to crack down on these influence marketers because it is illegal to not disclose that a tweet, Instagram post, or a product endorsement in a YouTube video is a paid promotion.[394] In a TV commercial, viewers know the celebrity is getting paid to talk about a product, but if someone on Twitter, Instagram, or YouTube posts about how 'great' a product is, nobody knows if they just want to tell their followers about something they think is cool, or if it's a commercial.

An investigation into the official Obamacare Facebook page in 2014 found that the majority of the over 226,838 comments were from just a small handful of users who were most likely paid shills to give the false impression that everyone loved the new law.[395] Barack Obama's "nonprofit" Organizing for Action declined to comment if they were paying people to post, but it's clear from the extraordinary number of posts from the same few accounts that this was an organized online campaign.[396]

---

[393] Gizmodo "Average Internet Celebrities Make $75,000 Per Instagram Ad and $30,000 Per Paid Tweet" by Matt Novak (August 30th 2016)

[394] Bloomberg "FTC to Crack Down on Paid Celebrity Posts That Aren't Clear Ads" by Sarah Frier and Matthew Townsend (August 5th 2016)

[395] Washington Times "Obamacare Facebook page comments mostly from small group of supporters" by Kelly Riddell (November 16th 2014)

[396] Washington Examiner "Obamascare: 60% of online Obamacare defenders 'paid to post' hits on critics" by Paul Bedard (February 25th 2017)

The government actually paid WebMD, the popular health and medical website, $14 million dollars to promote Obamacare.[397] Those payments weren't even kept secret and were listed in the budget of the Department of Health and Human Services. A private foundation called the California Endowment even paid $500,000 to television networks to incorporate pro-Obamacare plot lines into TV sitcoms and other shows.[398]

All of this makes for a fascinating and complex media landscape which is difficult to navigate without getting lost in an endless maze of hyperlinks, and millions of people and countless companies and organizations all simultaneously hoping to be seen, heard, followed, and believed.

In a rare interview Drudge Report founder Matt Drudge gave to Alex Jones in 2015, he warned people not to rely on Facebook and other social media companies to communicate with their friends, get your news from, or to build a business with because, "You're a pawn in their scheme."[399] To see what he is talking about let's take a closer and more specific look at several of the current top social media sites (Facebook and Twitter) to see how they can, and do, manipulate and censor what people post and what users see. And then we'll look at YouTube, Google, and Wikipedia to see how and why they do the same thing.

[397] The Hill "WebMD received $14M to promote ObamaCare" by Sarah Ferris (September 25th 2014)

[398] New York Post "Is there ObamaCare 'propaganda' on our favorite shows?" by Kyle Smith (October 19th 2013)

[399] The Alex Jones Show (October 6th 2015) Matt Drudge Interview

# Facebook

Facebook slowly morphed from a website people could use to look up old friends from high school or college and share photos with family members, to a place where most people now get much of their news and keep up with current events. At one time Facebook only showed users what their 'friends' were posting, but that changed when they added the trending module — and with this simple little box they harnessed the power to introduce their one billion users to news stories that their friends hadn't posted — stories the company feels users *should know* about, and overnight Facebook transformed from just a social networking site to a news company.

With this change, combined with the algorithms which filter out certain content people post by limiting its distribution, Facebook has become a powerful gatekeeper that can decide which stories will go viral, and which ones will remain virtually unknown. Facebook also poses a danger to free speech by policing and censoring what people post, and if something is deemed 'too politically incorrect,' then posts are automatically deleted and users may have their accounts completely shut down.

Most news websites now rely on Facebook for the majority of their traffic from users posting links to their articles. An Internet analytics firm showed that Facebook was responsible for driving 43% of web traffic to over 400 major sites in 2016.[400]

---

[400] Parse.ly "Facebook Continues to Beat Google in Sending Traffic to Top Publishers" by Allie VanNest (December 4th 2015)

According to their study, in 2014 Facebook was responsible for 20% of all traffic to news sites, and in just two years that figure more than doubled as people became accustomed to scrolling through their Facebook feeds to see what articles their friends had posted and because they were now 'following' news websites on Facebook instead of bookmarking the websites in their Internet browser and visiting them directly.[401]

CEO Mark Zuckerberg has said one of his goals is, "To build the perfect personalized newspaper for every person in the world."[402] Facebook even began hosting articles from major publishers so users who clicked on a link wouldn't leave the Facebook ecosystem and could now view the content within Facebook's app.[403]

The company wants to be the primary hub of the Internet, bypassing search engines and web browsers altogether.[404] For those who were using the Internet in the late 1990s and early 2000s, we recall most companies encouraging people to visit their websites at the end of their commercials, but those calls to action have been replaced by now encouraging people to follow them on Facebook instead, making Mark Zuckerberg one of the most powerful (and unnecessary) middlemen in the history of the Internet.

---

[401] Mashable "Why Facebook now sends more traffic to news sites than Google" by JP Mangalindan (August 19th 2015)

[402] Time "7 Things You Didn't Know About Facebook From Mark Zuckerberg's Q&A" by Jack Linshi (November 6th 2014)

[403] The Wall Street Journal "Facebook Begins Hosting News Articles From Nine Publishers" by Deepa Seetharaman (May 13th 2015)

[404] Vanity Fair "Mark Zuckerberg Wants to Beat Google at Its Own Game" by Maya Kosoff (February 24th 2016)

As the 2016 election approached, many media analysts and tech bloggers began to realize that with so many people relying on Facebook as their primary news aggregator, that the site could leverage their power hoping to influence the election. *New York Magazine* published an article which asked, "Could Facebook help prevent President Trump?" and went on to say, "Not through lobbying or donations or political action committees, but simply by exploiting the enormous reach and power of its core products? Could Facebook, a private corporation with over a billion active users, swing an election just by adjusting its News Feed?"[405]

Paul Brewer, a communications professor at the University of Delaware, said, "Facebook would, like any campaign, want to encourage turnout among the supporters of its preferred candidate, persuade the small number of genuinely uncommitted likely voters, and target apathetic voters who could be convinced to get out to the polls."[406]

Josh Wright, the executive director of a behavioral science lab, also admitted, "There's lots of opportunity, I think, to manipulate based on what they know about people."[407] Wright pointed out how the site could fill people's news feeds with photos or stories showing a particular candidate engaged in activities that Facebook knows they like in order to use "in-group psychology" to get people to identify with a candidate who shares some of their interests.

---

[405] New York Magazine "Could Facebook Swing the Election?" by Dan Nosowitz (April 27th 2016)

[406] Ibid.

[407] Ibid.

We tend to judge someone by what other people we like are saying about them, and so Facebook could highlight statements made by celebrities that people follow, or even our own friends, about a candidate in order to influence our opinion of that person. If you think Facebook wouldn't engage in this kind of personalized high-tech manipulation, you would be wrong, because they already have.

A secret study Facebook conducted during the 2010 midterm elections, with help from researchers at the University of California, San Diego, investigated what's called social contagion which is how behavior or emotions are copied by others. Facebook included over 60 million of their users in the experiment and found that they could influence people to actually get out and vote by showing people that their friends had voted, which then influenced others to go vote as well. "Our study suggests that social influence may be the best way to increase voter turnout," said James Fowler, a UCSD political science professor who conducted the study. "Just as importantly, we show that what happens online matters a lot for the 'real world.'"[408] Their experiment increased voter turnout by 340,000 people.[409]

Facebook obviously has a political agenda. They've hosted a Q & A for Barack Obama,[410] they hung a huge Black Lives Matter banner at their headquarters,[411] and

[408] UC San Diego News Center "Facebook Boosts Voter Turnout" by Inga Kiderra (September 12th 2012)

[409] Ibid.

[410] TechTimes "President Obama And Mark Zuckerberg To Talk Tech On Facebook Live" by Horia Ungureanu (June 23rd 2016)

[411] Fusion "Facebook just put up a huge 'Black Lives Matter' sign at its headquarters" by Kristen V. Brown (July 8th 2016)

Mark Zuckerberg has been very outspoken about his support of illegal immigration,[412] gay marriage,[413] and other liberal causes. The company conducts internal polls of employees where they submit questions and vote on them in hopes of getting Zuckerberg to answer, and one poll in March of 2016 showed that a bunch of employees asked if the company should be used to help prevent Donald Trump from winning the election.[414]

UCLA law professor Eugene Volokh told Gizmodo, "Facebook can promote or block any material that it wants. Facebook has the same First Amendment right as the New York Times. They can completely block Trump if they want. They can block him or promote him."[415] Technically the First Amendment only prevents the U.S. government from suppressing someone's speech, not a corporation.

Gizmodo's report on the political bias of Facebook pointed out, "Most people don't see Facebook as a media company — an outlet designed to inform us. It doesn't look like a newspaper, magazine, or news website. But if Facebook decides to tamper with its algorithm — altering what we see — it's akin to an editor deciding what to run big with on the front page, or what to take a stand on."[416]

---

[412] Newsweek "Mark Zuckerberg Files Brief Supporting Obama's Executive Actions on Undocumented Immigrants" by Seung Lee (March 8th 2016)

[413] Los Angeles Times "Facebook's Mark Zuckerberg joins San Francisco gay pride parade" by Salvador Rodriguez (July 1st 2013)

[414] Gizmodo "Facebook Employees Asked Mark Zuckerberg If They Should Try to Stop a Donald Trump Presidency " by Michael Nunez (April 15th 2016)

[415] Ibid.

[416] Ibid.

Whether they are legally allowed to do such a thing is one issue, whether such favoritism and censorship is deceptive and immoral is another.

"If Facebook decided to," professor Volokh says, "it could gradually remove any pro-Trump stories or media off its site — devastating for a campaign that runs on memes and publicity. Facebook wouldn't have to disclose it was doing this, and would be protected by the First Amendment."[417]

"If Facebook was actively coordinating with the Sanders or Clinton campaign, and suppressing Donald Trump news, it would turn an independent expenditure (protected by the First Amendment) into a campaign contribution because it would be coordinated — and that could be restricted," he said. "But if they're just saying, 'We don't want Trump material on our site,' they have every right to do that. It's protected by the First Amendment."[418]

## Censorship of Trending Topics

In May of 2016, tech blog Gizmodo confirmed what many had suspected and what was obvious to those with common sense — that Facebook was systematically suppressing news stories from conservative outlets and those which presented a positive conservative message.[419] "Facebook workers routinely suppressed news stories of interest to conservative readers from the social network's influential 'trending' news section, according to a former

[417] Ibid.

[418] Ibid.

[419] Ibid.

journalist who worked on the project," reported Gizmodo.[420]

The whistleblower revealed that the company suppressed stories about CPAC (the Conservative Political Action Committee conference), Mitt Romney, Rand Paul, and other topics from showing up on the trending module, even though they would have appeared there organically from so many people posting about them.

It wasn't just one whistleblower, but several, and they also revealed that employees would manually insert topics into the trending list that they wanted to get more attention. One former employee said that positive stories about Black Lives Matter were often inserted into the trending box to help them go viral when they didn't organically trend from people posting about them.[421]

"In other words," Gizmodo reported, "Facebook's news section operates like a traditional newsroom, reflecting the biases of its workers and the institutional imperatives of the corporation. Imposing human editorial values onto the lists of topics an algorithm spits out is by no means a bad thing — but it is in stark contrast to the company's claims that the trending module simply lists 'topics that have recently become popular on Facebook.'"[422]

They also called the news section "some of the most powerful real estate on the Internet" that helps dictate what hundreds of millions of people are reading. One of

---

[420] Gizmodo "Former Facebook Workers: We Routinely Suppressed Conservative News" by Michael Nunez (May 9th 2016)

[421] Ibid.

[422] Ibid.

the news curators said they used a notebook to document stories that were censored which included ones about Lois Lerner, the IRS official who targeted conservatives for audits; stories about the Drudge Report, Ted Cruz, Steven Crowder, and more.

A second curator said, "It was absolutely bias. We were doing it subjectively. It just depends on who the curator is and what time of day it is. Every once in a while a Red State or conservative news source would have a story. But we would have to go and find the same story from a more neutral outlet that wasn't as biased."[423]

If a story was on Breitbart, *The Washington Examiner*, Newsmax or other conservative sites and was going viral and qualified to be included in the trending module, curators would wait until an outlet like CNN or *The New York Times* covered the story before it would be allowed to show up as a trend. One insider revealed that Facebook injected the latest Black Lives Matter protests into the trending module, giving them special preference to further their cause. The editors also prevented negative stories about Facebook itself from showing up in the trending section.

The very next day after the story broke about Facebook manipulating the trending topics list, the US Senate Commerce Committee, which oversees interstate commerce and communications, sent a letter to Mark Zuckerberg with a list of detailed questions demanding answers about who determines which stories are included in the Trending Topics section. They also wanted to know details about the process of selection, oversight, and

---

[423] Gizmodo "Want to Know What Facebook Really Thinks of Journalists? Here's What Happened When It Hired Some" by Michael Nunez (May 3rd 2016)

wanting answers to the allegations of politically motivated manipulation.[424]

Mark Zuckerberg then invited several conservative media figures including Glenn Beck, Fox News host Dana Perino, Tucker Carlson, and others to Facebook's headquarters to try and save face, prevent conservatives from abandoning Facebook, and to 'talk about their concerns.' But since our world moves so fast most people quickly forgot all about the scandal and continue to blindly believe that what they see trending is what people are talking about most, not even giving a second thought about the legitimacy of what they are seeing.

## "Boosting" Posts

Most people think that what they and their friends post (and what news sites they follow post), shows up in their feed unless they choose to hide posts from a user they are still following, but Facebook openly admits limiting the distribution of posts unless users pay them (in most cases hundreds of dollars for each post). It's called "boosting" a post, and is mostly for people like me who have a "fan page" which is what all public figures, TV shows, news outlets, and bands use. It has a few more features than standard Facebook pages, such as not having to approve friend requests every time someone follows the page.

My page, at the time I'm writing this has about 500,000 followers. But each status update I post only shows up on a few thousand people's news feeds. This

---

[424] TechCrunch "Senate committee asks Facebook to answer questions about its Trending Topics" by Kate Conger (May 10th 2016)

isn't some conspiracy, it's just a method Facebook uses to generate money by encouraging administrators of fan pages to "boost" their posts, or pay to have them actually show up in the feeds of people who are following the page. For administrators of "fan pages," when we post something, we are alerted with a button that says "boost this post" which takes us to a checkout page showing various prices and the corresponding number of people Facebook will then allow to see the post.

For example to boost a post so that it will reach at least 100,000 of the 500,000 people following my page, the cost is $4,000.[425] That's for *one* status update. I mention this because a lot of people wonder why they miss posts from pages they follow, and this is the reason. You may only be seeing one out of every four posts because of the limitation Facebook puts on the posts that aren't being "boosted."

## Experimenting on Users

Aside from the previously mentioned secret study into Facebook's effectiveness of getting out the vote in the 2010 midterm elections by using 60 million users as unknowing guinea pigs,[426] Facebook has conducted other experiments on its users as well. In 2012 they manipulated the news feeds of 700,000 people by both limiting and boosting the number of positive and negative posts showing up in some people's feeds to determine whether they could alter their moods. They then

---

[425] As of October 9th 2017.

[426] Vox "Facebook's "I Voted" sticker was a secret experiment on its users" by Dara Lind (November 4th 2014)

monitored what those users posted to see if they were either more negative or positive as a result of what they were regularly seeing in their own feeds.[427] All Facebook users actually consent to this kind of manipulation by agreeing to the terms of service when they sign up.[428]

Leaked documents also revealed that Facebook experimented on what they considered to be emotionally vulnerable teenagers who felt "useless."[429] The documents show that the company's algorithms can determine which users are feeling "worthless," "insecure," "useless," "overwhelmed," and other depressed feelings, and then they use this assessment to allow advertisers to target those people with ads for products they think they will be able to get them to buy.[430]

Because of the continued instances of people committing horrific crimes while broadcasting them using Facebook's 'Live' feature, the company is developing an artificial intelligence system to watch live streams in real time, and monitor people's posts in order to remove any 'offensive' or violent content.[431] If their A.I. is able to monitor all posts and live streams in near real time, it opens the door for Orwellian censorship straight out of a

---

[427] The Guardian "Facebook sorry – almost – for secret psychological experiment on users" by Dominic Rushe (October 2nd 2014)

[428] The New York Times "Facebook Tinkers With Users' Emotions in News Feed Experiment, Stirring Outcry" by Vindu Goel (June 29th 2014)

[429] Ars Technica "Report: Facebook helped advertisers target teens who feel "worthless" by Sam Machkovech (May 1st 2017)

[430] Forbes "Facebook Is Helping Brands Target Teens Who Feel "Worthless"" by Paul Armstrong (May 1st 2017)

[431] Washington Post "AI may soon monitor your live videos on Twitter, Facebook" by Karen Turner (July 27th 2016)

science fiction film, because those who control the parameters for having content removed could choose to use the system to prevent the spread of certain political views, as we have already seen with the Trending Topics scandal.

In May of 2017, Facebook hired another 3000 people to monitor live streams, and other posts that are flagged for potentially violent or 'hateful' content in attempts to have such posts removed more quickly.[432]   So there is now a virtual army of moderators ready to not just delete posts or videos, but to shut down livestreams if someone is talking about an issue in a way Facebook deems 'sexist,' 'racist,' 'homophobic,' or any number of buzzwords that indicate 'Thought Crime.'

## A Threat to Free Speech

Relying on Facebook to communicate with friends and family has become a threat to free speech around the world as fewer people actually talk on the phone (let alone meet face to face).  People are now being arrested for 'hate speech' for posting criticism about their government's policies on Facebook.[433]   This isn't just happening in Third World countries or Orwellian dictatorships like Communist China or North Korea; it's

---

[432] Time "Facebook Is Hiring 3,000 Additional Content Monitors After Live-Streamed Murders" by Associated Press (May 3rd 2017)

[433] The Guardian "Man arrested for Facebook posts about Syrian refugees in Scotland" by Libby Brooks (February 16th 2016)

happening in England,[434] Scotland,[435] Germany,[436] Canada,[437] and other supposedly 'free' countries. Facebook also frequently deletes users' posts and locks people out of their accounts (or deletes their accounts entirely) for posting statements critical of illegal immigration, the LGBT agenda, and other policies Leftists are pushing.

These alleged 'terms of service' violations aren't for posting threats, they're for simply criticizing the liberal agenda, or for using certain words that social justice warriors deem 'hateful.' This kind of Orwellian censorship is the equivalent of your phone company listening to every conversation you have, and then turning off your phone if they didn't like what you were saying.

Facebook has deleted several of my posts and locked me out of my account for three days for such 'violations' after I criticized anti-white racism and a bizarre pro-transgender soap commercial. I expect that any day they may just delete my account altogether for what they will claim is a 'serious violation' of their terms of service.

When logging on one morning I was told, "We removed the post because it doesn't follow the Facebook Community Standards," and I found that Facebook had deleted a post I made that was critical of a Dove soap commercial featuring 'Real Moms' which included a

---

[434] Associated Press "In UK, Twitter, Facebook rants land some in jail" by Jill Lawless (November 12, 2012)

[435] Breitbart "UK Police Arrest Man For 'Offensive' Facebook Post About Migrants" by Liam Deacon (February 16th 2016)

[436] BBC "Facebook, Google and Twitter agree German hate speech deal" (December 15th 2015)

[437] Huffington Post "Think Canada Allows Freedom of Speech? Think Again" by Tom Kott (December 19, 2012)

transgender 'woman' holding 'her' new little baby, and the person 'identified' as the child's 'mother' even though he was the biological father. All I did was post a link to a story about the commercial, along with the comment, "Excuse me now while I go grab some Irish Spring to clean up my puke," a sarcastic joke, referencing Irish Spring, a competitor's soap.[438]

People often call this being put in "Facebook Jail" which means you can't log in or post anything for up to 30 days, depending on how many times you've been suspended for 'violating' their terms of service. Facebook has suspended people for simply posting Bible verses that are critical of homosexuality.[439] Other posts critical of illegal immigration, black crime, LGBT extremists, or radical Muslims are regularly deleted as well.[440]

Facebook employees have actually pressured Mark Zuckerberg to delete some of Donald Trump's posts for violating their 'hate speech' rules for his stance on immigration.[441] Again, imagine the phone company canceling your service because they didn't like what you and your friends talked about. That's basically what Facebook and the other social media giants are doing by policing what people post and then shutting down their

---

[438] Breitbart "Facebook Suspends YouTuber for Disliking 'Transgender Mother' Commercial" (April 15th 2017)

[439] Christian Post "Facebook Suspends Christian Homeschool Mom's Account Over Posts Citing Bible on Homosexuality" by Samuel Smith (February 21st 2017)

[440] https://twitter.com/lauren_southern/status/902007443143712768?lang=en

[441] The Wall Street Journal "Facebook Employees Pushed to Remove Trump's Posts as Hate Speech" by Deepa Seetharaman (October 21st 2016)

pages if they feel something is too 'offensive' or violates their terms of service.

Facebook quietly admits censoring content for the Chinese government.[442] The website was banned in China in 2009, so Facebook developed new censorship tools to appease the Communist government there, and so they allowed the website back.[443] The day before Prince William and Kate Middleton's wedding in the UK, Facebook suspended a bunch of pages of people and groups they suspected were going to 'cause trouble' during the event.[444] And Mark Zuckerberg has admitted working with various European countries in order to censor criticism of the mass influx of Muslims into Britain, France, Germany, and Sweden.[445]

Some are calling for Facebook (and other social media services, including search engines like Google) to be treated as public utilities.[446] One of the arguments is that using them in today's society is as necessary as having access to traditional utilities like the telephone, water, electricity, and natural gas.[447]

After the historic flooding in Houston after Hurricane

---

[442] BBC "Facebook 'made China censorship tool'" by Dave Lee (November 23rd 2016)

[443] New York Times "Facebook Said to Create Censorship Tool to Get Back Into China" by Mike Isaac (November 22nd 2016)

[444] The Guardian "Activists claim purge of Facebook pages" by Shiv Malik (April 29th 2011)

[445] The Guardian "Facebook accused of removing activists' pages" by Shiv Malik (April 29th 2011)

[446] Fast Company "Maybe It's Time To Treat Facebook Like A Public Utility" by Cale Guthrie Weissman (May 1st 2017)

[447] Fortune "Steve Bannon Wants to Regulate Facebook and Google as Utilities" by David Z. Morris (July 29th 2017)

Harvey in 2017, many victims took to social media begging to be rescued, posting their address and pictures of the rising floodwater, and many were rescued by local volunteers this way. One may argue that banning people from such sites could put lives at risk, and is one more reason Facebook, Twitter, and other social media services should be considered utilities that can't be shut off just because someone is posting things the companies don't agree with.

## The Future of Facebook

Not only does Facebook want to be the middleman of all Internet traffic, but they're getting into commerce by enabling financial transactions, original content creation like Amazon and Netflix, and they hope to lead the virtual reality revolution. Mark Zuckerberg has even created flying solar-powered Wi-Fi routers to bring the Internet to remote parts of Africa,[448] and envisions a world where instead of physically going to a friend's house to watch a football game, everyone will stay at their own homes and put on their VR headsets to watch television 'together' while communicating with each other through avatars. They're calling it Facebook Spaces.[449]

If you're starting to think Facebook's vision of the future looks like something right out of *The Matrix*, you wouldn't be wrong. Zuckerberg himself says that in 50 years we'll all be "plugged into the Matrix" through his mind-reading machines and using virtual reality headsets

---

[448] CNET "Facebook's self-flying, solar-powered, Wi-Fi airplane nails first flight" by Xiomara Blanco (June 21st 2016)

[449] USA Today "Facebook Spaces is where real and virtual worlds collide" by Edward C. Baig (May 1st 2017)

as part of our daily lives. He said, "I think you're going to be able to capture a thought [and take] what you're thinking or feeling, in its kind of ideal and perfect form in your head, and share that with the world."[450]

Such themes have been explored in science fiction films like *Surrogates* (2009), *eXistenZ* (1999), and *The Thirteenth Floor* (1999), all of which warn about the dangers of this kind of society, but Zuckerberg is determined to make such thing a reality.

---

[450] Washington Post "Here are Mark Zuckerberg's full remarks about how much he'd like to (literally!) read your thoughts" by Caitlin Dewey (June 14th 2016)

# Twitter

Twitter is often the Internet's equivalent of a wall in a gas station's bathroom stall. Anonymous idiots write all kinds of garbage for the sole purpose of entertaining themselves for a few seconds by trying to shock those who read it. It's also a place for people to engage in hate-filled arguments with random people over the latest political or pop culture story that's trending. Twitter is also a way for people to try to get the attention of their favorite (or most hated) celebrities since many of them do engage with their fans there.

Unlike Facebook, (at least at the time I'm writing this) Twitter doesn't have a real name policy and thrives on users being able to remain anonymous so what they say can't be tied to them, where they live, where they work, or their picture. This anonymity encourages people to tweet the most vile, hateful, and threatening things they can imagine while hiding behind their computer (or phone).

Tweets consist of short statements that can't exceed 140 characters and thus Twitter is called a 'micro blogging' site. While people can post lengthy essays on Facebook, Twitter is mostly for very short, often very blunt statements, and is a very fast-paced social networking site with the flow of new tweets never ending.

Despite the mudslinging and constant trolling, somehow (at least at the moment) Twitter does have a measurable influence on our society. It is perhaps best known for what's trending on the site and was the first major social media platform to include a trending topics list. The trending box allegedly shows the list of the top 10 topics that people are tweeting about, and a look at it on any given day reveals what is most important to the people using Twitter. This is usually celebrity gossip, sports entertainment news, or tweets about the latest liberal causes or complaints. Often what's trending on Twitter then gets picked up by mainstream media as a topic they see of interest to report on.

Twitter has become a place where celebrities release public statements on whatever scandal they may be involved in, and random things they say are often turned into meaningless little stories on celebrity gossip sites. As you know, President Trump likes to tweet and often goes on 'Twitter rants' about the media, the Democrats, and Deep State operatives within the government trying to sabotage his administration.

## The Trending Topics

As I covered in the previous chapter, Facebook was exposed for manipulating the trending topics box by not only censoring certain stories and topics from being included on the list, but also artificially inserting topics into the module that they wanted to promote.[451] And knowing what we know about technology and these major social media companies, it would be foolish to think that Twitter doesn't do exactly the same thing. In fact, in a now deleted tweet, a Clinton insider named Peter Daou tweeted to CEO Jack Dorsey asking him to remove "Words That Don't Describe Hillary" from trending,

---

[451] Gizmodo "Former Facebook Workers: We Routinely Suppressed Conservative News" by Michael Nuez (May 9th 2016)

saying that Twitter was, "providing a platform for pure misogyny" by allowing it to stay on the trending list.[452]

When President Obama did a live Q & A with Twitter in 2015 using the hashtag #AskPOTUS [POTUS is short for President of the United States], the CEO asked his team to implement an algorithm to filter out "abusive" tweets that contained the hashtag.[453] A few years later they would roll out this feature for everyone, allowing people to manually input any words, phrases, usernames, and even emojis they want automatically filtered out from their feed.[454] The muting is even case sensitive. For example, you can now literally put the words "President Trump" in your filter, and if someone tweets at you a message that contains those words, you won't even see it.[455]

In June of 2015, when the Supreme Court ruled that gay marriage had to be accepted as legal in all 50 states, the hashtag #LoveWins was instantly trending and included a rainbow heart emoji.[456] Twitter automatically includes a custom emoji when certain hashtags are tweeted if the hashtag is sponsored by a company or an

---

452 Gateway Pundit "Clintonista Complains to Twitter Co-Founder That Hillary-Mocking Hashtag is 'Pure Misogyny'" by Kristinn Taylor (January 26th 2016)

453 FrontPage Magazine "Twitter CEO Ordered Censoring Anti-Obama Tweets" by Daniel Greenfield (August 11th 2016)

454 Ttwitter.com Help Center - Advanced muting options on Twitter

455 Washington Post "Twitter introduces a mute button for trolls as it struggles to fight online abuse" by Hayley Tsukayama (November 15th 2016)

456 Observer "If You Tweet Using #LoveWins, Twitter Will Ad a Rainbow Heart" by John Bonazzo (June 26th 2015)

organization.[457] It appears that President Obama was one of the first people to start using the hashtag, showing that it (along with the custom 'gay' emoji) was preplanned.[458] Twitter even introduced a special Black Lives Matter emoji consisting of the "black power" fist the day after a Black Lives Matter activist shot twelve police officers, killing five of them in an ambush during one of the movement's marches.[459]

It's not just the top trending topics that are manipulated, but also their associated results. When you click on one of the top 10 topics, you are brought to a page that shows what people are led to believe are the top tweets or photos using those hashtags or words in a tweet. In theory, if a tweet has 5,000 likes, then it is one of the first tweets shown in the results for the topic, but this isn't actually the case. It has been documented that what Twitter features as the top results for various trending topics appear to be manipulated at times to cast them in a certain light.

For example when a secret service agent tackled a *Time* magazine photographer at a Trump campaign rally, a photo showing the photographer with his hand grabbing the throat of the agent was the top result connected to the trending topic "Secret Service," but that photo was later

---

[457] TechCrunch "Twitter's Custom Emojis Make Their Debut As An Ad Unit With #ShareACoke" by Drew Olanoff (September 17th 2015)

[458] The Hill "Obama hails ruling: '#LoveWins'" by Jordan Fabian (June 26th 2015)

[459] Town Hall "24 Hours After the Dallas Shooting, Twitter Creates Black Power Symbol" by Justin Holcomb (July 9th 2016)

replaced by another one showing the photographer lying on the ground after having been tackled by the agent.[460]

A Trump rally in Chicago had to be canceled in March of 2016 because an angry mob of violent protesters were getting more out of control by the minute and local police advised the campaign to call off the event. That night "Trump Rally" was the top trend on Twitter, and when it first began trending, all of the top tweets included photos of a bloody police officer who had been smashed in the head with a bottle along with pictures of protesters blocking traffic, but those top results were soon replaced with pictures of KKK rallies and links to news articles attacking Trump.[461]    Many people started tweeting the hashtags #TwitterCensorship or #TwitterCensoring as a result.

While Twitter remains silent on the issue, Instagram openly admits that they delete hashtags and censor certain search results in order to, as they claim, "hide inappropriate content."[462]    Sometimes they just temporarily censor hashtags when a certain topic they feel is "inappropriate" becomes associated with a benign hashtag.  It's not just NSFW (not safe for work) hashtags like #RussianMilf or #Cumfession, that they censor, it has

---

[460] YouTube "Twitter Censoring Photographer Assaulting Secret Service Agent (February 29th 2016)

[461] YouTube: "News of Violent Anti-Trump Protesters Being Censored by Twitter to Manipulate Public Opinion" (March 11th 2006)

[462] Gizmodo "10 Normal Hashtags That Instagram Bans for Some Weird Reason" by Casey Chan (August 26th 2013)

also been hashtags like #Kansas, #AmericanGirl, and even #Brain.[463]

Hillary Clinton's campaign was accused of paying Twitter to inject the hashtag #BernieLostMe into the top trend hoping to erode support for Bernie Sanders during the primaries. The #BernieLostMe hashtag was number one despite having just a few thousand people tweeting it, while other topics that were ranked lower on the list had more than ten times as many people tweeting about them.[464] 'Influencers' are often chosen to simultaneously start tweeting hashtags as part of political propaganda campaigns because their fans will mindlessly follow their lead and can quickly cause certain topics to trend.

Twitter has also allowed disgusting topics to trend like, "Rape Melania,"[465] and #GoldenShowers.[466] The day President Trump was inaugurated, over 12,000 tweets called for his assassination and "Assassinate Trump" trended.[467] The same threats flooded Twitter the day after

[463] Breitbart "The Craziest Hashtags that Instagram Restricts from User Search" by Tom Ciccotta (May 12th 2006)

[464] YouTube.com/MarkDice "Hillary Paid Twitter to Inject Hashtag As Top Trend" (May 18th 2016)

[465] Breitbart "Twitter Allows 'Rape Melania' to Trend After Site Explodes with Trump Assassination Threats" by Katie Mchugh (November 16th 2016)

[466] Mediaite "#GoldenShowers Trends on Twitter Following Unverified Trump Intel Dump" by Justin Baragona (January 10th 2017)

[467] Mashable "Over 12,000 tweets are calling for Trump's assassination. Here's how the Secret Service handles it" by Sasha Lekach (February 2nd 2017)

the election when unhinged liberals couldn't contain their violent hatred for the new president.[468]

## President Trump on Twitter

President Trump's use of Twitter has been called the modern day equivalent of President Franklin D. Roosevelt's fireside chats, when he used the new media of his time — radio — to speak directly to the American people. We really take for granted how amazing most of our technology is today, and before FDR's fireside chats if someone wanted to listen to a president's speech, they had to actually be at an event in person. Instead of Donald Trump going to a radio station, or holding a press conference in the Rose Garden in front of all the different television cameras, he can just pick up his phone and type a message directly to his 30 million Twitter followers.

"Trump's tweets" have become legendary for their bluntness and controversial nature, but the power of him being able to get his message directly to people through Twitter instead of relying on television networks, radio stations, or newspapers to relay it, is truly remarkable. In an interview with *The Financial Times*, he said, "Without the tweets, I wouldn't be here...I have over 100 million followers between Facebook, Twitter [and] Instagram. Over 100 million. I don't have to go to the fake media."[469]

Twitter co-founder Evan Williams actually apologized

---

468 New York Post "Assassination threats against Trump flood Twitter" by Joshua Rhett Miller (November 11th 2016)

469 Financial Times "Trump on Merkel, Twitter and Republican infighting — FT interview" by Lionel Barber, Demetri Sevastopulo and Gillian Tett (April 2nd 2017)

for Twitter's role in getting out his message, and when asked about Trump crediting Twitter with helping him win the election, Williams responded, "It's a very bad thing, Twitter's role in that. If it's true that he wouldn't be president if it weren't for Twitter, then yeah, I'm sorry."[470]

## Banning and Censoring Users

The most popular case of someone being banned from Twitter is when Breitbart's Milo Yiannopoulos was permanently banned after teasing *Saturday Night Live* cast member Leslie Jones about the new all-female remake of *Ghostbusters* which was derided by critics for its gratuitous pro-feminist agenda.[471] Milo tweeted Leslie a link to his review which was published on Breitbart, and the two went back and forth insulting each other.[472] Leslie Jones had her feelings hurt by Milo's 'trolling' which his followers joined in on, and tweeted, "I leave Twitter tonight with tears and a very sad heart. All this cause [sic] I did a movie. You can hate the movie but the shit I got today…wrong."[473]

Twitter CEO Jack Dorsey responded to her saying "Hi Leslie, following, please DM me when you have a moment,"[474] trying to head off the bad PR of having

---

[470] Fox News "Twitter co-founder apologizes for helping elect Trump" (May 21st 2017)

[471] Adweek "Reactions to the All-Female Ghostbusters Trailer Prove It'll Be the Most Polarizing Movie of the Year" by David Grinder (March 3rd 2016)

[472] CNN "Twitter permanently removes Milo Yiannopoulos from its platform" by Sara Ashley O'Brien (July 20th 2016)

[473] https://twitter.com/lesdoggg/status/755271004520349698

[474] https://twitter.com/jack/status/755235268056092672

another celebrity quit Twitter after getting tired of being trolled. Then, even though Milo hadn't threatened her, or used any language that's not commonplace on Twitter, his account was banned. Many were stunned by this because Twitter is mostly known for being a place to trash-talk others. Many saw the ban being politically motivated because Milo had become a vocal critic of social justice warriors and was becoming quite an Internet celebrity.

Even Wikileaks tweeted to CEO Jack Dorsey seeking some answers. First they called him out saying, "Cyber feudalism. @Twitter founder Jack banned conservative gay libertarian @Nero for speaking the 'wrong' way to actress @Lesdoggg."[475]

Jack responded, "@Wikileaks we don't ban people for expressing their thoughts. Targeted abuse & inciting abuse against people however, that's not allowed."[476]

Wikileaks responded, "@Jack Like this?" and included a link to an archive of tweets from Leslie Jones doing just that. She had also said on *Late Night with Seth Meyers* that she uses her fans to go after people on Twitter who say things to her she doesn't like. "And I'll blow you up too, so if you tweet me thinking I'm the only one who's gonna get it, I retweet it so all my followers can see it, and get on your punk [ass]."[477]

Wikileaks continued to press Jack, asking "@Jack Who has access to justice? Many have had vastly worse.

[475] https://twitter.com/wikileaks/status/756206619860561920

[476] https://twitter.com/jack/status/756212232841596928

[477] Late Night with Seth Meyers "How Leslie Jones Handles Her Twitter Haters - Late Night with Seth Meyers "May 12th 2015)

What's the appeal mechanism? What's the transparency of the process?"[478]

They went on, "@Jack Because it appears that a politically aligned famous American actress has access to ban-power that everyone else does not."[479]

They continued, "@Jack It is time @Twitter got out of the censorship/justice game. Let users create communal filter lists if need be."[480]

"@Jack a punitive mechanism leads to a flood of manipulative score settling & eventual defensive pre-emption just like #TurkeyPurge & 1937."[481]

"@Jack We will start a rival service if this keeps up because @Wikileaks & our supporters are threatened by a space of feudal justice."[482]

Jack Dorsey finally responded, "@Wikileaks all fair points. We are working to get here."[483]

Before they had actually banned Milo, Twitter "unverified" his account,[484] removing the coveted blue checkmark found on celebrities' social media accounts which confirm that it is in fact them and not a fan account or someone impersonating them. Having a verified social media account has some prestige to it because the person is seen as popular enough or "important" enough to

---

[478] https://twitter.com/wikileaks/status/756215642597056517

[479] https://twitter.com/wikileaks/status/756216881556643840

[480] https://twitter.com/wikileaks/status/756217834947088384

[481] https://twitter.com/wikileaks/status/756229517371281408

[482] https://twitter.com/wikileaks/status/756230470472433664

[483] https://twitter.com/jack/status/756237056280522752

[484] Business Insider "Twitter 'unverified' the right-wing writer Milo Yiannopoulos and nobody is behaving in a reasonable or sober manner about it" by Jim Edwards (January 10th 2016)

warrant having such special treatment.[485] So unverifying Milo was a step trying to take away from his status and growing popularity.

Meanwhile, countless Black Lives Matter supporters call for killing cops, and crazy liberals repeatedly called for mass shootings at Donald Trump campaign events and for killing white people; and even to assassinate President Trump.[486] Throughout 2016 I documented repeated instances like this on my YouTube channel.[487]

Twitter was sued by an American woman whose husband was killed by an ISIS attack in Jordan where he was working as a contractor for what she alleged was providing material support to terrorists because so many radical Muslims were posting ISIS propaganda. The lawsuit claimed, "Without Twitter, the explosive growth of ISIS over the last few years into the most feared terrorist group in the world would not have been possible."[488] Twitter even verified the account of the Muslim Brotherhood which has been designated a terrorist organization in several countries, and allows an account dedicated to Hamas, the radical Palestinian Sunni-Islamic organization which has almost 50,000 followers.[489]

---

[485] CNBC "Does being verified on Twitter really matter?" by Michelle Castilo (May 19th 2015)

[486] New York Post "Assassination threats against Trump flood Twitter" by Rhett Miller (November 11th 2006)

[487] YouTube.com/MarkDice "Death Threats to Donald Trump" Playlist

[488] USA Today "Twitter sued by widow for alleged aid to ISIL" by Jessica Guynn (January 14th 2016)

[489] https://twitter.com/HamasInfoEn

When rapper Azealia Banks threatened to have Sarah Palin gang raped by a bunch of black men, Twitter didn't penalize her account.[490]   Banks had also bullied and harassed a child actor from the Disney Channel, but again there was no action taken to even temporarily suspend her account.[491]   It was only after she called One Direction singer Zayn Malik a "faggot" that her account was suspended.[492]

Meanwhile, after I posted a meme saying there were only two genders, I was sent an email from Twitter's Support department encouraging me to delete the tweet and saying my account was under review to see if I violated their no "hateful conduct" policy.

James O'Keefe had his account temporarily suspended shortly after he announced he would release a new undercover investigation into a democrat candidate for the U.S. Senate.[493]   O'Keefe's Project Veritas organization would later release damning footage of democrat operatives discussing voter fraud and planning to use stink bombs at an inaugural ball which led to several arrests.[494] The Drudge Report's tweets have been

[490] New York Daily News "Rapper Azealia Banks calls for 'burliest blackest' men to 'run a train' on Sarah Palin, who threatens suit" by Meg Wagner and Nancy Dillon (April 5th 2016)

[491] Metro "Azealia Banks just made another racist dig at 14-year-old Disney star Skai Jackson" by Ann Lee (March 15th 2016)

[492] Vulture "Azealia Banks Has Finally Been Suspended From Twitter" by Dee Lockett (May 12th 2016)

[493] Newsmax "Twitter Suspends Activist James O'Keefe After Posting Clinton Video" by Joe Crowe (October 14th 2016)

[494] Washington Times "Police: Arrested activist featured in Project Veritas inauguration video" by Andrea Noble (January 20th 2017)

censored using the "sensitive content" filter,[495] and at least 32 of Donald Trump's tweets encouraging people to get out the vote in key battleground states like Florida and Wisconsin vanished shortly after he posted them and couldn't be seen unless you had their exact URLs.[496]

Twitter suspended World Net Daily's account for 12 hours because of a tweet including a link to a story they wrote about former DNC chair Donna Brazile allegedly being upset that a private investigator had been hired to look into the murder of Seth Rich. He was a DNC staffer who many suspect may have been the person who leaked DNC insider emails to Wikileaks shortly before the election.[497]

Twitter even suspended the account of a Christian mother for posting 'homophobic' remarks for denouncing an article in *Teen Vogue* instructing kids on how to have anal sex with each other.[498]

Since banning Milo Yiannopoulos caused #FreeMilo to become the number one trend from all his supporters tweeting their criticism of his ban, Twitter began "shadow banning" popular conservative accounts which covertly

---

[495] Breitbart "Twitter Temporarily Censored Drudge Report Tweets Behind 'Sensitive Content' Filter" by Allum Bokhari (March 27th 2017)

[496] Gateway Pundit "TWITTER Censors 32 of Donald Trump's GOTO Battleground Tweets! ...Deletes Another!" by Mike Garcia (October 7th 2017)

[497] World Net Daily "Twitter suspends WND for Seth Rich report" by Bob Unruh (May 24th 2017)

[498] Breitbart "Twitter Bans Christian Mom for Calling Out Teen Vogue's Push of Underage Sodomy" by Thomas D. Williams (September 4th 2017)

limits the visibility of their tweets to others.[499] It's a more subtle way of censoring someone since their account isn't getting shut down and specific tweets aren't causing their account to get suspended, so the tactic of shadow banning quietly restricts the reach that the user has. This seems to be the new preferred method of cracking down on conservatives because this "soft censorship" doesn't raise as many alarms because as you can imagine when a popular user gets suspended, people notice and then start aggressively spreading the word on Twitter about the latest victim of censorship.

Twitter also experimented with locking accounts temporarily if people tweeted profanity to celebrities.[500] They appear to have abandoned this method in favor of enabling mute lists and automatic profanity filters that users can activate which will prevent any tweet with profanity or custom words or phrases of their choice from showing up in their feed.

They also enabled block lists, which have been compiled by different groups, and once added to a person's account automatically block hundreds, or even thousands of users, based on any number of criteria.[501] If someone blocks you, then they won't get any notifications when you tweet to them, and you can't access their feed to see their tweets. Some people I'm blocked by include

---

[499] Breitbart "EXCLUSIVE: Twitter Shadowbanning 'Real and Happening Every Day' Says Inside Source" by Milo Yiannopoulos (February 16th 2016)

[500] The Verge "Twitter is locking accounts that swear at famous people" by Russell Brandom and Casey Newton (February 24th 2017)

[501] Slate "Beware the Blocklists" by David Auerbach (August 11th 2015)

Rosie O'Donnell, CNN's Jim Acosta, actress Leslie Jones, singer John Legend, model Chrissy Teigen, *Tonight Show* band leader Questlove, the DJ Moby, rapper Ice T, Andrew Dice Clay, Amy Schumer, and many more.

## Bots

Twitter admitted to the U.S. Securities and Exchange Commission that they estimated over 23 million of their active user accounts were "bots," or fake accounts run by automated computer programs which then post spam or are used by people who buy followers so they can look more popular than they are.[502]   A later study put the number at almost 48 million bots, or between 10% to 15% of the active accounts on the platform.[503]

A lot of bots have an attractive and scantly clad girl as the profile picture and do nothing other than respond to tweets which use certain keywords by posting a scripted message along with a link to a porn site, or have the porn site linked up on the account's bio hoping to dupe people into visiting it after getting their attention from the bot responding to their tweets. Of course Twitter attempts to detect and shut down these porn bot accounts, but it is an ongoing battle.

After Bruce Jenner announced 'her' new name, someone set up the @She_Not_He bot on Twitter which would tweet a response to anyone who referred to Caitlyn

---

[502] Bloombert "Beware of Twitter Robots Telling People How to Vote by Mark Buchanan" by Mark Buchanan (July 18, 2016)

[503] ZDNet "Twitter has a spam bot problem — and it's getting worse" by Zack Whittaker (April 23rd 2017)

Jenner as a he, to "politely correct" them.[504]  About 10,000 tweets were sent from the account before it was shut down.[505]  This bot was obviously created by a social justice warrior who wanted to defend 'Caitlyn' Jenner and shows how they can be used for propaganda purposes.

Bots are also used by services that sell 'likes' and 'retweets' that some people buy hoping to appear as if they have more 'fans' than they actually do.[506]  In the social media world, how many 'likes' a post has is often seen as a measuring stick of how 'popular' someone is, and people looking to build up their personal "brand" sometimes resort to these deceptive practices by using bots or 'click farms' located in poor countries which literally just pay people to like and retweet things.[507]  The more "engagement" a tweet has, the more likely Twitter's algorithm is to place it at the top of search results for certain keywords or when someone clicks on a link to one of the top ten trending topics.  Unlike bots, click farms use actual humans to do the 'liking' and retweeting, but the effect is the same.  They give the false impression that posts are more popular than they actually are.

The more bots that tweet out a certain keyword or hashtag, the more likely those topics will start trending. So if a person, a political activist group, or a marketing agency wanted a certain topic to show up on the top ten

---

[504] Time "This Twitter Bot Corrects You If You Misgender Caitlyn Jenner" by Matt Vella (June 1st 2015)

[505] BBC "Twitter bot corrects Caitlyn Jenner references from 'he' to 'she'" (June 2nd 2015)

[506] CBS 60 Minutes "Bots have big effect on Scott Pelley's Twitter" (March 24th 2017)

[507] Metro "Behind the big business of selling Twitter followers and Facebook likes" by Haden Smith (February 11th 2014)

trending list, then using bots could likely help make that happen. Then the issue, topic, or wannabe celebrity's name would be brought before the eyes of everyone who happens to look at the trending module.

Brad Hayes, a computer scientist at MIT, explained, "A bot army can be utilized for a number of dishonest purposes, chief amongst them, misrepresenting public sentiment about whichever topics the controller has interest in. If 3 million people started tweeting in favor of or against a particular topic, would it shift public perception? What if those same 3 million people targeted every source you use for information? It's fair to say that this kind of written 'show of force' can certainly alter perceptions."[508]

A Latin American political operative named Andrés Sepúlveda admits he has used bots to influence people in the build-up to major elections in Mexico, Colombia, and Nicaragua. In 2014 he was sentenced to ten years in prison for espionage, using malicious software, and conspiracy, but from his prison cell he gave an interview to Bloomberg News where he said, "When I realized that people believed what the Internet says more than reality, I discovered that I had the power to make people believe almost anything."[509] He concluded, "I worked with presidents, public figures with great power, and did many things with absolutely no regrets because I did it with full

---

[508] New York Daily News "Trump Twitter bots, numbering in millions, could be used to blanket internet with weaponized false info" by Adam Edelman (June 3rd 2017)

[509] Bloomberg "How to Hack an Election" By Jordan Robertson, Michael Riley, and Andrew Willis (March 31st 2016)

conviction and under a clear objective, to end dictatorship and socialist governments in Latin America."[510]

A study at Oxford University in England looked at bots tweeting just before the UK-EU Referendum which resulted in Britain voting to leave the European Union and found that of 300,000 Twitter accounts they included in their study, one percent of them were responsible for one third of all the tweets about the Brexit debate.[511] Such a high level of activity from such a small sample led the researchers to believe that the accounts were run by bots. They said there were some bots tweeting support for Remain, and other bots tweeting support for Brexit.[512]

It's pretty much expected in today's social media world that some marketing firms may use Twitter bots to generate the appearance of "buzz" about the little-known singers or albums they are hired to promote. Bots are most likely used by marketing agencies to promote the albums of some well-known singers and television shows on major networks. One blogger posted screen shots of dozens of Twitter accounts tweeting exactly the same thing at exactly the same time, all promoting Rachel Maddow's show on MSNBC along with the hashtag #Maddow.[513]

---

[510] Ibid.

[511] SSRN "Bots, #Strongerin, and #Brexit: Computational Propaganda During the UK-EU Referendum" by Philip N. Howard and Bence Kollanyi (June 20th 2016)

[512] New Scientist "Beware the Brexit bots: The Twitter spam out to swing your vote" by Chris Baraniuk (June 21st 2016)

[513] NewsBusters "Did Rachel Maddow Use Multiple Fake Twitter Accounts to Boost Her MSNBC Show?" P.J. Gladnick (March 2nd 2013)

To 'trend' on Twitter is seen as a sign of success in the entertainment and news business, and most people would probably do anything to make it happen. Of course Twitter is trying to eliminate the use of bots, but it is unknown how effective they are at filtering them out.

## Correct The Record

A Super PAC supporting Hillary Clinton called Correct the Record, founded by David Brock, who also started the left-wing Media Matters 'watchdog group,' released an army of paid trolls onto the Internet during the 2016 election to tweet and comment on Facebook (and in the comment sections of news websites) about how great Hillary Clinton was, and to respond directly to people criticizing her.

*The Los Angeles Times* noted, "In effect, the effort aims to spend a large sum of money to increase the amount of trolling that already exists online."[514] During the election Trump's support online was tremendous, and his use of Twitter has become a part of the daily news cycles. Bernie Sanders had legions of social media savvy millennials who constantly defended and promoted him online, but Hillary's supporters were much older and didn't use social media or the comment sections of websites, so the Super PAC decided to artificially create the online support for her.

"It is meant to appear to be coming organically from people and their social media networks in a groundswell of activism, when in fact it is highly paid and highly tactical," said Brian Donahue, CEO of Craft Media/

---

[514] Los Angeles Times "Be nice to Hillary Clinton online — or risk a confrontation with her super PAC" by Evan Halper (May 9th 2016)

Digital, a political consulting company.[515] "That is what the Clinton campaign has always been about," he said. "It runs the risk of being exactly what their opponents accuse them of being: a campaign that appears to be populist but is a smokescreen that is paid and brought to you by lifetime political operatives and high-level consultants."[516]

David Brock, the man behind the trolling program, is known for his political dirty tricks, and so this plan was right up his alley. On a side note, Super PACs are prohibited by law from working directly with campaigns and are supposed to be completely independent entities, but Wikileaks emails revealed that Hillary's campaign was working with David Brock's Correct The Record in an apparent violation of federal law.[517]

Actor Tim Robbins, who supported Bernie Sanders, once tweeted, "Dear @CorrectRecord operatives, Thank you for following today's talking points. Your check is in the mail. Signed, @davidbrockdc," in a response to what he thought were replies to his tweets by the paid trolls.[518] He later deleted the tweet. David Karpf, a professor of media and public affairs at George Washington University, appeared to defend the paid trolling effort, saying the Super PAC was, "using the tools they have at

---

[515] Ibid.

[516] Ibid.

[517] The Intercept "Hacked Emails Prove Coordination Between Clinton Campaign and Super PACs" by Lee Fang and Andrew Perez (October 18th 2016)

[518] Los Angeles Times "Be nice to Hillary Clinton online — or risk a confrontation with her super PAC" by Evan Halper (May 9th 2016)

their disposal" and that, "In this day and age of campaigning, they absolutely have to do it."[519]

Unfortunately, that's the society we're living in now, where paid trolls and bots are being used to promote or defend certain causes or political candidates online in order to artificially screw the appearance of what people are thinking and saying on social media. It's truly a Brave New World.

---

[519] Ibid.

# YouTube

YouTube is the second most popular website in the world according to Alexa, the industry standard in web traffic analytics,[520] and it is so large that every minute over 400 hours of video is uploaded there.[521] It was launched in 2005 and for years most people just saw YouTube as a place to post funny cat videos, or "fail" videos of people slipping and falling or getting injured when attempting stupid stunts; but others saw it as a powerful platform to share news and commentary.

Google bought YouTube in 2006 for $1.6 billion dollars,[522] and it quickly became the most popular video sharing site in the world. For years it functioned primarily as a user-generated platform, meaning it hosted amateur videos posted by average every day people. Independent content creators, often called "YouTubers" would soon build huge grass roots followings with very little cost by making videos ranging from vlogs telling stupid stories, product reviews, do it yourself home improvement, and news and commentary. The videos are monetized through Google's AdSense, which places small banner ads on them or short "pre-roll" ads that play before the videos. For each ad that's shown, the creator gets a fraction of a penny. While it's difficult to make enough

[520] http://www.alexa.com/topsites

[521] Tubefilter "YouTube Now Gets Over 400 Hours Of Content Uploaded Every Minute" by Bree Brouwer (July 26th 2015)

[522] New York Times "Google to Acquire YouTube for $1.65 Billion" by Andrew Ross Sorkin and Jeremy W. Peters (October 9th 2006)

money to pay your bills doing this, a few of the top creators earn millions of dollars a year.[523]

As of April 2016 there were over 2000 YouTube channels with at least a million subscribers,[524] and channels like PewDiePie (57 million), Watchmojo (15 million), Ryan's Toys Review (9 million), Philip DeFranco (5 million) and others get more viewers per video than many major television shows.

My channel now has over a million subscribers and other conservative channels have recently been thriving like Next News Network, Infowars, Steven Crowder, Rebel Media, and Paul Joseph Watson. Many young female conservatives have gained large followings as well, like Lauren Southern, Lauren Chen, and Candace Owens.

*The New York Times* lamented, "For the New Far Right, YouTube Has Become the New Talk Radio," saying, "They deplore 'social justice warriors,' whom they credit with ruining popular culture, conspiring against the populace and helping to undermine 'the West.' They are fixated on the subjects of immigration, Islam and political correctness. They seem at times more animated by President Trump's opponents than by the man himself, with whom they share many priorities, if not a style."[525]

---

[523] Forbes "The Highest-Paid YouTube Stars 2016: PewDiePie Remains No. 1 With $15 Million" by Madeline Berg (December 5th 2016)

[524] TubeFilter "There Are Now 2,000 YouTube Channels With At Least One Million Subscribers" By Sam Gutelle (April 4, 2016)

[525] New York Times "For the New Far Right, YouTube Has Become the new Talk Radio" by John Herrman (August 3rd 2017)

YouTube has changed the world. Sociologist Philip N. Howard quoted an Arab Spring activist on the power of YouTube back in 2010 as saying activists used, "Facebook to schedule the protests, Twitter to coordinate, and YouTube to tell the world."[526] This was before Facebook (and Twitter) enabled users to upload and share videos directly there as well, and while we may now take for granted the ability to upload videos online and share them with the world, YouTube first put this power in the hands of ordinary people, and it was truly revolutionary.

The mega-viral *Kony 2012* video, which received over 100 million views, was credited with encouraging the U.S. Senate to introduce a resolution against African warlord Joseph Kony, which they did just two weeks after the video was posted.[527]

A YouTube video is even said to have cost Mitt Romney the 2012 election after his comments at a $50,000 per plate dinner were secretly recorded by a bartender at the event, where Romney complained that 47% percent of Americans would never vote for him because they're dependent on the government for handouts.[528] That video was posted on YouTube just a month and a half before the election and immediately went viral, changing the entire tone.

While it started as primarily a user-generated content platform, once major corporations realized the power of YouTube, they started focusing on getting in on the

---

[526] The Guardian "Egypt five years on: was it ever a 'social media revolution'? " by Maeve Shearlaw (January 25th 2016)

[527] CBS News "Congress pushes to raise reward for Joseph Kony" by Associated Press (April 18th 2012)

[528] Bloomberg "Today, Mitt Romney Lost the Election" by Joshua Barrow (September 17th 2012)

action. It took a while for major media companies to see the potential and significance of it, but eventually the major news and entertainment networks began using the platform and were given favoritism and special features by YouTube, like anti-piracy monitoring (Content ID), and the ability to edit videos after they were already posted.[529] The home page now mostly consists of corporate sponsored videos, and what was once a community of small and independent video producers has been completely hijacked by the big media corporations.

As with Facebook and Twitter, YouTube has a Trending tab which features the *supposedly* most watched videos of the day, but just a quick look at the ranking of the videos and the amount of views they have can tell you that their Trending section is censored and manipulated too, or as a YouTube spokesman calls it, "a little human curation."[530] A brief look at the tab on most days shows many videos which hardly have any views but are manually placed on the list, hoping to artificially cause them to go viral because they promote political or social agendas that YouTube wants to further.

YouTube has also admitted that they manipulate the search results for certain topics to favor news reports from mainstream media channels over regular, independent ones.[531] They did this to put "more reliable and trustworthy" videos at the top of the page after

---

[529] Rolling Stone "Katy Perry Removes Islamic Symbol From 'Dark Horse' Clip After Protest" by Kory Grow (February 27th 2017)

[530] Venture Beat "YouTube's new trending tab shows you viral videos 'as they take off'" by Harrison Weber (December 9th 2015)

[531] USA Today "YouTube alters algorithm after searches for Las Vegas shooting turn up conspiracy theories" by Jessica Guynn (October 5th 2017)

"conspiracy" videos populated the top spots for certain searches.[532] Previously, the most-watched videos, or videos with the most engagement (comments and likes) were the top search results, no matter what channel they were from, but that is no longer the case. YouTube is now playing favorites with the major media companies, even if their videos barely have any views.

## Not Just Entertainment Anymore

While most people just saw YouTube as a place to upload funny videos of their pets or their kids (remember *Charlie Bit My Finger?*), others saw the amazing power in being able to upload news segments so they could email the links to their friends — and when social media would come on the scene, share them there as well. There were also people like myself who started making our own videos giving our analysis of current events and uploading them to share our thoughts with anyone who would watch.

When I first got started making YouTube videos in 2006, smartphones didn't have video cameras in them, so the only people making YouTube videos were those who had camcorders, and to make the videos look and sound like they weren't shot in your basement, you had to have lighting kits, external microphones, and editing software; all of which cost money. Today a single smartphone has a high enough quality camera and microphone for anyone to record a vlog or an interview, and it looks and sounds pretty good, but in the early days of YouTube it took some

---

[532] The Verge "YouTube changes search algorithms after misinformation during Las Vegas shooting" by Thuy Ong (October 6th 2017)

equipment, money, and know-how to be able to make videos.

Now anyone with a cellphone can record a high quality video of anything — from a protest, or an interview with someone, to just a simple commentary on a current event, and it can be seen by just as many people as something that airs on the major television networks. What once took millions of dollars of equipment and infrastructure, not to mention a staff of skilled people, can now be accomplished by one person using a device that fits in the palm of their hand.

As YouTube "stars" got larger followings than many actors on network television, the sharks smelled blood in the water, and began circling. The Hillary Clinton campaign began recruiting YouTubers to encourage their audience to support her in the 2016 election since they had so much influence over their fans. *Vanity Fair* wrote, "The Clinton Campaign Deploys Its Secret Weapon: YouTubers," and pointed out that they recruited three popular YouTubers to help her appeal to voters in swing states just a week and a half before the election.[533]

The Clinton campaign got YouTubers to make endorsement videos for her in Pennsylvania, Ohio, and Florida. One of the videos, shot by Todrick Hall, who has two and a half million subscribers, consisted of him "surprising" a fan of his who said she wasn't sure if she was voting, so he decided to visit her and encourage her to vote for Hillary Clinton. "I'm partnering with Hillary Clinton for America, because I want everybody to come

---

[533] Vanity Fair "The Clinton Campaign Deploys Its Secret Weapon: YouTubers" by Richard Lawson (October 27th 2016)

out and vote, and I want everyone to make the right vote, and I believe the right vote is Hillary Clinton," he said.[534]

Another YouTuber, GloZell Green, who has 4.5 million subscribers but can barely get 20,000 views on a video because her novelty skits of eating gross foods quickly wore off, also posted a video which consisted of her meeting a "super fan" to talk to her about why she should vote for Hillary Clinton.[535] Barack Obama also met with YouTubers hoping to help Hillary. He sat down for live interviews with several popular YouTubers, one of which was also GloZell Green, who is best known for taking a bath in a tub full of milk and cereal.[536] While many YouTubers aren't household names, their fans can be very dedicated and easily influenced, which is why both Hillary and Obama tried to tap into their audiences.

As independent content creators began dominating the platform and amassing huge followings of millions of people, all while working from their basement or bedroom; the "powers that be" got so concerned that their information monopoly was collapsing, they had to do something to stop it. When channels like mine and Alex Jones, and Next News Network are getting more viewers than CNN, MSNBC, and other major 'news' networks, you know that industry insiders are panicking, not only because they're losing millions of viewers, but because they're losing the ability to control the narrative surrounding major issues.

---

[534] TodRickHall "We're #StrongerTogether" (October 27th 2016)

[535] GloZell Green "#StrongerTogether Super Fan Cereal Surprise! - GloZell" (October 27th 2016)

[536] Washington Times "Obama slammed for YouTube talks with GloZell, a woman who ate cereal from tub" by Cheryl Chumley (January 23rd 2015)

Censorship is a problem that slowly kept creeping up on YouTube in the form of giving channels "Community Guidelines strikes" and deleting videos their moderators thought constituted 'hate speech' or 'bullying,' but as channels like mine began getting millions of views a week, YouTube began to regret the 'monsters' that they helped to create, and new Orwellian censorship tactics were implemented.

## YouTube is Over Party

Philip DeFranco, a popular YouTuber with over five million subscribers, posted a video titled "YouTube is Shutting Down My Channel and I'm Not Sure What to Do About It" on August 31st 2016 which started the "YouTube is Over Party" sarcastic hashtag to trend on social media from people talking about the new restrictions on content being rolled out. YouTubers like myself had noticed our videos were getting regularly demonetized — meaning no advertisements were allowed to run on them if they included certain keywords in the title or description. Words like 'war,' '9/11,' 'police shooting,' 'ISIS,' 'terrorism,' 'sex,' 'drugs,' etc. It didn't matter the context, they automatically got demonetized, but you wouldn't notice unless you looked closely at the analytics since there was no notification about it.

What brought this to Philip DeFranco's attention was that YouTube finally started emailing people when their videos were demonetized instead of just doing it without notice. One's first thought to get around this would be to just avoid using certain keywords in the titles, descriptions and tags of videos, and that solved the problem — at least for a little while — but YouTube's system kept getting more sophisticated by the day and now appears to analyze the transcripts of all videos uploaded. In 2009 YouTube began using voice recognition software and creating automatic transcripts for videos, and while not being 100% accurate, it is eerie to see that YouTube knows what the people in a video are saying because their servers are now "listening" to every word that is said in every video.[537]

## PewDiePie Under Attack

A few months after the 'YouTube is Over' demonetization scare, the *Wall Street Journal* would target YouTube's biggest channel, PewDiePie, which has over 57 million subscribers, and claim he's making money by posting 'racist' and 'anti-Semitic' videos. PewDiePie, whose real name is Felix Kjellberg, is a 27-year-old guy from Sweden who started off as a "gamer" (a person who literally plays video games while other people watch) and later branched out into comedy skits and social commentary, and is a huge star rivaling many Hollywood A-listers in terms of popularity.

"Disney Severs Ties With YouTube Star PewDiePie After Anti-Semitic Posts," was the *Wall Street Journal's* headline where they boasted that they asked Disney about videos of his which they claimed included "Anti-Semitic jokes or Nazi imagery"[538] Their story cast him in a false light and gave the impression that he might be racist or

---

537 Google Blog "Automatic Captions in YouTube (November 19th 2009)

538 Wall Street Journal "Disney Severs Ties With YouTube Star PewDiePie After Anti-Semitic Posts" by Rolfe Winkler, Jack Nicas, and Ben Fritz (February 14th 2017)

anti-Semitic because of some jokes he made in his videos. *The Wall Street Journal* even put out a video of their own to accompany their story which showed PewDiePie dressed as a soldier sitting in front of his computer watching an Adolf Hitler speech while smiling and nodding in agreement. What they failed to mention was this scene was from a skit he shot in response to previous false claims by the mainstream media which accused him of being racist, so he made the Hitler video as a joke making fun of their ridiculous claims.

This *Wall Street Journal* article on PewDiePie poured gasoline on what were just smoldering embers, and it blew up into a huge forest fire that would be used as a token example that advertisements for major brands were being shown on YouTube videos that were 'racist,' 'inappropriate' or 'offensive.' *Wired* magazine then ran the headline, "PewDiePie Was Always Kinda Racist, But Now He's a Hero to Nazis,"[539] and when they tweeted out the link they added the comment, "White supremacists have a new hero, and his name is PewDiePie."[540] After facing major backlash from their defamatory title, they later changed it to "PewDiePie's fall shows the limits of 'LOL JK.'"[541]

His original series *Scare PewDiePie* on YouTube Red (a subscription service similar to Netflix) was immediately canceled, and YouTube pulled his channel from their premium advertiser program costing him a

---

[539] http://archive.is/U9QDe

[540] https://twitter.com/wired/status/832237289795354624?lang=en

[541] https://twitter.com/Sharp_tK/status/832312667771633664

massive drop in income.[542]    Major YouTubers rallied behind him showing support, including Jewish ones,[543] but the war against YouTubers was just beginning.

## News Channels Targeted

BuzzFeed, the infamous clickbait bottom feeders of the Internet, published an article titled, "How YouTube Serves As The Content Engine Of The Internet's Dark Side," pressuring YouTube to start demonetizing videos about 'conspiracy theories.'[544]    The story began, "Everyone knows that Twitter and Facebook spread bad information and hate speech.  But YouTube, which pays for conspiracy theories seen by millions, may be even worse."[545]

They named one particular conspiracy channel with 150,000 subscribers and said that, "His videos, usually preceded by pre-roll ads for major brands like Quaker Oats and Uber, have been watched almost 18 million times, which is roughly the number of people who tuned in to last year's season finale of NCIS, the most popular show on television."[546]

BuzzFeed continued, "In the aftermath of the 2016 presidential election, the major social platforms, most

---

[542] Variety "YouTube Cancels PewDiePie Show, Pulls Channel From Ad Program After His 'Death to All Jews' Stunt" by Todd Spangler (January 14th 2017)

[543] Ibid.

[544] BuzzFeed "How YouTube Serves As The Content Engine Of The Internet's Dark Side" by Joseph Bernstein (February 24th 2017)

[545] Ibid.

[546] Ibid.

notably Twitter, Facebook, and Reddit, have been forced to undergo painful, often public reckonings with the role they play in spreading bad information...And yet there is a mammoth social platform, a cornerstone of the modern Internet with more than a billion active users every month, which hosts and even pays for a fathomless stock of bad information, including viral fake news, conspiracy theories, and hate speech of every kind — and it's been held up to virtually no scrutiny: YouTube."[547]

The article goes on to complain about what they called the "conspiracy-industrial complex" on the Internet, "which has become a defining feature of media and politics in the Trump era," and says it "would be a very small fraction of itself without YouTube."[548]

They said the Internet's biggest "conspiracy-news stars" live on YouTube and named a few channels like Alex Jones, Paul Joseph Watson, and Sargon of Akkad. The writer then reminisces about the good old days of YouTube, but says, "Today, it fills the enormous trough of right-leaning conspiracy and revisionist historical content into which the vast, ravening right-wing social Internet lowers its jaws to drink."[549]

"Frequently, the videos consist of little more than screenshots of a Reddit 'investigation' laid out chronologically, set to ominous music," he says. "Other times, they're very simple, featuring a man in a sparse room speaking directly into his webcam, or a very fast

---

[547] Ibid.

[548] Ibid.

[549] Ibid.

monotone narration over a series of photographs with effects straight out of iMovie."[550]

The articles goes on to lament, "Sometimes, these videos go hugely viral," and mentions a few including one that is critical of the mass immigration of Muslims into Europe which had been viewed over 4 million times. "That's roughly as many people as watched the *Game of Thrones* Season 3 premiere," it says.[551]  "So what responsibility, if any, does YouTube bear for the universe of often conspiratorial, sometimes bigoted, frequently incorrect information that it pays its creators to host, and that is now being filtered up to the most powerful person in the world?"[552]

It concludes by asking, "But morally and ethically, shouldn't YouTube be asking itself the same hard questions as Facebook and Twitter about the role it plays in a representative democracy?  How do those questions change because YouTube is literally paying people to upload bad information?"[553]

Alex Jones' channel, which has over 2 million subscribers, was then targeted by Media Matters hoping to get all advertisements removed.  They wrote up an entire article titled, "Google Is Funding Alex Jones' Harassment And Hate On YouTube" where they claimed his videos, "often violate YouTube's policies for its advertising partners," and "frequently appear with ads for brands such

---

[550] Ibid.

[551] Ibid.

[552] Ibid.

[553] Ibid.

as Trivago, PlayStation, and a corporation that is contracted by the state of Hawaii to promote tourism."[554]

They went on to say, "Jones has also made numerous disparaging comments about LGBTQ people," and that, "He has also said that Chelsea Clinton looks like Mister Ed the Horse and made numerous other sexist comments about women and their looks."[555] They concluded, "It would appear to be consistent with YouTube's existing policies to pull advertising from Jones' videos. If YouTube fails to take action, advertisers can request to have their ads removed from videos appearing on Jones' channel."[556]

## Advertisers Boycott "Offensive Content"

After *The Wall Street Journal* was done investigating PewDiePie and falsely claimed he was posting 'racist and 'anti-Semitic' videos, they continued searching for 'offensive' content that had advertisements on it. They found two racist videos from unknown random channels which were monetized and had Coca-Cola ads running before they played, and instead of just doing a story about this, they contacted Coca-Cola to get a statement from them, or as many believe, to bully the company into pulling their advertising from YouTube.

Jack Nicas, who wrote the story, appeared to brag on Twitter, saying, "Google has lost $26B in market value

---

[554] Media Matters "Google Is Funding Alex Jones' Harassment And Hate On YouTube" by Brennan Suen and Katie Sullivan (March 27th 2017)

[555] Ibid.

[556] Ibid.

over this ad controversy in the past week."[557]   And later tweeted, "Update: Coca-Cola is pulling all non-search ads with Google in response to our story. Two separate Coke ads played before this racist video."[558]

*The Daily Mail* opined that, "Netflix, Guess, Trivago, Opodo, Asus and SunLife insurance have adverts alongside videos published by conspiracy theorists on Google's YouTube platform."[559]   *The Guardian* then reported, "PepsiCo, Walmart Stores and Starbucks on Friday confirmed that they have also suspended their advertising on YouTube after the *Wall Street Journal* found Google's automated programs placed their brands on five videos containing racist content. AT&T, Verizon, Johnson & Johnson, Volkswagen and several other companies pulled ads earlier this week."[560]

Walmart released a statement saying, "The content with which we are being associated is appalling and completely against our company values."[561]   AT&T said, "We are deeply concerned that our ads may have appeared alongside YouTube content promoting terrorism and hate. Until Google can ensure this won't happen again, we are

---

[557] https://twitter.com/jacknicas/status/845405516306116608

[558] https://twitter.com/jacknicas/status/845383192274092032

[559] Daily Mail "Jihadi terror manuals on how to use a car as a 'tool of war' for mass murder can be found in just two minutes on Google and Twitter" by Paul Bently, Glen Keough, and Sam Greenhill (March 23rd 2017)

[560] The Guardian "Starbucks and Walmart join growing list of advertisers boycotting YouTube" (March 25th 2017)

[561] Ibid.

removing our ads from Google's non-search platforms."[562]

Of course, these same brands don't have a problem advertising on network television or cable shows that glorify crime, sex, and drugs. When CNN goes to a commercial after breaking news about the latest mass shooting or terrorist attack, these brands don't have a problem being associated with that. Local news stations across the country report on horrific crimes like rape, child abuse, and murder every single night, and then casually cut to a commercial paid for by these same mega corporations.

Since cable news channels have many of the same advertisers which are used as pre-roll ads before YouTube videos, why are companies okay with running their ads on graphic and disturbing stories on cable news and adult dramas, but not on smaller independent YouTube channels? Another "investigation" into the matter by *The Australian Financial Review* reported, "a number of local companies — including Holden, Kia, Wesfarmers-owned hardware retailer Bunnings and electronics chain JB Hi-Fi — had video advertisements playing in front of men's rights and anti-feminist content on YouTube."[563] It appears they contacted Kia to tattle, and the company's spokesman said, "As of now, programmatic advertising has been suspended until such time as we can meet with

---

[562] Advertising Age "Now AT&T Halts YouTube Ad Buys Over Brand Safety Concerns" (March 22nd 2017)

[563] Australian Financial Review "Holden and Kia pull ads from YouTube as Google boycott widens" by Max Mason (March 26th 2017)

Google to further clarify the application of this advertising."[564]

*The Financial Review's* report said, "The series of videos by one YouTube user centered around a men's rights movement known as MGTOW (Men Going Their Own Way) — a group of straight men who will not date women and believe feminism has ruined society...One included an edited segment from Ten Network's Studio 10 that showed an interview with controversial author Peter Lloyd, who wrote the book *Stand by Your Manhood*. The video insults the Ten hosts, including calling former Australian of the Year Ita Buttrose a 'hag.'"[565]

It's completely understandable that companies wouldn't want their ads to run on ISIS propaganda videos, or porn, but these isolated instances of 'racist' videos being monetized that were dug up by the papers caused the entire Ad Sense program to be put under a microscope. For over a decade since the monetization program had been put in place YouTube was like the wild west, where (within reason) just about any video could be monetized and advertisers didn't care about the content, but almost overnight all that changed.

## New Advertising Policies

Google's chief business officer Philipp Schindler explained that, "It has always been a small problem" with a "very very very" few number of ads being shown on videos that aren't "brand-safe" but "over the last few weeks, someone has decided to put a bit more of a spotlight on the problem."[566]

A Google spokesperson said that the error rate was less than 1/1000th of a percent, meaning that their algorithms automatically identified most racist or 'objectionable' content and wouldn't place advertisements on it.[567] But YouTube immediately announced that changes were coming to the platform and they would begin removing advertisements on all 'non advertiser-friendly' content (like mine). They posted a letter for their advertisers saying, "Recently, we had a number of cases where brands' ads appeared on content that was not aligned with their values. For this, we deeply apologize. We know that this is unacceptable to the advertisers and agencies who put their trust in us. That's why we've been conducting an extensive review of our advertising policies and tools, and why we made a public commitment last week to put in place changes that would give brands more control over where their ads appear."[568]

"We know advertisers don't want their ads next to content that doesn't align with their values. So starting today, we're taking a tougher stance on hateful, offensive and derogatory content. "This includes removing ads more effectively from content that is attacking or harassing people based on their race, religion, gender or similar categories. This change will enable us to take action, where appropriate, on a larger set of ads and sites."

---

[566] RedCode "Google says its YouTube ad problem is 'very very very small' but it's getting better at fixing it anyway" by Peter Kafka (April 3rd 2017)

[567] Ibid.

[568] Google Blog "Expanded Safeguards for Advertisers" by Phillip Schindler (March 21st 2017)

It concluded saying, "The YouTube team is taking a hard look at our existing community guidelines to determine what content is allowed on the platform — not just what content can be monetized."[569]

And then the mass demonetization began. On March 29th 2017, Ethan Klein of H3H3 Productions, a channel with over 3 million subscribers, tweeted that, "YouTube has demonetized everything from 'Vape Nation' to 'Thank You for 3 million' with no notification and no option to appeal."[570]  Jenna Marbles, who has over 17 million subscribers, responded "I've also had a bizarre selection of videos demonetized with no notification or option to appeal."[571]

YouTubers large and small began posting screen shots showing their videos had been demonetized in bulk, along with screen shots of emails from YouTube rejecting their appeals. Internet sensation Diamond and Silk, the duo of African American sisters who post videos supporting Donald Trump, reported that 95% of their videos were demonetized.[572]

My revenue dropped 90% and at the time I had just under one million subscribers, so you can imagine how much the smaller channels were hurt by this. The mass-demonetization just kept coming as YouTube implemented new algorithms to search through older videos and demonetizing them. As Patreon co-founder

---

[569] Google Blog Post "Expanded Safeguards for Advertisers" by Philipp Schindler - Chief Business Officer. (March 21st 2017)

[570] https://twitter.com/h3h3productions/status/847200160560140288

[571] https://twitter.com/Jenna_Marbles/status/847202902837829632

[572] Washington Times "Diamond and Silk rip YouTube, say 95% of videos demonetized over Trump support" by Douglas Ernst (August 10th 2017)

and CEO Jack Conte said, "It sucks that it's 2017 and you've got creators with millions of fans getting paid a few hundred bucks a month. That sucks."[573]

Patreon is a new website where viewers can support their favorite YouTubers by chipping in a dollar a month or whatever they want in order to supplement the loss of revenue from the issues with demonetization, so if you enjoy watching my videos, I hope you'll look me up there or visit my page at Patreon.com/MarkDice.

Videos that talk about certain subjects are now automatically demonetized the moment they're uploaded since the autogenerated transcripts allow YouTube to know exactly what is being said in the videos themselves, so if people avoid certain titles, descriptions, or tags hoping to slip past their system, that will no longer work.

And while I've had tons of videos demonetized for "not being advertiser friendly," videos on big liberal channels like The Young Turks or CNN and MSNBC which cover the same story are often still allowed to be monetized. Not to mention trash channels BuzzFeed and Feminist Frequency.

## YouTube Removing Videos

Aside from just demonetizing videos and not letting them earn any revenue for the person who posts them, YouTube often just removes videos completely, claiming they violate their terms of service or places them in a

---

[573] Interview with The Rubin Report on YouTube (Streamed July 31st 2017) titled "Patreon CEO Jack Conte LIVE: Lauren Southern, IGD, and Free Speech"

"limited state" so you can only watch them if you have the exact URL because they don't show up in searches.[574]

The Colin Flaherty channel has had multiple videos removed which show anti-white hate crimes being committed by blacks.[575] Another channel had a video removed which showed a compilation of women violently assaulting men to show that domestic violence isn't just a one way street and that women do in fact attack men.[576] A University of Toronto professor, Jordan Peterson, who refuses to acknowledge transgender people by their "preferred pronouns" had his entire channel removed without explanation.[577] Prager University's videos were age restricted, meaning only people 18 or older could watch them, even though they just talk about politics, economics, and science from a conservative perspective.[578]

YouTube locked one of my videos on private so nobody could watch it, saying that it was "deceptive." The video was actually me exposing how deceptive CNN

---

[574] Engadget "YouTube will isolate offensive videos that don't violate policies" by Mallory Locklear (August 1st 2017)

[575] World Net Daily "YouTube bans proof of black-on-white violence" (August 15th 2015)

[576] Red Pill Philosophy "CENSORED By YouTube/Facebook: WATCH the Viral "Anti-Feminist Gender Equality" Video" by Chris Delamo (November 24th 2015)

[577] Washington Times "Jordan B. Peterson's YouTube account locked during biblical lecture series: 'No explanation'" by Douglas Ernst (August 1st 2017)

[578] Washington Times "YouTube muzzles PragerU's conservative content, group 'no option but to go public'" by Douglas Ernst (October 11th 2016)

is, so the censorship couldn't be more ironic."[579]  I've also had videos placed on age-restricted status, and the channel is under a constant threat of receiving "community guideline" strikes and being shut down (again) completely.   My entire channel and all of my videos were deleted in 2014.[580]  At the time I had 265,000 subscribers, and only after a wave of public pressure and me luckily being able to reach one of the heads of their news division did they restore everything.

Videos showing black teens attacking random white people, a viral trend known as 'polar-bear hunting' to the thugs, are often removed for what the site claims are violations of their policy against posting violent content. Author Colin Flaherty has documented black on white violence for years to raise awareness of the problem and YouTube regularly removes his videos despite them being posted not to glorify violence, but to show people one of the problems plaguing many communities.   If people aren't able to see what kind of anti-white hate crimes are happening on the streets in cities like Baltimore, St. Louis, Milwaukee, and others, how will people know to take precautions?

YouTube even deleted a video of mine about an anti-white hate crime, in which a black man shot up a predominantly white church in Tennessee to get 'revenge' for when white supremacist Dylann Roof did the same thing to a black church two years earlier in Charleston,

---

[579] Infowars "YouTube CENSORS Video For Criticizing CNN" by Paul Joseph Watson (July 19th 2017)

[580] Infowars "YouTube Censors Major Anti-Obama Channel" by Paul Joseph Watson (March 23rd 2014)

South Carolina.[581]   Not only was mainstream media ignoring the story, but then my video on it (which got over 300,000 views in 48 hours) was censored and a penalty placed on my channel in the form of a Community Guidelines strike.   I appealed the removal, and after it was further reviewed, the video was restored, but the fact that the moderators took it down in the first place shows how vulnerable YouTube videos are to political censorship.   YouTube has also deleted viral videos from black conservatives who criticized the Black Lives Matter movement, claiming they violate their terms of service.[582]

Many videos are also automatically deleted without issuing the channels which post them a "community guidelines violation" by identifying them through the Content ID system, which scours through all videos to find specific clips using visual and audio printing technology and removes them without warning and with no recourse to have them restored.   Hollywood studios use the Content ID feature to have clips of TV shows and movies automatically blocked, sometimes even if they're used in accordance with fair use laws.[583]

Liberals love to claim YouTube is a "private business" and say they can decide what to allow on their site and what not to, but when a Christian bakery refuses to use their artistic talent to make a special gay wedding cake with two men painted in frosting or saying

[581] New York Times "Suspect in Tennessee Church Shooting Cited Revenge for Charleston Massacre" by Serge F. Kovaleski and Alan Blinder (September 29th 2017)

[582] https://twitter.com/RedPillBlack/status/903027170460803072

[583] Variety "Despite YouTube's Emmy, Google Still Has a Long Way to Go" by Todd Spanger (October 24th 2013)

"Congratulations Adam and Steve," then liberals want that business sued and shut down for 'discrimination.'[584]

Gays cried 'censorship' after they noticed many LGBT videos were placed on restricted mode, which is meant to filter out adult content for parents, schools, and public libraries.[585] They posted videos about strange gay sex practices and then complained when YouTube didn't allow them to be seen by children. As a result, YouTube apologized and 'fixed' their algorithm so that the adult content filter would ignore most LGBT videos so kids can now watch them.[586]

Transgender activist Riley Dennis, who argues that women can have penises and says people are 'transphobic' if they don't want to have sex with trannies,[587] made a Facebook post on March 5th 2017 saying 'she' "Spent the entire day watching videos of people calling me a stupid regressive snowflake tranny faggot retarded SJW, so that I could compile a list of channels that harass me, so I can make the argument to YouTube that we have to do something about it."[588]

'She' then proceeded to report the videos to YouTube alleging they were 'bullying her' and there were reports

---

[584] The Oregonian "Christian bakers take fight over same-sex wedding cake to Oregon appeals court" by Casey Parks (March 2rd 2017)

[585] USA Today "YouTube under fire for LGBTQ video filtering" by Jefferson Graham (March 20th 2017)

[586] CNET "YouTube apologizes for blocking LGBT videos" by Kate Collins (March 20th 2017)

[587] The Blaze "Transgender 'feminist' lays down the law: 'Some women have penises'" by Dave Urbanski (March 23rd 2017)

[588] Cowger Nation "EXPOSED: Screenshot from Riley's private Facebook reveals he engages in censorship" by Hunter Avallone (April 1st 2017)

that the videos were then removed.[589] So just criticizing a radical transgender activist on YouTube is now considered to be 'hate speech' or 'bullying.' Of course, liberals can post videos saying the most hateful things one can imagine about Christians, and that's celebrated as 'free speech' (which it is), but that same protection does not exist the other way around.

In 2015, a Christian singer named Joyce Bartholomew sued YouTube after they removed one of her music videos of her singing a song with a pro-life theme. The video, titled *What Was Your Name*, was uploaded to YouTube in April of 2014 and quickly gained over 50,000 views but then YouTube removed it claiming it violated their terms of service. She sued them for defamation, arguing that by YouTube saying she violated their terms of service when she did not, they had damaged her reputation by making false statements about her.[590] The video was later re-uploaded, and at the time I'm writing this, has over 500,000 views.[591]

Singer Elton John and his 'husband' were involved in a sex scandal in the UK when it came to light that their 'marriage' was really just a sham and that they had engaged in threesomes with other men.[592] And after news of this broke in the British tabloids, Elton John got a court

---

[589] Cowger Nation "Riley J. Dennis: His disturbing control over the Internet." by Hunter Avallone (March 17th 2017)

[590] LifeSiteNews "Youtube banned this powerful pro-life music video. Then the artist sued" by Pete Baklinski (December 18th 2015)

[591] https://www.youtube.com/watch?v=6zQOV3GSWfM

[592] Daily Mail "Injunction farce deepens as German and Spanish media name married celebrity who had threesome in their reports on how he CAN'T be identified over here" (by Keiligh Baker and Martin Robinson (May 19th 2016)

order to block every news outlet in England from reporting on the story.[593]

After I posted a YouTube video about the legal threats I received after tweeting about the censorship, the video was soon blocked in the UK as well. Fans from England sent me screenshots showing my video was blocked in their region after they clicked on the link I posted on my Facebook page. Anyone living in the UK who went directly to my YouTube channel (YouTube.com/MarkDice) just simply didn't see the video at all. It's an ongoing battle for many of us YouTubers to keep our videos (and our entire channels) from being deleted. I wasn't given any warning for this, but since I was aware that Elton John was silencing the media in the UK, and having Twitter send out legal threats to people tweeting about it, it was pretty clear what was happening.[594]

People and companies often abuse YouTube's copyright policy and file DMCA [Digital Millennium Copyright Act] takedown notices on peoples' videos when they include clips of their content for purposes of criticism, which is fully allowed under fair use laws, but sometimes people file these false copyright claims in attempts to have the criticism removed.[595] Various social justice warriors have been accused of filing false DMCA claims against their critics, and even some videogame

---

[593] The Telegraph "Celebrity 'threesome' identities revealed across the globe but Supreme Court still considering case - everything you need to know" by Tom Morgan, Nicola Harley, and David Barrett (April 27th 2016)

[594] TechDirt "Why Is Twitter Sending Legal Letters Warning People About Tweeting About The Gagged Topic Of A 'Celebrity Threesome'" by Mike Masnick (May 20th 2016)

[595] Channel Awesome "Where's The Fair Use? - Nostalgia Critic" (February 16th 2016)

developers have been accused of abusing DMCA takedowns to have negative reviews of their games deleted.[596]

## The Future of YouTube

It is possible that the constant pushback against the politically correct 'Thought Police' may eventually cause advertisers and YouTube to loosen their restrictions on 'offensive' or 'controversial' content, but it's an uphill battle and one that at this point we are losing by a landslide. The days of most smaller conservative YouTubers being able to make a living using the website is probably a thing of the past.[597] And even for larger channels like mine, it's a constant struggle.

You may be wondering, 'doesn't YouTube need to make money from advertisers?' 'Wouldn't demonetizing so many videos cost them money as well?' At this point there may be so many 'brand friendly' videos that it won't matter to YouTube if they don't run ads on channels like mine, because there are so many others available that they see as being 'safe.' It also appears that YouTube has changed its revenue model, so they no longer need content creators to make videos to place ads on like they once did.

Shortly after the "Ad-pocalypse" (the advertiser apocalypse as we call it), YouTube announced YouTube TV and started going after cable TV providers like Cox,

---

[596] TechDirt "Copyright As Censorship Again: Game Developer Takes Down Scathing YouTube Review" by Mike Masnick (October 21st 2013)

[597] TubeFilter "The #Adpocalypse Is Here To Stay" by Tristan Snell (May 11th 2017)

Time Warner, and Dish Network, by offering people the same basic cable service through the YouTube TV app on their smart TVs, tablets, and phones.[598] Like a parasite that sucked the blood out of its host until it died, YouTube has simply moved on to other ways to generate money, and left thousands of full-time content creators in the dust — people like me who had largely relied upon revenue from making YouTube videos to pay our bills.

YouTubers franticly scrambled to try and stay afloat and many went to a fan-funded model though Patreon or started making money from livestreaming through Super Chat donations, where users pay to ask them questions. Many started asking for direct donations through PayPal, Bitcoin, and other crowdsourcing methods. Others started selling merchandise like T-shirts and coffee mugs or began getting their own sponsors through MCNs (Multi Channel Networks) or 3rd party ad agencies.

In previous generations most kids wanted to grow up to be a professional athlete, a rock star, or an actor; but the millennial generation and generation Z all wanted to be YouTubers because it seemed like a life of freedom, fun, and easy money; but the heyday of truly independent YouTubers who do and say whatever they want is over. With the wheels having fallen off the gravy train for many, what was once a dream job has become more of just a job, or even a hobby now that many have had to get 'real jobs' to pay their bills since YouTube's monetization program has collapsed. As bad as all this is, unfortunately YouTube continues to tighten the restrictions on what people are allowed to post even if it's not monetized.

---

[598] Fortune "YouTube Is In a Race With Facebook, Netflix, and Amazon Over TV's Future" by Mathew Ingram (May 5th 2017)

YouTube announced they were going to further censor 'controversial' content and teamed up with the ADL [Anti-Defamation League] a 'civil rights' agency which has the sole purpose of 'fighting bigotry' — an organization whose standards for what is 'extremist' content is so low that they labeled Pepe the Frog, a cartoon character used in pro-Trump memes, a 'hate symbol.'[599]

In a blog post YouTube admitted, "We've started rolling out features from Jigsaw's Redirect Method to YouTube. When people search for sensitive keywords on YouTube, they will be redirected towards a playlist of curated YouTube videos that directly confront and debunk violent extremist messages. We also continue to amplify YouTube voices speaking out against hate and radicalization through our YouTube Creators for Change program."[600]

Of course, to YouTube it is considered 'extremist propaganda' if someone says that there are only two genders, or if they say it's disgusting to allow a man who thinks he's a woman to shower in the girl's locker room, or if someone doesn't support gay marriage, or if they want to secure the U.S./Mexico border and deport criminal illegal aliens from the United States.

In an interview with CNN, YouTube's CEO Susan Wojcicki was asked if she had experienced any "sexism" in the tech industry since it is dominated by men, and after thinking silently for a moment — not wanting to disappoint the interviewer with a "no," she responded that

---

[599] USA Today "Pepe the Frog declared a hate symbol by Anti-Defamation League" by Mary Bowerman (September 28th 2016)

[600] YouTube Official Blog "An Update on Our Comittment to Fight Terror Content Online" (August 1st 2017)

she has experienced sexist "microaggressons" such as when men "interrupt" her while she's talking, or when men say something that "annoys" her.[601]  Those were literally her examples of "sexism" in Silicon Valley, so you can see why the company considers videos criticizing feminists and other aspects of the Leftists' agenda as "hate speech."

Many viewers who have seen her interviews wonder how she could possibly be the CEO of any company, let alone YouTube, because she seems like a complete idiot. Many suspect nepotism is the reason she got the job because her sister married Google's co-founder Sergey Brin.[602]  (Google is the parent company of YouTube — or was — now it's Alphabet Inc., which is the new parent company due to corporate restructuring.)

In July of 2017, just as the crackdown on conservative channels was ramping up, she tweeted out a photo of herself meeting with The Young Turks host Cenk Uyger, the biggest liberal 'news' channel on the platform, thanking him for stopping by YouTube's headquarters.[603] So it's clear that she's playing favorites, and you can see which team she is on, and that the liberal rot at YouTube is coming directly from the head.

Some people are turning to other platforms, including decentralized peer-to-peer file sharing networks and even blockchain technology to avoid YouTube censorship.  So if my channel ever gets deleted, check out my Facebook page or Twitter feed (if they're still up) so you can find

---

[601] CNN "YouTube CEO Susan Wojcicki: Don't interrupt me" by Sara Ashley O'Brien (May 8th 2017)

[602] New York Times "Silicon Valley Wide-Eyed Over a Bride" by Katie Hafner (May 29th 2007)

[603] https://twitter.com/SusanWojcicki/status/890654400192028672

links to my videos (wherever they're being hosted) and see where I've moved to, if it comes to that. But in the meantime, I hope you'll subscribe to me at YouTube.com/MarkDice and visit the channel regularly for new videos.

# Google

Google is more than just a search engine. It is the closest thing to an all-powerful information monopoly the planet has ever seen. Not only does it account for 90% of Internet searches in most countries,[604] and run the Android operating system on 80% of the world's smartphones and tablets,[605] and own YouTube — the largest video sharing site in the world; but the company is also trying to give birth to the world's first artificial intelligence. They're even hoping to make humans immortal.[606] In 2015 Alphabet Inc. was created as part of a corporate restructuring and is now the parent company of Google and its many subsidiaries.

As you know, Google has become a verb and is a synonym for "looking something up" online, but when so much of the world relies on a single source for accessing their information, there are inherent dangers of censorship and political favoritism regarding the massive amount of content they control. Beneath the surface of being "just a search engine," Google has a very deep and far-reaching political agenda and their control over so much of the Internet and their ability to manipulate how billions of people see the world has dramatic implications.

---

[604] The Guardian "Google dominates search. But the real problem is its monopoly on data" (April 19th 2015)

[605] The Statistics Portal "Share of Android OS of global smartphone shipments from 1st quarter 2011 to 1st quarter 2017"

[606] CNN "How Google's Calico aims to fight aging and 'solve death'" by Arion McNicoll (October 3rd 2013)

Most people treat Google like a magic eight ball which answers any question they ask since it is literally as convenient as clicking a few keys (or today, using Okay Google or Siri voice recognition search systems) which most people blindly trust "tells the truth." Because Google's algorithms are considered trade secrets it's difficult for most people to understand how they work or see how they favor certain people, issues, websites, and political viewpoints over others. But while it's difficult, it's not impossible. In this chapter we'll take a look at some of the examples that researchers have discovered and the concerns they raise.

It's also important to point out that people's long-term memories are actually becoming atrophied and aren't retaining information like they used to in the recent past since their brains don't make it a priority to store a lot of information anymore because people can just "Google it."[607] It's a cliché but true, that as computers got smarter, most people got dumber.

As the war against 'fake news' and 'offensive' content heated up after the 2016 presidential election, of course Google jumped on the bandwagon and used the moral panic as an excuse to expand their censorship under the disguise of this new moral crusade.

CEO Eric Schmidt said, "We're very good at detecting what's the most relevant and what's the least relevant. It should be possible for computers to detect malicious, misleading and incorrect information and essentially have you not see it. We're not arguing for censorship, we're

---

[607] New York Post "How Google is making you stupid" by Larry Getlen (July 17th 2016)

arguing just take it off the page, put it somewhere else...make it harder to find."[608]

If you're wondering where Schmidt's political allegiance lies, he was with Barack Obama on election night in 2012,[609] and "helped recruit talent, choose technology and coach the campaign manager," Obama operative David Plouff admitted.[610] And where was he on election night in 2016? He was at Hillary Clinton's party, where he was photographed wearing a "staff" badge.[611]

The visitor logs during the Obama administration show that Google's lobbyist had visited the White House 128 times between January of 2009 and October of 2015.[612] That was more visits than lobbyists for Comcast, Verizon, Facebook, and Amazon combined.[613] That same year Google spent $16 million dollars on lobbying, the most out of any tech company.[614] Why would a search engine need to work so closely with the Obama administration?

---

[608] CNBC "Alphabet Chairman Eric Schmidt: We 'can't guarantee' ads won't appear next to offensive content" by Anita Balakrishnan (March 23rd 2017)

[609] New York Post "Google controls what we buy, the news we read — and Obama's policies" by Kyle Smith (March 28th 2015)

[610] Ibid.

[611] FreeBeacon Google's Eric Schmidt Wore 'Staff' Badge at Hillary Clinton Election Night Party" by Joe Schoffstall (November 16th 2016)

[612] Fox News "Visitor logs show Google's unrivaled White House access" by Johnny Kampis (May 17th 2016)

[613] Ibid.

[614] ConsumerWatchdog.org "Google's 2015 Spending On Lobbying Tops $16 Million For Second Year, Leading 16 Tech And Communications Companies; Facebook, Amazon, Apple Post Records" by John M. Simpson (January 21st 2016)

## Manipulating Top Search Results

Google's secret algorithms determine which webpages will show up and in what order when someone looks something up. While you will get thousands, perhaps hundreds of thousands of results for any given topic, SEO (search engine optimization) experts have conducted studies which show that over 90% of people click on something that's on the first page of those search results.[615]

If you sell things online, like every major retailer does — from Best Buy to Advance Auto Parts, or run a news site, you want your website to show up as one of the first results when someone searches for something relevant to your work. Having a first-page result is what makes or breaks many online businesses, and it's entirely up to Google which pages will show up, in what order, or even if they'll show up at all, no matter how relevant they are to your search.

"Google, Inc., isn't just the world's biggest purveyor of information; it is also the world's biggest censor," declared *US News and World Report* after a 2016 investigation.[616] Their report highlights the little-known fact that Google has nine different blacklists (that we know of), and have created censorship tools for various repressive governments around the world to keep

---

[615] Search Engine Watch "No. 1 Position in Google Gets 33% of Search Traffic [Study]" by Jessica Lee (June 20th 2013)

[616] US News & World Report "The New Censorship" by Robert Epstein (June 22nd 2016)

information hidden from their people no matter how detailed their searches are.[617]

Their report pointed out, "When Google's employees or algorithms decide to block our access to information about a news item, political candidate or business, opinions and votes can shift, reputations can be ruined and businesses can crash and burn. Because online censorship is entirely unregulated at the moment, victims have little or no recourse when they have been harmed. Eventually, authorities will almost certainly have to step in, just as they did when credit bureaus were regulated in 1970."[618]

Their report concludes that, "Google has rapidly become an essential in people's lives — nearly as essential as air or water. We don't let public utilities make arbitrary and secretive decisions about denying people services; we shouldn't let Google do so either."[619]

When you Google a person, on the right hand side of the page there are several boxes which usually include a photograph of them, along with a few sentences describing them using information taken from Wikipedia. If you lookup a product, it may give you the supposed satisfaction ratings along with some other information about it like the price. These "Knowledge Panels" were introduced in 2012, and as one writer pointed out, "materialize at random, as unsourced and absolute as if

---

[617] CNN "Google: The reluctant censor of the Internet" by David Goldman (January 4th 2015)

[618] US News & World Report "The New Censorship" by Robert Epstein (June 22nd 2016)

[619] Ibid.

handed down by God."[620]   They show results for almost anything you look up, from what the capital of a city is, to the best restaurant in town.

A researcher from the University of Technology in Austria pointed out that, "Google has become the main interface for our whole reality.  To be precise: with the Google interface the user gets the impression that the search results imply a kind of totality.  In fact, one only sees a small part of what one could see if one also integrates other research tools."[621]

## Redirecting Search Results

Google doesn't just play favorites with the top search results; their control goes much deeper than that.  An interesting example of Google admitting they are manipulating the search results can be found in what they call their Redirect Method, which they admit was implemented in 2016 when they created an algorithm to show search results of imams [Muslim religious leaders] denouncing ISIS along with videos of former extremists denouncing their past beliefs whenever someone was searching for ISIS related material.

"This came out of an observation that there's a lot of online demand for ISIS material, but there are also a lot of credible organic voices online debunking their narratives," said Yasmin Green, Google's head of research

---

[620] Washington Post "You probably haven't even noticed Google's sketchy quest to control the world's knowledge" by Caitlin Dewey (May 11th 2016)

[621] Report on dangers and opportunities posed by large search engines, particularly Google, H. Maurer (Ed), Graz University of Technology, Austria, September 30, 2007, page 187

and development. He went on to admit, "The Redirect Method is at its heart a targeted advertising campaign: Let's take these individuals who are vulnerable to ISIS' recruitment messaging and instead show them information that refutes it."[622]

One specific example of this is a video showing long breadlines in Raqqa, the ISIS capital, which was chosen to come up as one of the top results when people search for certain travel routes to Syria. The idea is Google hopes to show potential ISIS fighters that the Islamic State isn't the paradise they thought it might be, and are trying to put their curiosities to rest. The Redirect Method proves that Google is actively manipulating the search results in hopes of influencing the way people think and the actions they do or do not take as a result of their Google searches.

What other topics are they specifically redirecting search results for? The Pandora's Box of possibilities is limitless. And while it may be a noble cause to redirect search results to paint the Islamic State in a negative light, what other issues are they trying to carefully frame in a certain way? The Second Amendment? Abortion? Immigration? Taxes? Socialized healthcare? Climate change? It would be extremely naive to think they were only using their Redirect Method to skew the search results for only one issue. Google has already been accused of suppressing websites and articles which refute climate change alarmists' allegations.[623]

---

[622] Wired "Google's Clever Plan to Stop Aspiring ISIS Recruits" by Angry Greenberg (September 7th 2016)

[623] WUWT "Caught Red-Handed: Google Search Suppresses Climate Realism" by Leo Goldstein (July 22nd 2017)

In April 2017, Google rolled out a new "fact checking tool" which includes a tag next to some search results that declares whether they are 'true' or 'false,' using sources like Snopes.com, PolitiFact.org, FactCheck.org, *The Washington Post*, and *The New York Times* as the 'fact checkers.'[624]   Google's blog explained, "Even though differing conclusions may be presented, we think it's still helpful for people to understand the degree of consensus around a particular claim and have clear information on which sources agree."[625]

For example, a search for "Obama born in Kenya" brings up results including the "fact checking snippet" saying "Fact Check by Snopes: False." Searching for "15 million undocumented immigrants" brings up the result "Three Pinocchios" by *The Washington Post*, and "Pants on Fire" by PolitiFact, even though the number was said to be 11.4 million back in 2012 according to the government's own statistics.[626]

## Manipulating Elections

Researchers at the American Institute for Behavioral Research and Technology published a study showing that Google could influence how people thought about different candidates in an election by serving up mostly

---

[624] Bloomberg "Google Brings Fake News Fact-Checking to Search Results" by Mark Bergen (April 7th 2017)

[625] Google Blog "Fact Check now available in Google Search and News around the world" by Justin Kosslyn and Cong Yu (April 7th 2017)

[626] PewResearchCenter "Unauthorized immigrant population stable for half a decade" by Jeffrey S. Passel and D'Vera Cohn (September 21st 2016)

positive or negative articles about them when people searched for certain topics. "We estimate, based on win margins in national elections around the world, that Google could determine the outcome of upwards of 25 percent of all national elections," said Robert Epstein, who helped conduct the study. [627]

The amount of influence doesn't even have to be all that great, because when you consider that most elections have fairly close margins, if Google can increase or decrease the positive or negative feelings about a particular candidate or issue by just a small percentage, it could be enough to change the outcome of a race.

During the 2016 election, a *New York Times* tech writer named Farhad Manjoo actually suggested that Google should filter out search results to videos and articles which raised questions about Hillary Clinton's health problems. "Google should fix this," he said in response to Rudy Giuliani encouraging people to look up "Hillary Clinton illness." He added, "It shouldn't give quarter to conspiracy theorists."[628] Just three weeks later Hillary would be caught on video collapsing as she was leaving the 9/11 memorial at Ground Zero where she had to be carried away by her staff, confirming what many had been suspecting — that she was not well.[629]

Just a month after the election *The Guardian* actually claimed that search results were, "being manipulated and controlled by rightwing propagandists," because a

---

[627] Wired "Google's Search Algorithm Could Steal the Presidency" by Adam Rogers (August 8th 2015)

[628] Breitbart "New York Times Tech Columnist Calls on Google to Hide Hillary Health Info" by Patrick Howley (August 21st 2016)

[629] WABC-TV "Video shows Hillary Clinton appearing to faint while getting in van" by September 11th 2016)

journalist didn't like some of the results that came up when searching for 'Muslims,' 'Jews,' and 'women.'[630] "[Google] simply can't go on pretending that it has no editorial responsibilities when it is delivering these kinds of results," the article says. "It [Google] is simply not defensible for it go on claiming 'plausible deniability.' It has clearly become a conduit for rightwing hate sites and it must urgently take action."[631]

Shortly after Donald Trump's book *Crippled America* came out, a Google search for the title brought up pictures of Adolf Hitler's book cover *Mein Kampf*.[632] And for some period of time a search for "When Hitler was born" resulted in photos of Hitler, but also of Trump. After these and other strange search results began making headlines, Google quietly fixed the issue.

If you go to the Google News page you'll find a series of articles they have aggregated from various sources, and of course their editors have chosen which ones to feature as the "Top Stories" and what news outlets they come from. The page consists simply of links to articles from news outlets like the *Washington Post*, the *New York Times*, and other mostly liberal papers. The stories chosen to be featured there are obviously going to reflect the political leanings of Google, and from my own experience the top stories are almost always anti-Trump and frame conservative issues in a negative light.

---

[630] The Guardian "Google 'must review its search rankings because of rightwing manipulation'" by Carole Cadwalladr (December 5th 2016)

[631] Ibid.

[632] Fox News "Google search connects Trump's book to Hitler's 'Mein Kampf'" (July 28th 2016)

## Autocomplete

It's not just the search results that are manipulated (or completely hidden), Google also manipulates search *suggestions* as well. As you have likely noticed when you begin typing something into Google it will give you a list of what it thinks you are searching for (or what it *wants* you to search for).

For example if you just type in "When is," it will suggest four different options depending on what time of year it is, or what other users tend to put after those words. When I just typed "when is" into Google, it came up with "When is Mother's Day" as one, "When is Mother's Day This Year 2017" as the second, "When is Easter" as the third, and "When is the Kentucky Derby" as the fourth autosuggestion. Mother's Day is just a week away as I'm writing this, and the Kentucky Derby was just yesterday.

But after a close look at this autocomplete or "suggested search" feature, it becomes clear that certain autosuggestions are regularly censored so they don't show up. Google has admitted they filter out certain phrases from the autocomplete suggestions if they are "potentially inappropriate."[633] Currently, typing in "Islam is" brings up "a religion of peace" as the top autosuggestion. "Islam is Peace" is the second, and "Islam is not a race" is the third. Meanwhile one of the autosuggestions for Christianity is "Christianity is dying."

Currently, when "Hillary Clinton cri" is typed in, Google suggests "Hillary Clinton credentials," "Hillary Clinton creme brulee," and "Hillary Clinton crazy laugh,"

---

[633] BBC "Is Google autocomplete evil?" by Tom Chatfield (November 6th 2013)

but the same search on Yahoo brings up "Hillary Clinton crying," "Hillary Clinton crimes," "Hillary Clinton criminal," and "Hillary Clinton crimes list." Microsoft's Bing brings up "Hillary Clinton crying," "Hillary Clinton criminal," "Hillary Clinton crooked," and "Hillary Clinton crazy."

A search for "Hillary Clinton ind" on Google brings up "Hillary Clinton India," "Hillary Clinton Indiana," and "Hillary Clinton individual donors." On Microsoft's Bing the recommendations are: "Hillary Clinton indictment," "Hillary Clinton indicted," and "Hillary Clinton indictment update."

On Yahoo they are: "Hillary Clinton indictment," "Hillary Clinton indictment coming," and "Hillary Clinton indictment coming NY Times."

Autosuggestions involving Hillary's health were also censored when I tested this. Google's autosuggestions for "Hillary Clinton's health" are "Hillary's Clinton's health plan," "Hillary Clinton's healthcare plan," and "Hillary Clinton's healthcare plan 1993."

On Bing, a search for "Hillary Clinton's health" brings up "Hillary Clinton's health issues," "Hillary Clinton's health problems," and then third is "Hillary Clinton's health care plan."

These autosuggestions may have changed by the time you are reading this book, but others and myself have documented the clear protection of Hillary Clinton's autosuggestions by Google during the time period surrounding the 2016 election.[634] If Google manipulated the autosuggestions to protect Hillary Clinton during the

---

[634] Washington Free Beacon "Here Are 10 More Examples of Google Search Results Favorable to Hillary" by Bret Scher and Elizabeth Harrington (June 10th 2016)

election, which all evidence indicates they did, they are most likely doing it for other people, issues, and topics as well.

## Un-Googleable

They don't just manipulate the top search results for various topics for their own financial interest or political reasons — sometimes Google outright hides what would be results for certain topics so nothing shows up at all. Sometimes these censored pages are the result of DMCA takedown complaints; sometimes they're the result of a court order which is fairly common in England with their "right to be forgotten laws" that mandate Google hide certain pages from their index; and sometimes it's just because Google feels it's the 'right thing to do.' These topics are considered to be "un-Googleable."

Due to laws in the U.K., Google must remove certain search results when someone obtains a court order to enforce their "right to be forgotten law" which prevents not only the media from reporting on certain facts, but also prevents Google from including them in the search results in all countries that are part of the European Union as well.[635]

As I discussed previously, singer Elton John was able to obtain a court order to silence the British media about him and his 'husband's' fake marriage and deviant lifestyle, as well as remove tweets on Twitter (and videos on YouTube) that mentioned their names in connection with their sex scandal, and that censorship was also implemented on Google as well. Any article mentioning

---

[635] Fortune "Google Blacks Out More Sites Under 'Right to Be Forgotten'" by Jeff John Roberts (March 7th 2016)

the keywords "celebrity threesome sex scandal" and Elton John's name were dumped down a memory hole and don't show up for people in Europe.[636]   Google has different filters in different countries, so in the United States pages will still show up, but in Europe Google has to follow the law and censor such results.[637]

Sky News found that one of their articles about Kelly Osbourne getting sick on the set of her show *The Fashion Police* was removed from Google in Britain (Google.co.uk).[638] This was just two months after the "right to be forgotten" law had passed, enabling people to request the removal of search results they claim are "outdated or damaging" to their character.

*The Guardian* found that stories about a former Scottish soccer referee who admitted lying about the reason for rescinding a penalty issued to a team had been removed.[639]   *The Telegraph* had stories of theirs hidden about the former president of the British Law Society who made fake complaints about a colleague of his hoping to get him fired.[640]   The BBC (British Broadcasting Corporation) reported that shortly after the law was put in

---

[636] The Telegraph "Celebrity 'threesome' injunction: Google blocks search results" by Patrick Foster (April 14th 2016)

[637] The Guardian "Google to extend 'right to be forgotten' to all its domains accessed in EU" by Samuel Gibbs (February 11th 2016)

[638] Sky News "Google Starts Erasing Disputed Search Results" (July 3rd 2014)

[639] The Telegraph "Max Mosley, a former Scottish referee and the Law Society chief: the Telegraph story links deleted by Google" by Rhiannon Williams (July 3rd 2014)

[640] Ibid.

place Google had censored at least a dozen links to some of their stories as well.[641]

In 2013 when sexually explicit selfies of dozens of A-list celebrities were hacked from their iCloud accounts and posted online, Google made most of the direct links to the photos un-Googleable, and removed the pictures from their Google Image search.[642]

The Church of Scientology has used a number of DMCA (Digital Millennium Copyright Act) takedown notices to have information about their 'scriptures' removed which reveal the strange beliefs of high-level Scientologists about the "Lord Xenu" and the creation myth founder L. Ron Hubbard (a former science fiction writer) concocted for his cult.[643] Scientology has also had search results blocked in the EU by using the right to be forgotten statutes.[644]

Google has admitted censoring results for the Chinese government and other oppressive regimes around the world. For example, until 2010 Google had filtered out all websites supporting the independence of Tibet and Taiwan, and even any search results about the infamous Tiananmen Square protests in 1989 where hundreds, possibly thousands, of student protesters were killed by

---

[641] BBC "List of BBC web pages which have been removed from Google's search results" by Neil McIntosh (June 25th 2015)

[642] ZDNet "After legal threat, Google says it removed 'tens of thousands' of iCloud hack pics" by Liam Tung (October 3rd 2014)

[643] CNET "Google pulls anti-Scientology links" by Evan Hansen (April 22nd 2002)

[644] Reuters "EU judges to tackle 'right to be forgotten' again" by Julia Fioretti (May 16th 2017)

the Chinese government during a pro-democracy demonstration.[645]

Websites and articles in Australia, Israel, Canada, France, Germany, India, and others have also been censored — either due to court orders, or to comply with those countries 'hate speech' laws.[646]   And of course Google Earth and Google Street view have removed images that governments consider matters of national security.

## FTC Investigation

People within the Federal Trade Commission have actually recommended filing a lawsuit against Google for their search manipulation.[647]   In 2012 the FTC ended a two year investigation into Google after repeated complaints that their dominance gives them an unfair advantage over other companies because they aren't just in the search engine business, they're in the cell phone business (Android), and also sell books, music, and movies through their Google Play store.

Google even has their own product and restaurant reviews that are in direct competition with Yelp, which they have threatened to remove from their search results altogether.[648]   The Federal Trade Commission

---

[645] CNN "Google to censor itself in China" (January 26th 2006)

[646] The Guardian "Google can be forced to pull results globally, Canada supreme court rules" via Reuters in Otttawa (June 29th 2017)

[647] Wall Street Journal "Inside the U.S. Antitrust Probe of Google" by Brody Mullins, Rolfe Winkler, and Brent Kendall (March 19th 2015)

[648] Business Insider "Google threatened to remove websites from its search engine unless they let Google use their content" by Matt Rosoff (March 20th 2015)

investigation revealed that Google had placed restrictions on search results for content from their competitors, but despite high level staff members at the FTC wanting to file an antitrust suit against them because they were using their monopoly to cause "real harm to consumers and to innovation" through anticompetitive tactics, the commission surprisingly did nothing.[649]   Google did however agree to make some voluntary changes in the way they run the algorithms, trying to appease the FTC.

FTC senior advisor Tim Wu admitted Google is "reducing consumer welfare."[650]  And during the antitrust hearing Senator Richard Blumenthal (D-Conn.) said that, "While the company is a great American success story, their position in the marketplace has led to legitimate questions about whether they have used their market power to disadvantage competitors unfairly and ultimately limit consumer choice."[651]

A few years later the European Union charged Google with antitrust violations for unfair business practices and fined the company $2.7 billion dollars.[652]   One of the officials involved in the decision said, "Google has given its own comparison shopping service an illegal advantage by abusing its dominance in general Internet search.  It has promoted its own service, and demoted rival services. It has harmed competition and consumers.  That's illegal

---

[649] The Wall Street Journal "Inside the U.S. Antitrust Probe of Google" by Brody Mullins, Rolfe Winkler, and Bret Kendall (March 19th 2015)

[650] Politico "Sources: Feds taking second look at Google search" by Nancy Scola (May 11th 2016)

[651] Ibid.

[652] Tech Crunch "Google fined $2.7BN for EU antitrust violations over shopping searches" by Natasha Lomas (June 27th 2017)

under EU antitrust rules…Google has come up with many innovative products and services that have made a difference to our lives. That's a good thing. But Google's strategy for its comparison shopping service wasn't just about attracting customers by making its product better than those of its rivals. Instead, Google abused its market dominance as a search engine by promoting its own comparison shopping service in its search results, and demoting those of competitors."[653]

## Privacy Concerns

Aside from manipulating and censoring search results, Google is engaged in more disturbing and dangerous activities — putting people's personal information, their homes, and even their lives at risk.

Google keeps a log of everything that everyone searches for and puts tracking cookies (small files) on your computer. Such information is sold to advertisers. This means Google (and anyone they sell that information to) knows about people's possible health problems from them looking up their symptoms, as well as any personal interests that may be embarrassing if made public. They even know people's political leanings, which could be used to discriminate against them by a current or potential employer.

Google's terms of service have changed over the years, at one time the tracking cookies 'expired' after 31 years,[654] but more recently they claim the cookies will

---

[653] Ibid.

[654] PC World "Privacy Watch: How Much Does Google Know About You?" by Andrew Brandt (February 21st 2006)

now expire after two years.[655]   The advocacy group Privacy International said Google was "hostile to privacy" and gave them their lowest ranking of any company in their assessment.  Even browsing in 'incognito' mode on Google Chrome is not private as most people are led to believe.[656]   Google knows what you've been looking up, and so do countless advertising agencies, political organizations, law enforcement, and anyone else Google wants to give that information to.

For years Gmail users had the content of their emails scanned and read by Google in order to use them to show people advertisements based on what they were writing about.[657]  Users consented to this when they agreed to the terms of service which hardly anyone even reads or thinks twice about.   After word of this creepy tactic started making headlines, Google announced that they would stop doing so.

In response to critics about their privacy concerns CEO Eric Schmidt, declared, "If you have something that you don't want anyone to know, maybe you shouldn't be doing it in the first place."[658]   An interesting statement from a man who allegedly has an open marriage and had his $15 million dollar Manhattan penthouse soundproofed, which *New York Magazine* called a

[655] ZDNet "Google now expires cookies after 2 years, not 31" by Garett Rogers (July 16th 2007)

[656] VPN Express "Google Chrome Inconito Mode" by Alvin Bryan (August 8th 2013)

[657] Ad Week "Google Plans to Stop Scanning Users' Emails for Ad Targeting" by Marty Swant (June 23rd 2017)

[658] Computer World "Google CEO: if you want privacy, do you have something to hide?" by Richi Jennings (December 11th 2009)

"depraved sex palace" for him and his presumed mistresses.[659]

Google Street view allows anyone to get photos of your home, which is just as easy as looking up pictures of just about anything else. When gathering the 360 degree images of every street in America for the Street View feature Google also collected names, addresses, passwords, emails, text messages, hardware IDs, and browsing histories through people's home WiFi routers if they weren't password protected.[660]

Burglars often use Google Street View to conduct reconnaissance on homes and garages before breaking into them.[661] One survey showed that 80% of burglars use social media and Google Street View to case houses they're planning on burglarizing.[662] Police in Chicago say that a burglar suspected of breaking into at least eight different homes used Google Maps to find expensive houses located on a highway (for an easy escape) and then further cased the homes using Google's Satellite View of those properties.[663]

As Google grows more powerful and as their products and services become more ingrained in society, the dangers will likely grow in step. Many have voiced

---

[659] New York Magazine "Inside Google Chairman Eric Schmidt's Lavish Sex Palace" by Dan Amira (July 25th 2013)

[660] Wired "An Intentional Mistake: The Anatomy of Google's Wi-Fi Sniffing Debacle" by David Kravets (May 2nd 2012)

[661] The Telegraph "Google Street View 'led burglars to target my garage'" (April 12th 2010)

[662] ZDNet "Infographic: 80% of robbers check Twitter, Facebook, Google Street View" by Boonsri Dickinson (November 1st 2011)

[663] Business Insider "This Is Why You Need To Protect Your Home From A Google Maps Burglar" by Jill Krasny (September 28th 2011)

concerns about Google Home, which can enable hackers to listen in on people in their living rooms or bedrooms, and similar 'smart home' devices allow hackers to remotely open people's doors making them easy targets for burglars.[664]

## Is Google Becoming a God?

Alphabet Inc. (Google's parent company) CEO Eric Schmidt admitted the plan is to have Google think *for* people, saying, "The goal is to enable Google users to be able to ask the question such as 'What shall I do tomorrow?' and 'What job shall I take?'"[665]   Three years later he doubled down on his assertion that Google would think *for* people, telling *The Wall Street Journal,* "I actually think most people don't want Google to answer their questions, they want Google to tell them what they should be doing next."[666]   Tell us what we *should* be doing?  As strange as this sounds their goals are far more disturbing than that.

Google's executives want the company to be more than just a search engine and smartphone operating system; more than an ebook store and a place to stream music and movies; more than something that runs smart home gadgets and medical devices; they want it to become an artificially intelligent, all-knowing 'God.' Then they want to wire it directly into the brains of

---

[664] Newsweek "Hackers Unlock Doors of Samsung 'Smart' Home" by Anthony Cuthbertson (May 3rd 2016)

[665] Financial Times "Google's goal: to organize your daily life" by Caroline Daniel and Maija Palmer (May 22nd 2007)

[666] Wall Street Journal "Google and the Search for the Future" by Holman W. Jenkins Jr. (August 14th 2010)

humans through what's called a neural interface or BMI (brain machine interface) to merge man with machine, creating a new hybrid species of cyborgs.[667] Their final plan is to then upload the totality of one's mind into the Cloud or a silicon-based hard drive that's attached to a robotic body, believing this is the key to 'immortality' and 'transcendence.'[668]

Google's director of engineering Ray Kurzweil actually said, "So, does God exist? Well, I would say, not yet."[669] He was hired by Google in 2012 to work full-time on artificial intelligence and is one of the most well-known proponents of transhumanism, which is the idea of merging man with machine to create superhumans. Kurzweil believes that by the year 2099, neural interfaces or BMIs (brain machine interfaces) will be surgically implanted into almost everyone, and that, "humans who do not utilize such implants [will be] unable to meaningfully participate in dialogues with those who do."[670] He and other transhumanists believe they will elevate humans to the level of gods in what they see as the final phase of humanity's physical and spiritual evolution as we merge into a cybernetic 'Borg.'

In a strange and creepy side note, Google reportedly owns P.O. Box 666 on the Caribbean island of Bermuda, which has a zero corporate tax rate, in an apparent effort

---

[667] The Verge "Elon Musk launches Neuralink, a venture to merge the human brain with AI" by Nick Statt (March 27th 2017)

[668] Time "2045: The Year Man Becomes Immortal" by Lev Grossman (February 10th 2011)

[669] Ray Kurzweil in documentary *Transcendent Man* (2009) by James Bedsole

[670] Kurzweil, Ray - *The Age of Intelligent Machines* page 234

to prevent paying taxes on about ten billon dollars in annual revenue.[671]


*Author's Note: Please take a moment to rate and review this book on Amazon.com or wherever you purchased it from to let others know what you think. This also helps to offset the trolls who keep giving my books fake one-star reviews when they haven't even read them. Almost all of the one-star reviews on my books are from NON-verified purchases which is a clear indication they are fraudulent, hence me adding this note. These fraudulent ratings and reviews could also be part of a larger campaign trying to stop my message from spreading by attempting to tarnish my research through fake and defamatory reviews, so I really need your help to combat this as soon as possible. Thank you!*

---

[671] Daily Mail "The post box in Bermuda numbered 666 which receives Google profits worth £8BILLION a year" by Tim Sculthorpe (January 31st 2016)

# Wikipedia

Wikipedia was launched in 2001 as an online encyclopedia that "crowdsourced" its articles by allowing anyone to write and edit them, a strange business model which has surprisingly led to them becoming the fifth most popular website in the world.[672] Its name derives from the words 'Wiki,' which is a website format that allows collaborative modifications, and 'encyclopedia.' It currently has over five million articles and is usually one of the top Google search results for most subjects entered into the search engine.

Unlike traditional encyclopedias, which are written and edited by experts in their field, pretty much anyone can add almost anything to Wikipedia articles, which are then read and believed by countless people. Since Wikipedia has become the most popular online "encyclopedia" and one of the most visited websites online, we must take a serious look at articles published on the site and how they are fact checked, edited, and censored.

Editors at most newspapers and traditional encyclopedia companies have names and titles, not to mention bosses and company policies they must abide by, but much of what happens on Wikipedia is a mystery, and most of the editors and writers are anonymous or only referred to by their online handles which rarely reveal any information about who they actually are or what credentials they have.

---

[672] Alexa "The Top 500 Sites on the Web" (as of August 12th 2017)

Since Wikipedia is free and there are no advertisements on the site, this leads to the question of who funds them? And how did an online 'encyclopedia' that was written by random anonymous people on the Internet come to be a trusted source of information by so many people? Their parent company, the Wikimedia Foundation, employs over 280 people and in 2016 they took in over $80 million dollars in revenue and now have over $91 million dollars in assets.[673] Where does all this money come from, and what are they doing with it since the articles are written and edited by random volunteers on the Internet who have too much time on their hands?

Apparently people just give them money, I'm not sure why, but they do — and a lot. In 2008 they got their largest donation to date, which was $3 million dollars from the Alfred P. Sloan Foundation, a philanthropic nonprofit organization founded by the former CEO of General Motors.[674] They would later give them millions more. Google has also given millions of dollars to them as well, so its no wonder that Wikipedia articles are usually one of the top search results for just about anything.

Google's co-founder Sergey Brin and his wife have given them hundreds of thousands of dollars of their own personal money, on top of the money Google gave them as a corporation.[675] All donations are tax deductible

---

[673] Wikimedia Foundation, Inc. Financial Statements June, 2016 and 2015

[674] Los Angeles Times "Wikipedia group gets a big boost" by Associated Press (March 26th 2008)

[675] Reuters "Google's Brin, wife donate $500,000 to keep Wikipedia going" (November 18th 2011)

because the Wikimedia Foundation is registered as a nonprofit organization.

Wikipedia has been involved in several lawsuits over defamation, and a substantial amount of their money has been spent defending them. One of their attorneys, Matt Zimmerman, admitted, "Without strong liability protection, it would be difficult for Wikipedia to continue to provide a platform for user-created encyclopedia content."[676]

Comedian Stephen Colbert once sarcastically praised Wikipedia for their 'quality' by pointing out that the article on Lightsabers (the handheld weapon from *Star Wars*) was longer than the article about the printing press.[677] Since its editorial policies and oversight are so flawed, the site has been called "the abomination that causes misinformation."[678]

Articles about controversial subjects like global warming, illegal immigration, and abortion all have massive liberal bias, and entries about living people, particularly conservative authors, journalists, and activists, are the most biased on the entire website.

Because Wikipedia has become the go-to place for most people when they want to look something up, major corporations use sock puppet accounts to edit pages about their companies and products trying to paint them in a favorable light and scrub criticism. Such edits have been traced back to people at companies like PepsiCo, Sea World, Walmart, Exxon Mobil, and others, since no

---

[676] The Telegraph "Wikipedia Fights Defamation Lawsuit" by Claudine Beaumont (May 11th 2008)

[677] Stephen Colbert. *The Colbert Report* episode 3109 (August 21, 2007)

[678] TektonTickeer "Wikgnosis" by JP Holding (December 23rd 2010)

company wants negative information about them or their products on an 'encyclopedia' article about them.[679]

In 2012 it was discovered that two employees of Wikipedia's parent company (the Wikimedia Foundation) also ran a public relations business which included editing and monitoring the Wikipedia pages of their clients.[680] In 2015 it was revealed that some Wikipedia editors had been running a coordinated blackmail and extortion racket by using their editorial powers to allow the defamation of public figures and businesses if they didn't pay them protection money.[681]

These editors would contact businesses and lesser-known 'celebrities' whose pages had been rejected due to lacking notoriety or for "excessive promotional content." As *The Independent* reported, "According to a Wikipedia insider, at this stage the scammers would demand a payment of up to several hundred pounds to successfully 're-post or re-surface' the article, and in some cases demanded an on-going monthly payment to 'protect' the articles."[682]

Before we look at the examples of censorship and liberal bias on Wikipedia as a whole, let's use my own page as an example. Since I'm a 'newsworthy' public figure there is an article about me, which (at the time that I'm writing this book) says that I'm an author and

---

[679] New York Times "Corporate editing of Wikipedia revealed" by Katie Hafner (August 19th 2007)

[680] Business Insider "I Get Paid To Edit Wikipedia For Leading Companies" by Mike Wood (January 9th 2013)

[681] The Independent "Wikipedia rocked by 'rogue editors' blackmail scam targeting small businesses and celebrities" by Jonathan Owen (September 1st 2015)

[682] Ibid.

"conspiracy theorist," best known for my "conspiracy theories" about secret societies like the Bilderberg Group and Bohemian Grove.

At one point in early 2017, the entry was updated to say that I'm an author and media analyst, and cited reports in *The Washington Times* and on Fox News, both calling me that. There was an editor war, and some people kept deleting the reference to me being a media analyst, and then others would change it back, and this continued until an editor locked the page which prevented anyone except approved Wikipedia editors from changing it. I then called out the founder of Wikipedia, Jimmy Wales, on Twitter for the censorship and the two of us exchanged messages privately though DMs and emails about the issue.

He surprisingly and graciously updated the article himself,[683] and used citations to reports from Fox News,[684] *The Washington Times*,[685] and *The Daily Caller* as the sources, all of which identified me as a media analyst.[686] Soon afterward some editors overruled him and deleted any reference to me being a media analyst,

---

[683] Jimmy Wales' username is Jimbo Wales (edit made on April 5th 2017)

[684] Fox News "WATCH: Hillary Supporters OK With Repealing the Bill of Rights" (August 6th 2015)

[685] Washington Times "Californians sign sham petition supporting 'Obama's preemptive nuclear strike' against Russia" by Jeffrey Scott Shapiro (June 11th 2015)

[686] Daily Caller "CNN's Chris Cuomo Wants Tolerance Of Naked Men In Women's Restrooms" by Betsey Rothstein (February 23rd 2017)

claiming the reason was that the citations were to "unreliable sources."[687]

Editors also deleted part of the article which said, "Dice runs a YouTube channel which has over 980,000 subscribers, and more than 300 million views," which is very strange because my YouTube channel is a large part of my career, and as you may know, I had become the most popular conservative YouTuber at the time.[688] The fact that Wikipedia wouldn't allow a reference to my YouTube channel or it's statistics is because they're trying to downplay my popularity and paint me as just some little known 'conspiracy theorist,' not wanting readers to know that I have a huge audience with millions of viewers a week.[689]

They also deleted a reference to a show on the Travel Channel that I had been featured on called *America Declassified*, even though I'm listed on the credits at IMDB, the Internet Movie Database, which is the industry standard for film credits.[690] The false categorizing of my work, and the deletion of prominent facts about my career and popularity are just the tip of the iceberg in terms of Wikipedia's manipulation of information and participation in spreading fake news.

Pages of popular conservatives often have large "Controversies" sections which contain long lists of every little thing they've said that liberals find objectionable or

---

[687] https://en.wikipedia.org/w/index.php?title=Talk:Mark_Dice&oldid=794882444

[688] Compared to Stephen Crowder, Next News Network, Paul Joseph Watson, Fox News Channel, and others as ranked on VidStatsX.com and SocialBlade.com in October 2017

[689] https://socialblade.com/youtube/user/markdice

[690] http://www.imdb.com/name/nm4412986/

want to amplify. Pages for Ann Coulter, Sean Hannity, Rush Limbaugh, and Michael Savage all have the "Controversy" section or equivalent which nitpick things they've said or done. Wikipedia has even been known to use unflattering photos of conservatives in their profiles.

Conversely, there are relatively few liberal journalists or talk show hosts who have a 'Controversy' section in their articles, or have much negative information about them even mentioned at all. For example, there is no mention on MSNBC's Lawrence O'Donnell's page about his conspiracy theories about President Trump, which got so outrageous that he even claimed Vladimir Putin orchestrated a false flag attack in Syria using chemical weapons to help President Trump's approval ratings.[691] There's not a single mention on Michael Moore's page, or Congresswoman Maxine Waters' page about their endless Russian conspiracy theories either. Maxine Waters even claims, among other strange things, that Russia coined the term "Crooked Hillary" for Donald Trump.[692]

Transgender TV star 'Laverne Cox' was born Roderick Cox, a man, but Wikipedia editors refuse to allow his birth name to be mentioned anywhere on his page.[693] Roderick was the first transgender person to appear on the cover of *Time* magazine and 'she' is hailed as a hero in the liberal media, but unlike every single other actor or actress on the planet who uses a stage name

---

[691] Washington Times "MSNBC host's conspiracy theory: What if Putin planned the Syrian chemical attack to help Trump?" by Avi Selek (April 8th 2017)

[692] Real Clear Politics "Rep. Maxine Waters: 'Crooked Hillary' and 'Lock Her Up' Memes Were 'Developed' By Putin" by Tim Hains (May 19th 2017)

[693] https://en.wikipedia.org/wiki/Laverne_Cox

(or legally changes their name), Wikipedia will not allow any mention of the fact that 'Laverne Cox' was born Roderick Cox.[694]

Many of Hollywood's biggest stars use stage names and while never mentioned in the traditional media, their real names are always included on their Wikipedia page, except for 'Laverne's.' Tom Cruise (real name: Tom Mapother), Nicholas Cage (real name: Nicolas Coppola), Katy Perry (real name: Katy Hudson), Demi Moore (real name: Demetria Guynes), Tina Fey (real name Elizabeth Fey), and every other 'cis gender' celebrity have their real names included on Wikipedia, but the site gives special treatment to 'Laverne Cox' (and probably other transgender people).

Liberal political figures also appear to get special treatment on Wikipedia by editors who carefully guard their pages, trying to keep them portrayed in a positive light. One investigation revealed that a single Wikipedia editor made 2,269 changes to Hillary Clinton's page over a ten year period from 2006 up until the time she announced she was running for president in 2016 in order to keep as much criticism off it as possible.[695] Wikipedia founder Jimmy Wales actually contacted Hillary Clinton's office to ask how she prefers to be named on the page, either "Hillary Rodham Clinton" or just "Hillary Clinton."[696]

Jimmy Wales' own page is heavily protected by the "edit protection mafia" as some people call them, who

---

[694] http://www.imdb.com/name/nm1209545/bio

[695] Business Insider "Meet the guy who has protected Hillary Clinton's Wikipedia page for almost a decade" by Maxwell Tani (May 15th 2015)

[696] Ibid.

guard it against criticism. Wales himself has even edited his own page, which is highly frowned upon according to Wikipedia policy, since all edits are supposed to be made only by "disinterested" 3rd parties to avoid conflicts of interest.[697]

He also used his administrative authority to scrub references to his connection to online porn.[698] In the 1990s he cofounded a website called Bomis, which started as a general interest informational site, but then became mostly about porn.[699] Several times he removed any references to pornography, and changed them to call the porn site the "Bomis Babes Blog" instead.[700]

He also made edits to remove any mention of Wikipedia's co-founder, Larry Sanger, after the two had a falling out.[701] After other editors reverted the changes, Wales again tried to remove the credit to his co-founder. When a technology writer caught the edits and contacted Sanger, he responded, "I must say I am amused. Having seen edits like this, it does seem that Jimmy is attempting to rewrite history. But this is a futile process because in our brave new world of transparent activity and maximum communication, the truth will [come] out."[702]

---

[697] Wired "Wikipedia Founder Edits Own Bio" by Evan Hanson (December 19th 2005)

[698] Ibid.

[699] Heat Street "FLASHBACK: Champion of Truth Jimmy Wales Edited Own Wiki Page to Remove Links to Porn Industry" by Kieran Corcoran (April 27th 2017)

[700] Wired "Wikipedia Founder Edits Own Bio" by Evan Hanson (December 19th 2005)

[701] Ibid.

[702] Ibid.

Allegations made by the site's co-founder Larry Sanger are so disturbing, I don't even want to discuss them. Just to give you an idea, he contacted the FBI in 2010 after he left the company to report certain kinds of images being published in the media section of the website he said Wikipedia was knowingly distributing.[703] After leaving Wikipedia, Sanger started a similar site called Citizendium, where writers have to reveal their real names to avoid many of the problems found on Wikipedia due to anonymous editors and anyone being able to write whatever they want.

For example, the Wikipedia page for *USA Today's* founding editor John Siegenthaler Sr. had once claimed he was directly involved in the assassination of John F. Kennedy and his brother Bobby.[704] The edit was made as joke by someone, but it stayed up, and when Siegenthaler learned of it he contacted Jimmy Wales, but at first the only thing Wikipedia did is correct the misspelling of a word in the entry. The false claim stayed on the website for four months before it was finally removed, but not before the claims had been repeated on other sites.[705]

A Turkish academic who traveled to Canada was reportedly detained for several hours by immigration officials because of a false claim someone added to his Wikipedia page.[706] Pro golfer Fuzzy Zoeller, who once

---

[703] Fox News "Wikipedia Distributing C**** P***, Co-founder Tells FBI" by Jonathan Winter (April 27th 2010)

[704] USA Today "Author Apologizes for Fake Wikipedia Biography" by Susan Page (December 11th 2005)

[705] USA Today "A False Wikipedia 'Biography'" by John Seigenthaler (November 29th 2005)

[706] The Volokh Conspiracy (Wikipedia and the Biograhy Problem" by Ira Matetsky (May 13th 2009)

won the U.S. Open and the Masters Tournament, sued Wikipedia after someone edited his page to say that he beat his wife and abused drugs, allegations which were then picked up by other websites.[707]

Just a few days before a Congressional mid-term election, someone changed the page of House of Representatives Majority Leader Tom DeLay to say that he was a "Grand Dragon" of the Republican Party, a reference to the title of the leader of the KKK. The IP address of the person who changed it was traced back to someone who reportedly worked for *The New York Times*.[708]

Because of the wild west nature of Wikipedia, people often change pages as a joke especially after a politician or a celebrity says something controversial. For example, after senator Ted Cruz got into an exchange on Twitter with the sports website Deadspin and hilariously 'owned' them with his response, someone changed the Wikipedia page for Deadspin, which usually reads that it's owned by parent company Gawker Media, to say it was owned by Ted Cruz.[709] While sometimes these kinds of edits are just harmless and funny pranks, they show the vulnerability of Wikipedia and the dangers of allowing anyone to make changes to articles without proper oversight.

People have changed the pages of celebrities to indicate that they have died, which has sometimes caused

---

[707] The Smoking Gun "Golfer Sues Over Vandalized Wikipedia Page" (February 22nd 2007)

[708] Ad Week "Fox News, New York Times Vandalizing Rivals' Wikipedia Entries?" (August 15th 2007)

[709] New York Post "Ted Cruz shows sense of humor, owns Deadspin in Twitter war" by Chris Perez (January 25th 2017)

the fake news to spread far and wide across the Internet. A sociology student actually added a fake quote to the Wikipedia page of French composer Maurice Jarre immediately after his death as an experiment to see if media outlets would pick it up in their obituaries and many did, including *The Guardian*.[710]

One study that measured how many people viewed pages that were "vandalized" with false information found that 42% of the "damage" was repaired almost immediately, but the majority of the edits which were not quickly corrected were viewed hundreds of millions of times before the articles had been fixed."[711]

Sometimes Wikipedia editors will even create an entire article about a topic or an issue hoping to shine a spotlight on it to further promote their political leanings. For example, there was a lengthy article titled "Criticism of George W. Bush," but the "Criticism of Barack Obama" page had been deleted four different times by Wikipedia editors who kept claiming the article "has no meaningful, substantive content," and called it an, "Attack page" that was "unsourced."[712]

After the edit wars continued, the site finally allowed the "Criticism of Barack Obama" page to stay, but renamed it to "The Public Image of..." and of course Obama's main page is mostly praise. The edit summary

---

[710] NBC News "Student Hoaxes World's Media on Wikipedia" by Shawn Pogatchnick of Associated Press (May 12th 2009)

[711] The Association of Computing Machinery - 2007 International ACM Conference on Supporting Group Work - "Creating, Destroying, and Restoring Value in Wikipedia" by Reid Priedhorsky, Jilin Chen, Shyon (Tony) K. Lam, Katherine Panciera, Loren Terveen, and John Riedl (November 4, 2007)

[712] Conservapedia "Examples of Bias in Wikipedia: Obama"

for the decision to rename and redirect the 'Criticism' section of Obama's page reads, "so the conservatards [conservative retards] won't get their knickers in a twist."[713]

The article about the United States Presidential Election of 2016 highlights liberals' conspiracy theories about Russian interference, and on Donald Trump's page in the section about his campaign for president it points out, "The alt-right movement coalesced around Trump's candidacy," and claims, "During the campaign, Trump was accused of pandering to white nationalists," and "Fact-checking organizations have denounced Trump for making a record number of false statements compared to other candidates."[714]

Editors have also been known to delete pages of conservatives who they don't feel warrant being mentioned on the site because when someone has a Wikipedia page, even if it is in a completely negative light, it gives the impression that the person is noteworthy or famous, and sometimes editors don't want to validate the person's success by dedicating a page to them. For example shortly after radio talk show host Wayne Dupree was named one of the Top 50 Influential Black Republicans for 2017, someone decided to create a Wikipedia page for him, but editors soon deleted it.[715] The gatekeepers don't want to let people know about black conservatives because liberals are trying to control

---

[713] Wikipedia "Criticism of Barack Obama: Revision history" by User Sceptre (March 16th 2009)

[714] Wikipedia entry on Donald Trump (May 2017)

[715] Newsmax "Newsmax's 50 Most Influential African-American Republicans" by Frances Rice (February 22nd 2017)

the narrative by continuing to perpetuate the myth that all black people are Democrats.

White, heterosexual, Christian men are usually demonized as the cause of every evil in the world by the liberal media today.[716] White people are held in such disdain by the liberal media that they are often told they should be ashamed of being white, and if they have any measure of success in life it's because they have "white privilege" which is said to be the primary reason for it, meaning they benefit from what liberals call an inherent white supremacist ideology incorporated into American society and its institutions.[717]

White people are being cast in such a negative light in the media and on college campuses today that they are encouraged to be ashamed of being white, and if any white person happens to be proud of their culture then they are painted as a racist and white supremacist. Every other race can be happy about who they are, except white people. A comparison between articles about White Pride, Black Pride, and Asian Pride on Wikipedia illustrates this double standard. For example, the White Pride article states, "White pride is a motto primarily used by white separatist, white nationalist, neo-Nazi and white supremacist organizations in order to signal racist or racialist viewpoints."[718]

---

[716] Daily Caller "Fancypants College Professor Blames 'White Heterosexual Male Privilege' For Trump Victory" by Eric Owens (January 18th 2017)

[717] EveryDayFeminism "10 Examples That Prove White Privilege Protects White People in Every Aspect Imaginable" by Jon Greenberg (November 26th 2015)

[718] Wikipedia entry for 'White Pride' (retrieved August 12th 2017)

Compare this to the article on Black Pride, which reads, "Black pride is a movement in response to dominant white cultures and ideologies that encourages black people to celebrate black culture and embrace their African heritage."[719]

The entry for Asian Pride reads that in the United States, "Asian Pride (also spelled AZN pride) is a positive stance to being Asian American."[720] The anti-white bias in the 'pride' articles is Cultural Marxism, which ironically Wikipedia calls a conspiracy theory.[721] Cultural Marxism is the use of the media to perpetuate Leftist ideologies such as political correctness, gender bending, and other sexual perversions as if they are normal and cool. Cultural Marxism uses pop culture and celebrity icons to promote regressive Leftist policies and behaviors to the masses so people will mimic these influencers by thinking their attitudes and actions are "cool." While Wikipedia calls Cultural Marxism a conspiracy theory, the Southern Poverty Law Center calls it a conspiracy theory with an "anti-Semitic twist."[722]

Wikipedia also uses their home page to highlight featured articles and have an "On This Day in History" section and other trivia boxes which all promote liberal causes, and progressive historical figures and activists. *Frontpage* magazine did an investigation into Wikipedia's liberal bias and published their results in a two part series titled "How the Left Conquered Wikipedia." It starts off

[719] Wikipedia entry for 'Black Pride' (retrieved August 12th 2017)

[720] Wikipedia entry for 'Asian Pride' (retrieved August 12th 2017)

[721] https://en.wikipedia.org/wiki/Frankfurt_School#Cultural_Marxism

[722] SPLC "'Cultural Marxism' Catching On" by Bill Berkowitz (August 15, 2003)

saying, "Finding examples of Wikipedia's bias is not difficult. One need only compare the entries of figures who do the same thing but from opposite sides of the political spectrum."[723]

They compared the pages of several prominent conservative political commentators like Ann Coulter to popular liberals like Michael Moore and found that the negative bias was overwhelming. At the time of their investigation the "Controversies and Criticism" section of Ann Coulter's page was over 35% of the article, where Michael Moore's was under 5% in terms of the word count.[724] The Criticism section on Keith Olbermann's page was also just 5% of the article.

Che Guevara's page had less than 2% dedicated to criticism. He's the Leftist communist revolutionary who is adored by liberals even though he oversaw the executions of at least one hundred political prisoners in Cuba.[725] Editors also guard the Southern Poverty Law Center's page, along with its founder Morris Dees. For example, information about Morris Dees' alleged abuse of his ex-wife and his supposed affairs keeps getting censored from his page.[726] The SPLC is the organization dedicated to painting conservatives as racists, homophobic, xenophobic, and anti-government extremists.

After Google put 'human rights activist' Yuri

---

[723] Frontpage Magazine "How the Left Conquered Wikipedia Part 1" by David Swindle (August 22nd 2011)

[724] Ibid.

[725] History.com "Che Guevara - Facts & Summary"

[726] Front Page Magazine "How the Left Conquered Wikipedia, Part II: Coddling Progressives" by David Swindle (August 31st 2011)

Kochiyama on their homepage in May of 2016 as a "Google Doodle," some media outlets pointed out that she openly admired Osama Bin Laden and other violent revolutionaries like Che Guevara and Fidel Castro.[727] Wikipedia editors quickly removed such information from her page and tried to hide the fact that she was a black supremacist. An edit war ensued and editors settled on having her page admit she supported black "separatism."

Breitbart News pointed out that the edit log showed the page had been edited more times in the 24 hours after she was featured on Google's home page than it had been edited in the last two years combined, and conclude that, "The Wikipedia edit log is a stark example of the lengths to which the left will go to rewrite history."[728]

A study of the demographics of Wikipedia editors found that over 85% of them were men with an average age of 27, most of whom do not have a girlfriend or any kids.[729] It appears many of them are loners trying to gain a sense of power by controlling how the world sees the people or issues they write about.

## WikiTribune

Wikipedia founder Jimmy Wales says that the day after the election of Donald Trump he came up with an idea for a news website to "combat fake news." A few

---

[727] Vox "Yuri Kochiyama, today's Google Doodle, fought for civil rights — and praised Osama bin Laden" by Dylan Matthews (May 19th 2016)

[728] Breitbart "Wikipedia Editors Scrub References To Activist's Bin Laden Praise Following Breitbart Article" by Mike Ma (May 20th 2016)

[729] https://en.wikipedia.org/wiki/File:WMFstratplanSurvey1.png

months later, the *WikiTribune* was announced. "That was when I really decided to move forward," he told *The Guardian*, speaking of Trump's victory.[730]

Wales said, "The news is broken and we can fix it. We're bringing genuine community control to our news with unrestricted access for all. We're developing a living, breathing tool that'll present accurate information with real evidence, so that you can confidently make up your own mind."[731]

It's paid for by crowdfunding and started with an initial staff of ten journalists.[732] *The Guardian* pointed out, "Those who donate will become supporters, who in turn will have a say in which subjects and story threads the site focuses on. And Wales intends that the community of readers will fact-check and subedit published articles."[733] So it sounds like the WikiTribune will have some of the same flaws as Wikipedia.

While it may have been a noble idea in theory that having a community of users who watch pages and are able to add to them or correct errors, as *Frontpage* points out, "Wikipedia in practice has strayed from these utopian ideas because of the ease with which political and social bias trumps altruism."[734]

---

[730] The Guardian "Wikipedia founder to fight fake news with new Wikitribune site" by Alex Hern (April 2nd 2017)

[731] Ibid.

[732] WikiTribune.com "A New Kind of Platform: 2: Free and Ad-Free"

[733] The Guardian "Wikipedia founder to fight fake news with new Wikitribune site" by Alex Hern (April 2nd 2017)

[734] Frontpage Magazine "How the Left Conquered Wikipedia Part 1" by David Swindle (August 22nd 2011)

The fact that Wikipedia is the default online encyclopedia is horrifying considering I've only mentioned a handful of the problems the site has. And with the ability to misinform so many people with bias or malicious information, it should not be considered a reliable source of information and should just be avoided altogether.

# CNN

CNN started out as the first cable news network, which is what CNN actually stands for, when it was launched in 1980 by entrepreneur Ted Turner. Back then it was revolutionary and changed the entire news industry by rapidly deploying correspondents anywhere around the world and covering breaking news as it happened, but today CNN is just a shell of its former self. As comedian Larry Wilmore once said, "I've been watching CNN a long time. Yep. I used to watch it back when it was a news network."[735]

As the 2016 election approached, CNN's coverage got more biased and absurd by the day, and after Trump won, they completely fell off the rails and lost any resemblance to a news network whatsoever. At first their pundits blamed Trump's victory on a "white lash" and "white supremacists," and then they veered off into the Twilight Zone, attacking President Trump for eating two scoops of ice cream and speculated that he may be "afraid of stairs" because he held onto the handrail when exiting Air Force One.

President Trump famously pushed back against their odd and obsessive attacks telling their White House correspondent Jim Acosta that CNN was "fake news" which caused the network to have even more animosity towards the new president.

Just two months after the election, with their reputation in shambles, CNN's president Jeff Zucker said

---

[735] Larry Wilmore at the White House Correspondents' Dinner 2016

he felt like his network's credibility "is higher than ever."[736] Let's not forget this is the network where host Fareed Zakaria boldly declared just before the election, "Trump will lose, and he will then destroy the Republican Party,"[737] and the tone of their coverage as the election approached gave the impression that Hillary's victory was inevitable.

CNN's reputation has been so damaged in recent years that host Jake Tapper was singled out by President Obama during the 2016 White House Correspondents Dinner when Obama joked that Tapper left journalism to join CNN.[738] Poor Jake even admitted that his own seven-year-old son now calls him 'fake news' to taunt him.[739]

For decades, CNN has been selling their anchors' likeness and their trademarked logo to be used in fake news segments in Hollywood films.[740] CNN's now defunct show *Crossfire* recorded a fake segment for Jody Foster's film *Contact* (1997); Larry King, once the face of the network, has played himself in various films where he staged discussions to make them look like they were part of his CNN show; Bernard Shaw, the network's lead news presenter for twenty years, recorded a fake news segment

---

[736] New York Magazine "CNN's Jeff Zucker on Covering Donald Trump — Past, Present, and Future" by Gabriel Sherman (January 18th 2017)

[737] Newsmax "Trump Will Lose and Take GOP Down" by Fareed Zakaria (October 14th 2016)

[738] Newsmax "CNN Irked at Obama's Jake Tapper Joke at Correspondents' Dinner" by Jason Devaney (May 2nd 2016)

[739] The Hill "Tapper: My son uses 'fake news' quip" by Mark Hensch (March 10th 2017)

[740] Entertainment Weekly "CNN in the Movies" by David Hochman and Carrie Bell (July 18th 1997)

for *Jurassic Park: The Lost World* (1997); and Anderson Cooper recorded a fake news segment for *Batman vs. Superman* in 2016.[741] So at this point it would be inaccurate to say that CNN *wasn't* producing fake news, but their unethical and deceptive actions go far beyond scripting fictional news segments for movies.

Like the time they conducted what looked like a live interview via satellite between Ashleigh Banfield and Nancy Grace using the standard split screen display with each of them appearing to be in different parts of the country, but some viewers at home happened to notice that the same cars, trucks, and even a giant bus were seen driving by in the background behind each of them, passing by one person then just a second or two later, the same vehicles would drive right past the other because they were standing right next to one another in the same parking lot.[742]

After a heroic firefighter saved an infant who had been abandoned in a hot car in a parking lot, he did a live interview with CNN's sister station HLN while wearing a "Trump" shirt and when the segment was replayed later in the day, which is common for cable news networks, they blurred out his T-shirt![743]

CNN was actually sued for reporting what the plaintiff claims was fake news about a hospital he ran as CEO after they aired a story depicting it as having an infant

---

741 The Wrap "Batman v Superman': 8 Real Media Stars Who Reported From Gotham and Metropolis" by Matt Donnelly (March 26th 2016)

742 Daily Mail "Bizarre moment CNN anchors unsuccessfully try to pretend they are not in the same parking lot" (May 9th 2013)

743 The Hill "HLN blurs out Trump T-shirt" by Joe Concha (September 1st 2016)

mortality rate of three times the national average, saying they intentionally manipulated statistics.[744] Exposing the fake news from CNN could fill an entire book itself, so in this chapter I'll just cover a few examples and some of the insane things their contributors regularly say. We'll also look at the claims that CNN has cozied up to dictatorships in hopes of getting interviews or to further CNN's business interests in certain countries.

## CNN's 2016 Election Aftermath

Just a few weeks before the election, when Trump was warning about possible hacking of electronic voting machines, CNN ran a story titled, "No, the presidential election can't be hacked,"[745] and dismissed Trump's concerns, but right after Hillary's devastating loss they published a story with the headline, "Where's the outrage over Russia's hack of the US election?"[746]

During one of their endless discussions on conspiracy theories about the Trump campaign 'colluding' with Russians to 'steal' the election from Hillary, they even used B-roll from a video game called Fallout 4 in a segment about "Russian Hackers."[747] B-roll, for those who don't know, is the stock footage that is played during

---

[744] Law Newz "Hospital CEO Wins Major Court Victory After Accusing CNN of False Reporting" by Rachel Stockman (February 15th 2017)

[745] CNN "No, the presidential election can't be hacked" by Tal Kopan (October 19th 2016)

[746] CNN "Where's the outrage over Russia's hack of the US election?" by Paul Waldman (December 10th 2016)

[747] CNET "CNN uses Fallout 4 screenshot in report on Russian hacking" by Alfred Ng (January 3rd 2017)

a news story while the reporter or anchor is talking about it. They literally used a clip from a video game during a 'news' story about their 'Russian collusion' speculation!

CNN contributor Bob Baer actually wanted an election "do over." When he mentioned this on air a surprised host asked, "Bob, if I'm hearing you correctly, you're saying we should have another election?"

Baer responds, "When a foreign country interferes in your election and the outcome is in doubt, the legitimacy of the government, I don't know how it works constitutionally, I'm not a lawyer, constitutional lawyer, but I'm deeply disturbed by the fact that the Russians interfered...I don't see any other way than to vote again."[748]

After Trump was elected, CNN's senior media analyst Brian Stelter asked, "Is this something of a national emergency?" and wondered if journalists were just "afraid to say so."[749] He also asked, "Do citizens in dictatorships recognize what's happening right here right now?" and wondered "Are they looking at the first two days of the Trump administration and saying, 'Oh, that's what my leader does?'"[750] Yes, he actually equated President Trump's inauguration with a dictator taking over.

Then later that day when it was learned that President Trump picked Frank Sinatra's *My Way* for the first dance at the Presidential Inaugural Ball, CNN reported that Sinatra's daughter Nancy was upset that Trump was using her father's song. The original headline to the story was,

---

[748] NewsBusters "CNN's Robert Baer: We Should Have Another Election" by Tom Blumer (December 11th 2016)

[749] NewsBusters "CNN's Stelter Frets 'National Emergency' of Trump Election, Ties to Russia" by Brad Wilmouth (December 11th 2016)

[750] CNN Transcripts Reliable Sources (January 22nd 2017)

"Nancy Sinatra Not Happy Trump Using Father's Song at Inauguration."[751]   She then responded on Twitter saying, "That's not true.   I never said that.   Why do you lie, CNN?"[752]

They then changed the headline and made major changes to the article and added an editor's note claiming they just "updated" it.[753]   How could they make such a huge mistake, causing Nancy Sinatra to not only say she never said such a thing, but to call CNN liars?   Most likely some editor probably voiced their opinion that they thought she would be upset about Trump's song choice, or said that they had 'heard' she was upset (which was just them hearing someone else's opinion that she might be) which they then decided to actually publish as if it were a real story.

## Hands Up Don't Shoot

CNN's fake news problem dates back at least several years, and one of the prime examples is them perpetuating the 'hands up don't shoot' hoax which largely gave rise to Black Lives Matter.   The saying was falsely attributed to Michael Brown, the six-foot-four three hundred pound thug who robbed a convenience store before attacking a police officer in Ferguson, Missouri in 2014 resulting in

---

[751] Mediaite "'I Never Said That': Nancy Sinatra Calls Out CNN For Saying She's Unhappy With Trump Using 'My Way'" by Justin Baragona (January 20th 2017)

[752] Fox News "Nancy Sinatra slams CNN for anti-Trump spin on story about her humorous tweet" (January 20th 2017)

[753] Mediaite "'I Never Said That': Nancy Sinatra Calls Out CNN For Saying She's Unhappy With Trump Using 'My Way'" by Justin Baragona (January 20th 2017)

him being shot and killed. After covering the protests one night, host Sally Kohn concluded her show saying "We want you to know, that our hearts are out there marching with them," and then she and her three other panelists all held up their hands in solidarity with the protesters who had adopted the gesture as a symbol of their cause.[754]

After the investigation into the shooting of Michael Brown was complete, even the most liberal of news outlets admitted the claim that he had his hands up when he was shot was a lie, and that narrative was ranked one of the biggest lies of the year, even by the far left *Washington Post*.[755] The damage had long been done though. 'Hands up don't shoot' had become the rallying cry of Black Lives Matter, and the slogan was printed on signs at protests and on people's t-shirts; and the lie that Michael Brown was an innocent victim, murdered by a racist police force had taken root.[756] Milwaukee Sheriff David Clarke would later say that fake news was born in Ferguson when the liberal media propagated the 'hands up, don't shoot' lie."[757]

---

[754] Washington Post "'Hands up, don't shoot' did not happen in Ferguson" by Michelle Ye Hee Lee (March 19th 2015)

[755] The Washington Post "The biggest Pinocchios of 2015" by Glenn Kessler (December 14th 2015)

[756] CNN "Why 'hands up, don't shoot' resonates regardless of evidence" by Emanuella Grinberg (January 11th 2015)

[757] Twitter: David A. Clarke, Jr. (@SheriffClarke) December 6, 2016 https://twitter.com/SheriffClarke/status/806075069961150465

## "Black People Can't Be Racist"

CNN's descent into the fake news swamp coincided with their alignment with identity politics and social justice warriors who see straight white men as being the source of all of society's problems. Many of their black contributors seem to harbor a deep resentment for white people and regularly make bizarre statements about race. CNN contributor Marc Lamont Hill actually denies that black people can be racist at all.

In one segment talking about Black Lives Matter he said, "To say that the Black Lives Matter movement is racist is bizarre to me," and continued, "not just because black people don't have the institutional power to be racist or to deploy racism, but because the movement has called for justice, it's called for demilitarization, it's called for nonviolence."[758] Such a claim is laughable considering they've chanted that they want more dead cops. Violence, looting, and rioting are often a regular feature at Black Lives Matter gatherings.[759]

This same contributor called black community leaders who met with President Trump shortly after the election to discuss how to help their communities, "mediocre negros."[760] This was just one day after Martin Luther

---

[758] Washington Times "Marc Lamont Hill, CNN commentator: Black people can't be racist" by Bradford Richardson (July 11th 2016)

[759] NPR "Riots Follow Fatal Police Shooting In Milwaukee" (August 14th 2016)

[760] Washington Times "CNN's Marc Lamont Hill: 'Bunch of mediocre Negroes' meeting with Trump" by Jessica Chasmar (January 17th 2017)

King the 3rd met with Trump,[761] and shortly after Steve Harvey, Pastor Darrell Scott, and Kanye West met with him too.[762] MLK's niece had publicly revealed that she herself had voted for Trump,[763] but the narrative CNN pushes is that only racist white people support President Trump and that black people should despise and fear him.

When one contributor mentioned that neither Hillary Clinton or Barack Obama had denounced the repeated incidents of violence at the hands of the anti-Trump protesters, calling the attacks politically motivated hate crimes, black CNN contributor Symone Sanders responded, "I'm sorry, hate crimes and protesting are not the same things. A hate crime is a crime that is committed against somebody because of their religion, because of what they look like, because of their sexual orientation. That's not the same thing as protesting."[764]

Panelist Carl Higbie answered, "What do you say to the people who dragged a poor white guy out of a car and beat him?"

She responded, "Oh my goodness, poor white people! Please!" she responded. "Oh my. Stop. Stop, Carl."

The puzzled-looking panelist responded, "That's not protesting! Dragging someone out of their car and beating them is not protesting."[765]

---

[761] USA Today "On King day, Trump meets with Martin Luther King III" by David Jackson (January 16th 2017)

[762] Ibid.

[763] Washington Times "Alveda King, MLK's niece: 'I voted for Mr. Trump'" by Jessica Chasmar (January 16th 2017)

[764] Mediaite "Dem Strategist Mocks Trump Supporter Beat Up By Mob: 'Oh My Goodness, Poor White People!'" by Alex Griswold (November 14th 2016)

[765] Ibid.

CNN's anti-white racial bias has become the norm at the network. After the Grammys in 2016 CNN asked, "Is racism why Adele beat Beyoncé at the Grammys?" and said, "Certainly for her diehard fan base known as the Beyhive — and for many music critics — Beyoncé's *Lemonade* was a creative masterpiece. But with its racial themes and imagery, some are questioning if the project was 'just too black' for Grammy voters."[766]

*The Daily Beast* (a website started by *Newsweek*) echoed this insanity and said Beyoncé was a "victim of racism," and that, "Once again, the Grammy Awards got caught with their pants around their ankles."[767]

CNN deceptively edited the statements of a black woman who encouraged angry protesters to go burn down homes and businesses in white suburbs to give the appearance that she had actually called for peace![768] After an armed thug named Sylville Smith was shot and killed by police in Milwaukee, Wisconsin, riots broke out with businesses looted and set on fire, and white people were targeted for assault by the angry mob of black thugs.[769] The next day the perpetrator's sister Sherelle Smith gave a statement to the media where she encouraged the mob to move from the black neighborhood into the white suburbs, saying, "Don't bring

---

[766] CNN " Is racism why Adele beat Beyoncé at the Grammys?" by Lisa Respers (February 13th 2017)

[767] Daily Beast "Beyoncé Falls Victim to the Grammy Awards' Racism" by Kevin Fallon (February 12th 2017)

[768] Washington Times "CNN edits out Milwaukee victim's sister calling for violence in 'the suburbs'" by Bardford Richardson (August 16th 2016)

[769] Daily Caller "Milwaukee Rioters Hunt Down, Attack Whites" by Blake Neff (August 14th 2016)

that violence here. Burnin' down shit ain't going to help nothin! Y'all burnin' down shit we need in our community. Take that shit to the suburbs. Burn that shit down! We need our shit!"770

CNN showed a brief segment of her statement and then muted her while the reporter did a voice over saying she called for peace. After the unedited video went viral online CNN issued an on-air apology the next day for their deceptive editing.771

## CNN on Wikileaks

After Wikileaks published Hillary's campaign manager John Podesta's emails, morning host Chris Cuomo discouraged people from visiting Wikileaks' website to read them, and claimed, "it's illegal to possess the stolen documents," but "it's different for the media. So everything you're learning about this, you're learning from us."772

In other words, don't read them yourself, just trust CNN to tell you what they say and what their significance is. While it is illegal to hack in and steal someone's emails, it's not illegal to read those stolen emails if the hacker gives them to you or even posts them online, as long as the person posting them wasn't conspiring with

770 Washington Times "CNN edits out Milwaukee victim's sister calling for violence in 'the suburbs'" by Bardford Richardson (August 16th 2016)

771 BET "Update: CNN Apologizes for Not Airing Sherelle Smith's Full "To The Suburbs" Statement" (August 16th 2016)

772 Washington Post "'Remember, it's illegal to possess' WikiLeaks Clinton emails, but 'it's different for the media,' says CNN's Chris Cuomo" by Eugene Volokh (October 17th 2016)

the hacker to get them. It's interesting to note that Chris Cuomo has over one million Twitter followers, but can barely get a dozen likes or retweets on most things he posts, and such low engagement is usually only found on accounts that have bought fake followers in order to give people the appearance of being more popular than they are.

This is the same host who said on several occasions that being called 'fake news' is the equivalent of being called the N-word,[773] and wants to teach young girls 'tolerance' so they don't get uncomfortable seeing naked men in women's locker rooms when biological males who 'identify' as women use the facilities.[774]

## Censoring Atrocities

CNN's chief war correspondent Christiane Amanpour admitted that reporters were self-censoring themselves in their coverage of the buildup to — and during — the Iraq War, and looking back on the events says that they weren't rigorous enough, didn't ask the right questions, and later characterized the Bush administration's reasons for going to war as "disinformation at the highest levels."[775]

Eason Jordan, their former chief news executive, admits censoring stories about the atrocities Saddam

[773] The Hill "CNN's Chris Cuomo: 'Fake news' label 'the equivalent of the N-word for journalists'" by Mark Hensch (February 9th 2017)

[774] Daily Caller "CNN's Chris Cuomo Wants Tolerance Of Naked Men In Women's Restrooms" by Betsy Rothstein (February 23rd 2017)

[775] USA Today "Amanpour: CNN practiced self-censorship" by Peter Johnson (September 14th 2003)

Hussein and his sons had committed in Iraq because the network didn't want their Iraqi CNN affiliates to face repercussions by the regime.[776]   Just after the Iraq War started in 2003, he wrote an op-ed for *The New York Times* titled, "The News We Kept To Ourselves," and tried to justify keeping various atrocities he knew of a secret because revealing them would have "jeopardized the lives of Iraqis, particularly those on our Baghdad staff."[777]   He said that some of the events he knew about still haunt him.

The Media Research Center, a conservative media watchdog group, asked, "If accurate reporting from Iraq was impossible, why was access to this dictatorship so important in the first place?   And what truths about the thugs who run other totalitarian states — like North Korea, Cuba and Syria — are fearful and/or access-hungry reporters hiding from the American public?"[778]

Former CNN reporter Peter Collins, who was in Baghdad during the buildup to the first Gulf War, said that he was with Eason Jordan and CNN's president Tom Johnson during meetings with Iraqi officials where they were hoping to get an interview with Saddam Hussein. Collins later revealed, "I was astonished.   From both the tone and the content of these conversations, it seemed to

---

[776] The New York Times "The News We Kept To Ourselves" by Eason Jordan (April 11th 2003)

[777] Ibid.

[778] Media Research Center "CNN Admits Honest Reporting Was Impossible, So Why Go To Baghdad?" by Katie Wright (April 11th 2003)

me that CNN was virtually groveling for the interview."[779]

A few months later he wrote an op-ed for *The Washington Times* about his experience titled "Corruption at CNN" where he said he felt CNN was broadcasting Saddam Hussein's propaganda for him in hopes of getting an exclusive interview with him (which they got scooped by CBS). "I thought long and hard; could I be comfortable with a news organization that played those kinds of games? I decided, no, I could not, and resigned."[780]

These aren't the only startling allegations of this kind. In 2012, former CNN journalist Amber Lyon went public with her experience of working for the network, giving details of what she said were more clear examples of them catering to dictatorships.[781]

"What CNN is doing is they are essentially creating what some people have termed 'infomercials for dictators.' And that's the sponsored content that they are airing on CNN International that is actually being paid for by regimes and governments," she said. "And this violates every principle of journalistic ethics, because we're supposed to be watchdogs on these governments. We are not supposed to allow them to be a paying customer as journalists. And that's the issue here — that CNN is feeding, then, this propaganda to the public and

---

[779] Washington Times "Corruption at CNN" by Peter Collins (April 15th 2003)

[780] Ibid.

[781] The Guardian "Why didn't CNN's international arm air its own documentary on Bahrain's Arab Spring repression?" by Glenn Greenwald (September 4th 2012)

not fairly disclosing to the public that this is sponsored content."[782]

## CNN Host Ate Human Brains

In March of 2017, CNN aired an episode of a reality show / documentary series titled *Believer* with host Reza Aslan, a former Christian turned Muslim, who traveled around the world exploring all sorts of bizarre religious practices. One of the groups he interviewed was a cannibalistic sect of Hindus in India called the Aghoris, who literally cook members of their tribe when they die and eat them. He didn't just interview them, he actually joined them around a bonfire where they cooked their friends' dead body and his brain.[783] When word began spreading online about this after the episode aired, many people (myself included) thought maybe he just sat there and observed their cannibal barbecue, but the host actually ate human brains too, and CNN really did air it.[784]

Just before the episode aired he posted on his Facebook page, "Want to know what a dead guy's brain tastes like? Charcoal. It was burnt to a crisp!"[785] Yes, the self-proclaimed "most trusted name in news" resorted to having one of their hosts eat dinner at a cannibal barbecue

[782] Interview with Amber Lyon on RT "'Bahrain buys favorable CNN content'" (October 3rd 2012)

[783] Fox News "Reza Aslan eats human brain on new CNN show 'Believer'" (March 10th 2017)

[784] New York Post "CNN Host Eats Human Brains, Sparking Outrage" (March 9th 2017)

[785] https://www.facebook.com/rezaaslanofficial/posts/ 1867367783509592

hoping to get people to tune in and watch. Reza Aslan was later fired for posting profanity-filled rants on Twitter aimed at the president and his children.[786]

## Employees 'Resign' Over False Stories

CNN's Trump/Russia conspiracy theories got so out of control that at one point a group of staffers 'resigned' after one of the stories put CNN at risk of being sued for defamation by one of Trump's associates who the report focused on.[787] He threatened to sue, and the story was not only retracted, but completely removed from CNN's website. In its place was a retraction, reading, "CNN.com published a story connecting Anthony Scaramucci with investigations into the Russian Direct Investment Fund. That story did not meet CNN's editorial standards and has been retracted. Links to the story have been disabled. CNN apologizes to Mr. Scaramucci."[788]

An executive editor then sent an internal memo to staff at CNN, which someone leaked, reading in part, "No one should publish any content involving Russia without coming to me and Jason first. This applies to social, video, editorial, and MoneyStream. No exceptions."[789]

---

[786] Breitbart "CNN Host Reza Aslan Calls Trump 'Piece of Sh*t' for Correctly Identifying London Terror Attack" by Lucas Nolan (June 3rd 2017)

[787] Politico "3 CNN staffers resign over retracted Scaramucci-Russia story" by Hadas Gold (June 26th 2017)

[788] CNN.com "Editor's Note (June 23rd 2017)

[789] Breitbart "Leaked CNN Memo: Top Execs to Review All Russia Stories After Very Fake News Retraction" by Lucas Nolan (June 25th 2017)

Their reckless editorial policy was coming back to bite them.

CNN's 'sources' became so bad that they reported former FBI Director James Comey would testify that he did *not* tell President Trump that he wasn't under a criminal investigation regarding the allegations of Russian interference in the election, but just a few hours later Comey's testimony proved CNN laughably wrong again.[790] Wolf Blitzer would later reprimand reporter Gloria Borger on air her for bad sources, saying that, "either they don't know what they're talking about or they're lying."[791]

The very next day after the group of staffers resigned when another conspiracy theory was debunked, CNN was hit by another devastating blow to their credibility when hidden camera footage was released showing a long-time producer making some stunning revelations that further called into question the network's integrity.

## Project Veritas

An undercover video of a CNN producer who worked at the network for almost fifteen years was published by the political activist organization Project Veritas showing him admitting that CNN's constant coverage of the Trump/Russia conspiracy theories was "mostly bullshit," just "for the ratings," and that he thought President Trump

---

[790] The Hill "CNN issues correction after Comey statement contradicts reporting" by Joe Concha (June 7th 2017)

[791] Daily Caller "Wolf Blitzer Humiliates Colleague Over Quality Of Her White House Sources [VIDEO]" by Chuck Ross (July 29th 2017)

was right to call it a "witch hunt."[792]  The producer also laughed about the 'ethics' of the news business today.

Another video was released by Project Veritas the following day showing CNN host Van Jones calling the Trump/Russia 'investigation' a "big nothing burger."[793]  A second producer was also caught on tape saying that 90% of the staff at CNN were anti-Trump, and that he thought the American people are "stupid as shit" for voting for him.[794]

*The Washington Post* published a story downplaying the significance of the footage and made an obviously false statement about it.  This led to the *Post* issuing a retraction about their own story trying to call into question the validity of the Project Veritas videos, making the whole thing look even worse for CNN.[795]

It's unclear if CNN can ever repair the damage to their brand, and based on their editorial policies in recent years they appear to have completely abandoned any desire to be an actual news network.  While many wonder if CNN will eventually go bankrupt due to destroying their once great reputation, they will likely stay in business and continue to function as a Leftist propaganda channel,

---

[792] Real Clear Politics "American Pravda: 'Project Veritas' Catches CNN Producer Admitting Russia Story Is "Mostly Bullshit," "About Ratings" by Tim Hains (June 27th 2017)

[793] Newsweek "CNN's Van Jones Calls Trump-Russia Story 'Nothing Burger,' Newest Project Veritas Video Shows" by Greg Price (June 28th 2017)

[794] Project Veritas "CNN Producer: Voters "Stupid as Sh*t"– American Pravda: CNN Part 3" (June 30th 2017)

[795] Washington Times "Project Veritas's James O'Keefe frames Washington Post retraction in latest video" by Valerie Richardson (July 7th 2017)

although with a much smaller audience than they once enjoyed during their prime.

# NBC News

One of the most shocking examples of fake news was when NBC aired a story about General Motors' trucks having faulty gas tanks that could rupture if they got into an accident and possibly explode. While this was a real concern, NBC actually staged a scene where they crashed a car into the side of a GM truck and blew it up. It turns out that NBC producers not only put the wrong gas cap on the truck so it would pop off causing fuel to squirt out, but they also attached lit flares underneath the car that crashed into the truck so when the fuel spilled out of the tank, it caught on fire and blew up.[796]

The scene was dramatic, with a huge fireball engulfing the two vehicles, and news of the exploding gas tanks was now everywhere. But General Motors was suspicious and obtained the vehicles from the junkyard and had them forensically analyzed.

GM sued NBC after the analysis revealed what actually happened and NBC later admitted they staged the whole thing. "We apologize to our viewers and to General Motors. We have also concluded that unscientific demonstrations should have no place in hard news stories at NBC. That's our new policy," they said in a statement.[797]

---

[796] New York Times "NBC Settles Truck Crash Lawsuit, Saying Test Was 'Inappropriate'" by Elizabeth Kolbert (February 10th 1993)

[797] Los Angeles Times "NBC Admits It Rigged Crash, Settles GM Suit" by Michael Parrish and Donald W. Nauss (February 10th 1993)

Another embarrassing and unethical blunder was accidentally exposed live on air when a reporter was shown in a canoe rowing down the middle of flooded streets in New Jersey after heavy rain. As soon as she began her segment the live shot looked like she was in six feet of water in the middle of a suburb, but then two men came walking by directly in front of her, showing the water was only ankle deep.[798]

Looking bewildered, anchor Matt Lauer asked what just happened, and the staff in the New York studio could be heard laughing off camera. "Are these holy men, perhaps walking on top of the water?" he joked, not sure what else to say. Years later Jimmy Fallon asked Matt Lauer about the incident when he was a guest on *The Tonight Show*, but he didn't want to talk about it and sarcastically said, "Thank you for bringing that up, James. I can't wait to check my email when I get done with this show."[799]

NBC has a history of deceptively editing people's comments which causes them to be misrepresented to the audience. One of the most well-known examples of this is when they edited George Zimmerman's call to 911 just before he got into an altercation with Trayvon Martin and ended up fatally shooting him. NBC's version of the call had Zimmerman on the phone with the operator saying, "This guy looks like he's up to no good. He looks black," but the actual conversation was Zimmerman saying, "This guy looks like he's up to no good. Or he's on drugs or

---

[798] AdWeek "Kosinki's Canoe Was A 'Today' Stunt" (October 15th 2005)

[799] Tonight Show with Jimmy Fallon "Matt Lauer Can't Deal with Fake Floods or New Zealand Outhouses" (April 28th 2016)

something.   It's raining and he's just walking around, looking about."[800]

The dispatcher then replies: "OK, and this guy — is he black, white or Hispanic?"

Zimmerman then responds, "He looks black."

Even *The Washington Post*, a far left newspaper, admitted, "No matter how you feel about Zimmerman, that bit of tape editing was unfair to the truth and to Zimmerman's reputation."[801]   Zimmerman sued the network for defamation with the lawsuit saying, "NBC saw the death of Trayvon Martin not as a tragedy but as an opportunity to increase ratings, and so set about to create the myth that George Zimmerman was a racist and predatory villain."[802]

After Rudolf Guiliani gave an interview on Fox News about President Trump's proposed travel restriction which would temporarily prevent immigrants from several countries plagued by terrorism from coming to the U.S., NBC aired a segment using an edited sound bite taken out of context in attempts to frame Guiliani's statements as if this was a 'Muslim ban' when he specifically said it was not.[803]

NBC also deceptively edited comments by Reince Priebus on the same issue, again giving the false

---

[800] Mediaite "NBC News Admits 'Error' In Editing George Zimmerman's 911 Call, Apologizes" by Meenal Vamburkar (April 3rd 2012)

[801] Washington Times "NBC issues apology on Zimmerman tape screw-up" by Erik Wemple (April 3rd 2012)

[802] CNN "George Zimmerman sues NBC Universal over edited 911 call" by Michael Martinez (December 7th 2012)

[803] NewsBusters "Fake News: NBC Deceptively Edits Giuliani Comments on Immigration Order" by Kyle Drennen (January 30th 2017)

impression that Trump was proposing to ban all Muslims from entering the U.S. when Priebus too said exactly the opposite. NBC's story was titled "Reince Priebus on Muslim Registry: 'Not Going to Rule Out Anything,'"[804] based on an interview he had with *Meet The Press* host Chuck Todd. NBC also tweeted that when Reince was asked by Todd, "Can you rule out a registry for Muslims?" he answered, "I'm not going to rule out anything." They actually cut his statement short to give readers the wrong impression, because he actually said, "I'm not gonna rule out anything, but we're not going to have a registry based on a religion."[805]

Surprisingly *New York Times* political correspondent Maggie Habernman called out NBC for the deceptive edit, saying that Reince's actual quote indicates the opposite of what NBC framed it.[806] Even BuzzFeed's senior technology writer Charlie Warzel said it was an "irresponsible half-quote [without] even a link for context."[807]

Perhaps Katie Couric, who worked as an anchor for NBC, learned the art of deceptively editing video clips in order to cast people in a false light there, because she was sued for twelve million dollars in 2016 by several people

---

[804] NBC News "Reince Priebus on Muslim Registry: 'Not Going to Rule Out Anything'" by Christina Coleburn (November 20th 2016)

[805] https://twitter.com/cwarzel/status/800374196295573504

[806] https://twitter.com/maggieNYT/status/800352195359207426

[807] Business Insider "NBC News under fire for misleading tweets about Trump chief of staff's answer on Muslim registry" by Oliver Darcy (November 20th 2016)

who claimed just that after they appeared in her anti-gun documentary *Under the Gun*.[808]

Trump once tweeted that NBC is the same fake news media that said there is 'no path to victory' for him during the election, and ridiculed them for pushing the phony Russian collusion stories.[809] NBC got so defensive over people calling them 'fake news' due to their obsession with conspiracy theories about Russia 'colluding' with the Trump administration that *Meet The Press* host Chuck Todd and others put together an article titled "Four Reasons Why the Russia Story Isn't Fake News."[810]

Just one month after Donald Trump took the oath of office, NBC News produced a segment called "Dear Mr. President: Kids Talk Donald Trump" which showed a bunch of young kids voicing their fears about the new president.[811] Instead of being just a cute segment of innocent kids asking questions about the presidency, it looked like a propaganda piece that North Korea would produce. Some of the statements the children made were: "Most of my family is black. I'm afraid that you're gonna hurt some of us blacks." "You are here, attempting to white-wash America." "I don't like your definition of American, because I don't seem to fit within it," and, "Some of my friends are really scared about you building

808 Washington Times "Katie Couric, Stephanie Soechtig sued for $12M for deceptive edits in anti-gun documentary" by Jessica Chasmar (September 13th 2016)

809 https://twitter.com/realDonaldTrump/status/848158641056362496

810 NBC News "Four Reasons Why the Russia Story Isn't Fake News" by Chuck Todd, Mark Murray, and Carrie Dann (May 9th 2017)

811 NBC News "Mr. President: Kids Talk Donald Trump" posted to the NBC News YouTube channel (February 20th 2017)

a wall and the travel ban, because a lot of their families live in different places."

It was clear the kids had no idea what they were talking about and their parents, who had to approve of their appearance, were behind the camera coaching them on what to say. The segment was widely denounced online for using children in an anti-Trump propaganda piece portrayed as 'news' by a major network.[812]

NBC actually had people dress up as Muslims and attend a NASCAR race in Virginia in order to attempt to spark negative reactions from the other attendees. NASCAR fans, as you probably are well aware of, are often stereotyped as racist rednecks, and so NBC thought they could easily find a few drunk hicks who would give dirty looks to the Muslims.[813] When their stunt was discovered many people denounced NBC for violating journalistic ethics. "It is outrageous that a news organization of NBC's stature would stoop to the level of going out to create news instead of reporting news," said NASCAR spokesman Ramsey Poston.[814] The segment never aired, likely because they didn't get the negative reactions they had hoped for.

This is the same network that still employs Brian Williams, even after his admittedly false claims about being under enemy fire while covering the Iraq War.[815]

---

[812] Fox News "NBC News video featuring kids terrified about Trump comes under fire" (February 23rd 2017)

[813] Washington Times "NASCAR riled by show seeking anti-Muslim bias" by Jerry Seper (April 6th 2006)

[814] ESPN "NASCAR outraged by 'Dateline' racial story approach" via Associated Press (April 5th 2006)

[815] New York Times "Brian Williams Admits He Wasn't on Copter Shot Down in Iraq" by Ravi Somaiya (February 4th 2015)

Perhaps they appreciate his ability to keep a straight face while mischaracterizing things and framing stories in a false light. President Trump can do nothing right in the eyes of NBC. After his first press conference Brian Williams categorized it as, "a live special television event brought to you by narcissism, thin skin, chaos and deeply personal grievances."[816]

Other NBC anchors just seem to complain about Trump instead of actually reporting on what he's doing. When Andrea Mitchell was the guest host of *Meet The Press* she mentioned that Trump's plan to fix Obamacare was just a bunch of white men who wanted to cut off healthcare for women.[817]

When their *Nightly News* anchor Lester Holt interviewed President Trump for the first time, he interrupted him nine times in just two and a half minutes, barely letting him finish a sentence before he would cut him off to challenge what he was saying, or ask him something else as if he didn't want him to finish his point.[818]

Every night on NBC News their disdain for President Trump is clear in how they frame their opening segment and cast their coverage of him in the most negative light possible. They too have long given up on objectivity in

---

[816] NewsBusters "Hypocrite: Brian Williams Bemoans 'Thin-Skinned' Trump's 'Narcissism' Living 'Through...Television'" by Curtis Houck (February 17th 2017)

[817] NBC Meet the Press with Guest Host Andrea Mitchell Interview with Tom Price, Health and Human Services Secretary (May 7th 2017)

[818] NBC News -Lester Holt Interview with President Trump About James Comey Firing (May 11th 2017)

exchange for being another weapon in the arsenal of the Liberal Establishment.

# CBS News

Shortly after the 'fake news' phenomenon swept the country, CBS actually changed their slogan to "Real News" in what many thought was a pathetic try-hard attempt hoping to somehow convince people they were a 'trustworthy' network. Many people joked that if a news station has to claim they're "real news" then there's a real problem. In this chapter you'll see just a sample of some of the fake news coming from CBS and why they're so defensive about being a 'real' news network.

One of the first of what would unfortunately become many instances of disturbing crimes being broadcast on Facebook Live was when four black thugs in Chicago broadcast themselves torturing a white mentally handicapped man.[819] He was bound, gagged, and had his clothes and hair slashed with a knife. National news outlets were hesitant to report on it at first, and it wasn't until the horrifying video went viral on social media that the major networks finally mentioned it. But a report that CBS aired about the incident is one of the most misleading segments produced by a national news outlet.

The report aired on CBS radio stations as part of the top of the hour newsbreak and began with the announcer saying, "The viral video of a beating and knife attack in Chicago suggests the assault had racial overtones. CBS's Dean Reynolds tells us the victim is described as a

---

[819] Chicago Tribune "Brutal Facebook Live attack brings hate-crime charges, condemnation from White House" by Jason Meisner, William Lee, and Steve Schmadke (January 6th 2017)

mentally-challenged teenager. In the video he is choked and repeatedly called the n-word. His clothes are slashed and he is terrorized with a knife. His alleged captors repeatedly reference Donald Trump. Police are holding four people in connection with the attack."[820]

While "technically" correct, there couldn't be a better example of a misleading report. In reality, the victim was white and the perpetrators were black, and while the attackers were "referencing Donald Trump" they were saying "Fuck Donald Trump, and fuck white people."[821] The victim was called a "nigga" because that term, as you likely know, is often used as both an insult and a term of endearment, and yes, black people call white people "nigga" as an insult and to intimidate them.

CBS never apologized for the misleading report after it was denounced online, they just ignored the criticism and pretended like nothing happened. Their report was so backwards that it couldn't have just been from a producer getting the basic facts wrong — it must have taken some serious mental gymnastics for them to twist the story around 180 degrees from what actually happened to give the listeners the impression that a group of racist Donald Trump supporters attacked a black man. The black perpetrators were charged with multiple felonies, including hate crimes for the attack.[822]

---

[820] Mediaite "CBS Radio Deceptively Implies Chicago Torturers Were White Trump Supporters, Victim Was Black" by Alex Greenwold (January 7th 2017)

[821] New York Magazine "4 People Charged With Hate Crime in Torture of Disabled Teen on 'Sickening' Facebook Live Video" by Jen Kirby (January 5th 2017)

[822] NBC News "Four Arrested in Facebook Live Torture Video Now Charged With Hate Crimes" by Erik Ortiz (January 5th 2017)

This is far from an isolated incident of CBS presenting stories in a false light to either protect liberals or smear conservatives. For example, CBS doctored an interview with Bill Clinton when he was asked about Hillary's infamous fainting incident in order to omit Bill's embarrassing gaffe that such a thing happened "frequently." On PBS, Charlie Rose asked him if it was something more serious than people thought, and Bill answered, "If it is, it's a mystery to me and all of her doctors, because frequently, not frequently — rarely — but on more than one occasion over the last many, many years, the same sort of thing has happened to her where she got severely dehydrated."[823]

When the same interview aired later that day on CBS, they deceptively edited out the part where Bill said "frequently." Because it would have been an obvious jump cut, they actually inserted a brief clip of Charlie Rose over the edit as a reaction shot so viewers wouldn't notice the quick edit.[824]

CBS News' Investigative Correspondent Sharyl Attkisson, who worked for the network for twenty years, resigned in 2014 citing the network's liberal bias.[825] She said that it was a "struggle" to get her reports on the air (i.e., to avoid the censorship of her stories by CBS) and later published a book titled *Stonewalled: One Reporter's Fight for Truth in Obama's Washington.*

---

[823] Washington Times "CBS News omits Bill Clinton gaffe that Hillary 'frequently' becomes faint" by Jessica Chasmar (September 13th 2016)

[824] The Hill "CBS News edits transcript, video clip of Bill Clinton discussing Hillary's health" by Joe Concha (September 13th 2016)

[825] Politico "Sharyl Attkisson resigns from CBS News" by Dylan Byers (March 10th 2014)

In the later part of her career she had investigated the Benghazi attack as well as Operation Fast and Furious, a covert gun-running scheme which transferred weapons to Mexican drug cartels in what many believe was a false flag operation to then blame American gun stores for firearms ending up in the hands of narco groups.[826] So, Sharyl wasn't just a reporter, she was investigating some very serious scandals the Obama administration didn't want people to know about. A year before her resignation she had learned, and CBS News confirmed, that her computer had been hacked into by a sophisticated hacker on multiple occasions when she was investigating the Benghazi cover-up.[827]

CBS confirmed, "Evidence suggests this party performed all access remotely using Attkisson's accounts. While no malicious code was found, forensic analysis revealed an intruder had executed commands that appeared to involve search and exfiltration of data. This party also used sophisticated methods to remove all possible indications of unauthorized activity, and alter system times to cause further confusion. CBS News is taking steps to identify the responsible party and their method of access."[828]

Just a month earlier it was revealed that Obama's Justice Department had secretly obtained the emails and phone records of Fox News' White House correspondent James Rosen trying to find out who his sources were. So it's likely that some Deep State operatives in the NSA or

---

[826] World Net Daily "'Fast and Furious' called false flag against gun dealers" by Taylor Rose (April 3rd 2013)

[827] CBS News "CBS News confirms Sharyl Attkisson's computer hacked" (August 7th 2013)

[828] Ibid.

CIA were snooping around in Sharyl Attkisson's computer to see what she was working on and who she was talking to.[829] The CIA admits they hacked into the computers of members of the Senate Intelligence Committee when they were investigating the CIA's detention and interrogations programs under the Bush administration.[830] Again, they wanted to know who their sources were and how much they knew.

So if the CIA would illegally hack into computers of the very Congressmen who are tasked with overseeing their activities, why wouldn't they hack into the computers of reporters who are also investigating their unethical and illegal actions? The fact that these crimes are all but ignored by mainstream news networks shows that they are complicit in the cover-up.

Just two months before the 2004 Presidential Election, CBS's show *60 Minutes* aired a fake news story about George W. Bush's military service record based on forged documents. The fake documents cast doubt on the quality of Bush's service in the Air National Guard and indicated he was given preferential treatment. Various bloggers immediately began scrutinizing them and found inconsistencies in the jargon as well as the typography between the fonts used in the documents versus the fonts that actual documents of that kind had.

If real, they would have been typed in the 1970s, but appeared to have been created using Microsoft Word. For two weeks CBS anchor Dan Rather stuck by his story but skepticism from those on the Internet kept growing,

---

[829] Fox News "Obama administration spying included press, allies, Americans" (April 4th 2017)

[830] New York Times "Inquiry by C.I.A. Affirms It Spied on Senate Panel" by Mark Mazzetti and Carl Hulse (July 31st 2014)

causing other news outlets to cover the controversy, and so CBS reluctantly had to finally address it.

CBS News President Andrew Heyward said, "Based on what we now know, CBS News cannot prove that the documents are authentic, which is the only acceptable journalistic standard to justify using them in the report. We should not have used them. That was a mistake, which we deeply regret."[831]

Dan Rather would later say, "If I knew then what I know now — I would not have gone ahead with the story as it was aired, and I certainly would not have used the documents in question."[832] The documents, it turns out, were a dirty political trick that CBS either willfully or negligently fell for.

As I mentioned in the introduction of this book, when CBS's flagship show *60 Minutes* did an 'investigation' into fake news they featured several websites as examples which were actually parody and satire sites, not actual fake news sites. Who could possibly not get the humor in a headline like, "After Colonoscopy Reveals Brain Tumor, Donald Trump Drops from Race" or reading the first two sentences in the article about "Donald Trump Caught Snorting Cocaine by Hotel Staff" where the 'eyewitness' says she mistook a dog lying on the floor for Donald Trump's hair!? To call parody and humor sites 'fake news' sites is not only disingenuous but it waters down the entire argument of those who are supposedly trying to prevent fake news from spreading.

---

[831] CBS News "CBS Statement On Bush Memos" by Jerrett Murphy (September 20th 2004)

[832] CBS News "Dan Rather Statement On Memos" by Jerrett Murphy (September 20th 2014)

After a left wing lunatic tried to assassinate Republican members of Congress while they were practicing for a charity baseball game during the summer of 2017, CBS News anchor Scott Pelley opened the broadcast that night saying the attack may have been "self-inflicted."[833] Congressman Tom Reed of New York denounced Pelley's comments as "beyond the pale" and said they "further proved that the Mainstream Media has completely lost any moral compass to guide its journalistic endeavors." Reed added, "Mr. Pelley should be ashamed of himself for doing the despicable deed of blaming the victim. He should never be employed in the media again by any forum or entity."[834]

The story of the ambush of Republican Congressmen on the baseball field was quickly dropped, because the liberal media didn't want people to keep using it as an example that their constant bombardment of fake news painting Donald Trump and his supporters as the resurgence of Hitler's Third Reich had incited a mentally unstable liberal to attempt to assassinate a group of Congressmen.

It might be interesting for people to know that the major shareholder of CBS's parent company Viacom is Sumner Redstone, who was once caught on tape trying to convince a reporter to reveal their source about an embarrassing leak within MTV (one of his networks). On the tape he can be heard saying, "We're not going to kill

---

[833] Washington Times "CBS News anchor Scott Pelley asks if GOP shooting was 'self-inflicted'" by Jessica Chasmar (June 19th 2017)

[834] Washington Examiner "Rep. Tom Reed: Scott Pelley should 'never be employed in the media again' after Scalise comments" by Sean Langille (June 19th 2017)

him. We just want to talk to him."[835] Redstone, who was 87-years-old at the time, also told the reporter he will be "well-rewarded and well-protected" if he gave up his source.[836] That's the kind of man who has been in control of CBS for decades — a man who bribes reporters in order to reveal their sources when they publish a report damaging to the network or their affiliates.

---

[835] Daily Beast "Sumner Redstone Offers Reward to Get the Electric Barbarellas Leak" by Peter Lauria (July 20th 2010)

[836] Adweek "Viacom CEO Tells Reporter To Give Up Source: 'You Will Be Well-Rewarded and Well-Protected'" by Joe Ciarallo (July 20th 2010)

# ABC News

Almost every single night, ABC News puts a liberal spin on their stories and carefully chooses topics that will further their cause, but ABC has also staged crime scenes, deceptively edited clips to give the opposite impression of what people said, and have been sued for almost two billion dollars by a company claiming their false stories destroyed their business.[837]

One shocking example of fake news on ABC was when a reporter set up her own "police line" for a live shot to make it look like she was reporting right in front of the crime scene with the yellow police tape swaying in the wind right behind her. They would have gotten away with it if it weren't for some locals who came out to witness the report and posted pictures online showing that the producers had put up their own police tape by tying it onto two different tripods that were off camera and out of the frame.[838]

After Dr. Drew expressed he was quite concerned about Hillary Clinton's health problems as the 2016 election approached, KABC Radio (a division of ABC Broadcasting) deleted the webpage about his interview in an apparent attempt to protect Hillary from the negative publicity it was generating. "Based on the information that she has provided and her doctors have provided, we

---

[837] Associated Press "ABC, meat company settle $1.9 billion 'pink slime' suit" (June 28th 2017)

[838] CNN "ABC News staged crime-scene shot, photograph shows" by Dylan Byers (November 4th 2016)

were gravely concerned not just about her health, but her health care," Dr. Drew said, giving more ammunition to those who were raising concerns about her diminishing health.[839]

The following week his show on CNN's sister station HLN, which had been on the air for five years, was canceled. Even the liberal *Washington Post* couldn't help but see the connection and published a story with the headline, "'Dr. Drew' show canceled days after host's negative speculation about Hillary Clinton's health."[840] He was also called a "conspiracy theorist" for thinking her health was failing and was labeled a "Hillary Clinton Health Truther."[841] Just two weeks later she completely collapsed and had to be carried away by her staff, confirming what many had been concerned about for some time.

ABC anchor and chief political correspondent George Stephanopoulos used to work as Bill Clinton's former communications director so he can't pretend to be an objective journalist when he was literally on the payroll of the Clintons and even donated $75,000 dollars to them through their sham charity. When his donation was discovered he apologized for not disclosing it to ABC News and its viewers.[842] He was then forced to drop out

---

[839] Washington Times "Dr. Drew 'gravely concerned' about Hillary Clinton's '1950-level' health care" by Jessica Chasmar (August 18th 2016)

[840] Washington Post "'Dr. Drew' show canceled days after host's negative speculation about Hillary Clinton's health" by Fred Barbash (August 26th 2016)

[841] Daily Beast "Dr. Drew Leads the Hillary Clinton Health Truthers" by Samatha Allen (August 18th 2016)

[842] The New York Times "George Stephanopoulos Apologizes to Viewers on Clinton Donations" by John Koblin (May 15th 2015)

from moderating one of the Republican presidential primary debates. Despite the obvious conflict of interest caused by him donating tens of thousands of dollars to the Clintons, ABC News called it "an honest mistake."[843]

After President Trump's controversial travel ban was blocked by an injunction from an activist judge appointed by President Obama, an Iraqi immigrant named Hameed Darweesh, who had just arrived to JFK airport in New York, was interviewed by the media. He was very gracious and said America is the greatest nation in the world and that he was happy to be here, but that's where ABC cut the clip they posted online. What they didn't show was that immediately after that, someone asked him, "What do you want to say to Donald Trump?" trying to tee him up to denounce the president's new travel screening.

Instead of criticizing the president, he responded that he likes Trump and was very understanding of the extensive screening he had to go through before being allowed into the United States.[844] If ABC showed him saying that he didn't have a problem with the increased travel restrictions, that would have contradicted the narrative the media was pushing at the time which was that it was 'anti-Muslim bigotry' and 'government-sanctioned discrimination.'[845]

---

[843] New York Times "George Stephanopoulos Acknowledges Giving Money to Clinton Foundation" by Gerry Mullany and Steve Eder (May 14th 2015)

[844] Information Liberation "ABC Cuts Footage Of Iraqi Detained At Airport Saying He Likes Trump" by Chris Menahan (January 29th 2017)

[845] Newsweek "Trump's Travel Ban, SCOTUS Decision Are 'Government-Sanctioned Discrimination,' Muslim-American Leaders and Allies Say" by Stav Ziv (June 27th 2017)

ABC issued an apology for deceptively editing former White House Press Secretary Ari Fleischer's comments about Trump's first few days in office after they cut him off mid-sentence in order to cast him in a false light. In a segment where ABC was complaining about the newly inaugurated president, Ari was shown saying, "It looks to me if the ball was dropped on Saturday," talking about the way Sean Spicer handled criticism about the size of the crowd at Trump's inauguration.[846]  The newscast continued to nitpick Trump's first week as president but after the segment aired, Fleischer tweeted, "*Nightline* proves Spicer right about MSM's [mainstream media's] dedication to negativity," adding, "If this is how the press reports, Trump is right to go after them." He concluded, "When the press distorts someone's quote and twists their words, we all have a problem."[847]

He said they twisted his words because they left out the rest of his sentence when he said, "Sean recovered it and ran for a 1st down on Monday." After being called out by Fleischer on the deception, ABC issue an on-air apology, saying, "*Nightline* aired a segment Monday night about the first three days of the new administration including Sean Spicer's statement to the press on Saturday. As part of the report, we interviewed former White House press secretary Ari Fleischer. In editing the piece for air, his quote was shortened and as a result his opinions mischaracterized. We are fixing the piece online

---

[846] Washington Times "ABC issues apology for misleading quote about Sean Spicer: 'We are fixing the piece'" by Douglas Earns (January 25th 2017)

[847] Ibid.

to include his full quote and context. We apologize and regret the error."[848]

ABC News was sued for $1.9 billion dollars by a South Dakota meat processing company for a series of reports calling their ground beef product 'pink slime.'[849] The company alleged that their revenue dropped 80% after the reports aired, causing word of the 'pink slime' to go viral online. ABC later settled the lawsuit for a reported $177 million dollars, which is close to an entire year's profit for the network.[850]

Stories showing behind the scenes activities of meat processing plants tend to be sensational and shocking, but it appears ABC went too far trying to scare up some viewers for their 'pink slime' exposé and it came back to bite them.

---

[848] ABC News "Nightline Correction" (January 24th 2017)

[849] Associated Press "ABC, meat company settle in $1.9 billion 'pink slime' libel suit" by James Nord (June 28th 2017)

[850] CBS News "Disney 'pink slime' lawsuit settled for whopping $177 million" by Jonathan Berr (August 10th 2017)

# MSNBC

Before the 2016 election season began, MSNBC's viewership was at historic lows with their prime time shows only getting between 25,000 to 103,000 viewers in their demo audience.[851] The "demo" audience is the key demographic advertisers are marketing to. The first quarter of 2015 MSNBC averaged only 316,000 total viewers during the day,[852] and by the fourth quarter they barely had 500,000 total viewers during prime time.[853]

With Trump's election victory and liberals getting whipped up into a frenzy hoping to find some dirt on him that would get him immediately impeached, MSNBC's viewership dramatically increased as the network became increasingly more radical with their anti-Trump agenda. The primary face of MSNBC is the butch lesbian Rachel Maddow, whose convoluted ramblings appear to be unprepared streams of consciousness she just comes up with off the top of her head once she's seated at her desk, but somehow her viewers are entertained by her scatterbrained diatribes.

Like CNN, MSNBC often grasps at straws trying to create artificial outrage over minor things — a business model that often just leaves them looking ridiculous.

---

[851] Mediaite "Thursday Cable Ratings: Ed Schultz Hits New Low of 25K in Demo" (May 15th 2015)

[852] Deadline "MSNBC Ratings Crater To All-Time Lows, Fox News Tops Q1 Results, CNN Up" by Dominic Patten (March 31st 2015)

[853] Ad Week "2015 Ratings: MSNBC Has Double Digit Declines in Demo" by Mark Joyella (December 30th 2015)

Since Donald Trump wouldn't release his tax returns during the presidential campaign, which is somewhat customary for candidates, the Democrats fixated on them thinking they must contain connections to Russia or that he somehow weaseled out of paying any taxes at all. Then, two months into the Trump administration, Rachel Maddow tweeted she was about to reveal a "bombshell" on her show.

She claimed to have obtained a copy of his tax returns and a countdown clock was put up on screen ticking down to the big moment he would be 'exposed.' When her show went to air she began rambling on, and on, for eighteen minutes without actually showing them, or even saying what was in them. The network then went to a commercial break and when the show returned, she revealed two pages of his 2005 returns which showed that he paid $38 million in taxes that year.

That's it. No bombshell. No controversial revelations. No nothing. In fact they actually debunked the rumors that he hadn't paid taxes for 'nearly two decades' as had been previously reported.[854] There hadn't been such an overhyped television event since Geraldo Rivera opened Al Capone's vault on live TV back in 1986 to find absolutely nothing, and Rachel Maddow became the laughing stock of the Internet and late night talk shows.[855]

One *Washington Post* reporter published an op-ed titled, "Rachel Maddow takes conspiracy theorizing

---

[854] NBC News "Trump Tax Return Shows He Could Have Avoided Taxes for 18 Years: NYT" by Phil Helsel (October 2nd 2016)

[855] Hollywood Reporter "Stephen Colbert Brutally Mocks Rachel Maddow's Lengthy Trump Tax Form Tease" by Patrick Shanley and Jackie Strause (March 15th 2017)

mainstream with Trump tax 'scoop,'" and said that after she rambled on for 20 minutes, "I realized that we weren't watching a news broadcast so much as a modern recreation of X's monologue from Oliver Stone's 'JFK.'"[856]

It's not just Rachel Maddow; other hosts on MSNBC comprise what is basically a conspiracy carnival on cable. After President Trump launched a few Tomahawk missiles and destroyed a Syrian airfield in response to Bashar al-Assad killing rebels with chemical weapons, MSNBC's Lawrence O'Donnell dedicated his opening monologue to his conspiracy theory that Vladimir Putin may have ordered Assad to launch the chemical attack to provoke President Trump into a military response to distract the media and "change the subject from Russian influence" on the election.[857]

It appears that nothing is too crazy for MSNBC. One of their contributors appeared to encourage the bombing of Trump Tower in Turkey.[858] Malcolm Nance, who is the channel's 'terrorism analyst,' tweeted, and then later deleted, a photo of Trump Tower in Turkey and added, "This is my nominee for the first ISIS suicide bombing of a Trump property"[859] He had previously called Trump the

---

[856] Washington Post "Rachel Maddow takes conspiracy theorizing mainstream with Trump tax 'scoop'" by Sonny Bunch (March 15th 2017)

[857] Mediaite "Lawrence O'Donnell Wonders: What If 'Vladimir Putin Masterminded the Last Week in Syria'?" by Josh Feldman (April 7th 2017)

[858] Washington Times "MSNBC terrorism analyst nominates Trump property for 'ISIS suicide bombing'" by Jessica Chasmar (April 19th 2017)

[859] Ibid.

"ISIS candidate" and said that the president is inciting Islamophobia. [860]

This is the same MSNBC contributor who insinuated that Donald Trump is a Russian KGB agent who was at some point "co-opted by Vladimir Putin," which caused him to "buy into" and "embrace" a "dictatorial ideology that was done by a spymaster of the KGB." He then said, "Ten years ago, twenty years ago, there would be treason trials at this point."[861]

One of their regular panelists, Donny Deutsch, actually issued a serious fight challenge to the president during one segment, saying, "Donald, if you're watching, we're from Queens. I'll meet you in the schoolyard, brother. You need to be schooled. No, I'm serious. This is where this needs to go. He's a coward! A coward!"[862] He wasn't fired, or even suspended; giving the impression that MSNBC endorses threats of violence against President Trump.

Host Mika Brzezinski once decried Trump's influence on Twitter, saying, "He is trying to undermine the media and trying to make up his own facts," and that "he can actually control exactly what people think. And that, that is our job."[863]

Another host apologized for fake news after she falsely claimed that Fox News was having their Christmas

---

[860] Ibid.

[861] https://twitter.com/richardhine/status/810165860488908800.

[862] Washington Times "Donny Deutsch issues Trump 'serious' fight challenge: 'I'll meet you in the schoolyard, brother'" by Douglas Ernst (June 30th 2017)

[863] Real Clear Politics "MSNBC's Brzezinski: Trump Thinks He Can "Control Exactly What People Think," But That's "Our Job"" by Tim Hains (February 22, 2017)

party at Donald Trump's new hotel in Washington D.C. which had recently just opened. "I mean, think about the hotel in Washington right now. The RNC is having their Christmas party there. Fox News had their Christmas party there. That doesn't feel a little hanky?"[864]

At the end of the show the host surprisingly apologized, saying, "This is some serious business that I need to share. I need to apologize to the audience. Earlier today in a segment I stated that the Fox network held their holiday party at Trump's D.C. hotel. I was wrong. We've since learned that neither Fox network nor an affiliate held any party at Trump's Washington hotel. I stand corrected. I apologize for the error. I am truly, truly sorry. The mistake entirely my fault. And of course, I wish all my friends over at Fox a very happy holiday no matter where you have your party."[865]

Of course she didn't say "Merry Christmas" because that might have offended some people, so instead she used the more "inclusive" phrase "happy holiday."

Host Chris Matthews said that President Trump's inauguration was "Hitlerian," meaning it reminded him of an Adolf Hitler rally, and aside from being obsessed with "possible Russian connections" for a year after the election, he has also compared Ivanka Trump and her husband Jared Kushner to Saddam Hussein's murderous sons, Uday and Qusay.[866] Chris Matthews is the same

---

[864] Free Beacon "MSNBC Anchor Falsely Claims Fox News Had Christmas Party at Trump's D.C. Hotel" by Cameron Cawthorn (December 9th 2016)

[865] Ibid.

[866] Washington Times "Chris Matthews compares Jared Kushner, Ivanka Trump to Uday and Qusay Hussein" by Jessica Chasmar (March 28th 2017)

guy who said he got a thrill up his leg from hearing Barack Obama speak.[867]

After a terrorist ran down pedestrians using a van on the London Bridge in England, killing eight people and injuring 48, MSNBC host Thomas Roberts suggested that President Trump was "trying to provoke a domestic terrorist attack" of a similar nature in the U.S. "to prove himself right" about the dangers of radical Islamic terrorism.[868] Such an egregious allegation should put an end to someone's career in the television news business, but these kinds of unhinged statements are a common occurrence on the network.

In the immediate aftermath of the bombing at an Ariana Grande concert in Manchester, England which killed twenty-two people, MSNBC briefly mentioned the attack but quickly cut away from the breaking news to continue covering what they said was "shocking news in Washington tonight" and went on as usual with their nauseating obsession with conspiracy theories about Russia and the 2016 election.[869] A bunch of children were blown up at a major pop star's concert by an ISIS terrorist, but MSNBC thought talking about six-month-old conspiracy theories was more important.

Anchor Katy Tur appeared to insinuate that she was concerned Trump may have journalists he doesn't like

---

[867] Huffington Post "Chris Matthews: "I Felt This Thrill Going Up My Leg" As Obama Spoke" by Danny Shea (May 25th 2011)

[868] Washington Times "MSNBC's Thomas Roberts suggests Trump trying to 'provoke' terrorist attack for political gain" by Jessica Chasmar (June 5th 2017)

[869] Daily Caller "MSNBC Ruthlessly Cuts To Trump Coverage As Manchester Victims Scream In Background [VIDEO]" by Rachel Stoltzfoos (May 22nd 2017)

assassinated, drawing parallels between Vladimir Putin, who is accused of having some of his most vocal critics killed. During an interview with Nebraska Senator Deb Fischer, Tur asked, "As we know, there's, since 2000, been a couple dozen suspicious deaths of journalists in Russia who came out against the government there. Donald Trump has made no secret about going after journalists and his distaste for any news that doesn't agree with him here. Do you find that this is a dangerous path he is heading down?"[870]

The fact that Katy Tur is put on air is a prime example of MSNBC's low standards and poor quality talent pool they have to work with. During an interview with Republican Congressman Francis Rooney of Florida, when Tur again was grasping at straws to keep the Trump-Russia conspiracy theories circulating, Rooney pointed out that it was President Obama who got caught on a hot mic telling the Russian president he'd have "more flexibility" after his election.[871]

Tur responded, "I'm sorry, I don't know what you're referring to, Congressman."

Rooney replies, "Remember when he leaned over at a panel discussion or in a meeting and he said, I'll have more flexibility after the election? No one really ever pushed the president on what he meant by that, but I can only assume for a thug like Putin it would embolden him."

---

[870] Washington Examiner "Did an MSNBC reporter just suggest Trump would have reporters assassinated?" by Becket Adams (February 6th 2017)

[871] Real Clear Politics MSNBC Host Can't Remember When Obama Promised Russians "More Flexibility" Atfer 2012 Election" by Tim Hains (February 20th 2017)

Tur then immediately ended the interview.[872]   Any journalist should have known what he was talking about since it was a pretty stunning exchange to have been caught on tape, and what Obama meant was that he didn't want to lose votes in his bid for re-election, so he had to wait until after the election to do what he really wanted with Russia.   In response to online criticism of her ignorance she tweeted, "To be fair, I didn't touch politics in 2012.  I almost exclusively covered fires and shootings in NYC area."[873]

This is the same 'journalist' who says that Trump has "weaponized" the term "fake news" and claimed that Trump had never denounced white supremacists during the 2016 campaign despite video compilations circulating on YouTube and Facebook showing him doing such things over and over again, as far back as the year 2000 when he denounced David Duke as a racist and a bigot.[874] Tur's father — it's interesting to note — is also a reporter who now identifies as a woman, and once threatened to 'curb stomp' conservative pundit Ben Shapiro for using the wrong pronoun during a panel discussion Mr. Tur was involved in when he was called 'sir.'[875]

MSNBC hasn't gotten as much heat as CNN since the 'fake news' backlash began because it is a liberal network, whereas CNN was supposed to be impartial, and

---

[872] NewsBusters "Katy Tur Doesn't Remember Obama Telling Russians He'd Have 'More Flexibility' After His Reelection" (February 20th 2017)

[873] https://twitter.com/KatyTurNBC/status/833814870646784000

[874] YouTube Video: "Trump Disavows Racists Over and Over Again - While Media Says Exactly the Opposite" (August 15th 2017)

[875] Fox News "WATCH: Transgender Reporter Threatens Breitbart's Shapiro" (July 23rd 2015)

has recently changed its format from covering breaking news around the world to being an extension of the Democrat Party and a mouthpiece for George Soros.

# Conclusion

The search for truth and investigating and verifying what a bona fide fact is, and what makes it different from a belief or an opinion has been an age-old philosophical quest known as Epistemology. What is knowledge? What is truth? How do we "know" something? While Socrates and Plato were searching for answers to these important questions over two thousand years ago, it's a strange situation we find ourselves in when the 'information age' has helped to cause millions of people to drown in misinformation. It's a paradox. Misinformation has become so pervasive in the information age that some say we're living in a 'post-truth' world.

The Oxford Dictionary defines post-truth as "Relating to or denoting circumstances in which objective facts are less influential in shaping public opinion than appeals to emotion and personal belief," and the constant flow of media that is carefully crafted from multibillion-dollar corporate conglomerates has gotten constructing a post-truth world down to a science. Millions of people are mesmerized by an endless amount of information that bombards us constantly; wanting our attention, wanting us to believe something, wanting us to buy something, and wanting us to be something. It's hard to tune it out and think for ourselves sometimes, and it seems that fewer people are even thinking at all.

Thankfully, however, many are waking up to this mass manipulation and have seen the new systems of media production and distribution as they were constructed, and remember what society was like before this information overload engulfed our world.

While some of the information I covered in this book may seem like common sense to those who have lived long enough to observe patterns over years or decades, it is important to clearly document what has happened so we can teach the younger generations about the details and the sophistication of information manipulation mechanisms and help them become media literate.

Even if you've suspected this kind of deception occurs, I'm confident that this book has provided you with countless pieces of evidence to prove beyond a shadow of a doubt that we are in an information war, and as technology advances, the tactics to abuse it will likely also continue to advance. Soon it may be difficult for even experts to prove that something is or is not true.[876] James Madison once said, "A popular Government, without popular information, or the means of acquiring it, is but a Prologue to a Farce or a Tragedy; or, perhaps both. Knowledge will forever govern ignorance: And a people who mean to be their own Governors, must arm themselves with the power which knowledge gives."[877]

Unfortunately people have always, and will most likely continue, to believe that some hoaxes are real, and that some real events are hoaxes. Millions of Americans believe President Trump is a white supremacist and that

---

[876] The Belfer Center for Science and International Affairs — *Artificial Intelligence and National Security* "The existence of widespread AI forgery capabilities will erode social trust, as previously reliable evidence becomes highly uncertain" by Greg Allen and Taniel Chan (July 2017) page 30

[877] U.S. Department of Justice "Celebrating James Madison and the Freedom of Information Act (March 13th 2008)

police departments across the country are dominated by racist white men who enjoy killing black people. A large number of people still believe the moon landing was faked, and Flat Earthers even made a resurgence in early 2016, despite having limitless scientific research at their fingertips, they actually believe the Earth is flat and that NASA is lying to us; so it's clear we have a serious problem with knowledge and information in today's society. Others are more concerned with celebrity gossip than actual issues which directly impact their lives.

One thing we can do is prevent this problem from getting worse by being aware of the dangers of clickbait journalism, and knowing how most 'news' websites make money today. People should know why old subscription models are better — when people paid for monthly or yearly subscriptions to newspapers and magazines they liked and trusted instead of these companies relying on people sharing their articles on social media which encourages websites to generate page views by any means necessary.

The more shocking and sensational the headlines, the more likely people will click the link, bringing traffic to the site and revenue from the advertisers. Social media platforms are now the lifeblood of most 'news' sites which rely on people sharing their articles on Facebook or Twitter in hopes of duping people into clicking on them.

Owners of major media companies see the power their empires hold and often choose to use their outlets to influence people instead of informing them. From activist journalists to senior editors to CEOs, many in the big media companies can't help but impose their personal political ideology on the world by using the infrastructure they have at their disposal. By building mountains out of molehills, through lying by omission, agenda-setting, framing stories and issues in a certain light, and by manipulating what is spread through social media by either limiting its reach or artificially amplifying it, the major media and tech companies try, and they do, influence the way people think and thus how they act.

As people have come to rely more and more on the media to think for them and don't use their own brains to remember things because they can "just Google it," many have continued to dull their own ability to think, reason, and remember. As 19th century Swiss writer Charles-Ferdinand Ramuz noted, "It would not be very difficult to show that the further man advances in the conquest of what we must call his secondary powers, which are of a mechanical nature, the more he regresses in the possession of his primary powers, which are of an intuitive nature, and thus he is constantly being weakened."[878]

The shift from print journalism to websites and Facebook pages doesn't just pose a danger to the distribution and verification of news, but it also puts our historical records at risk as well. Headlines and articles can now be changed without notice and information can vanish down a memory hole with little to no trace of its existence. With digital forgeries getting more sophisticated, how will we be able to verify that a document is actually authentic, especially if there are no physical documents anymore? Most people don't backup their own files locally anymore on external hard drives, and instead rely on cloud services. Many people don't even own software anymore, and instead pay monthly

---

[878] Quoted in *The Powers of Hypnosis* preface by Jean Dauven (Stein and Day 1971)

subscription fees for applications like Photoshop, Microsoft Office, and others.

Paperback books and magazines have become less and less popular since the creation of e-books and tablets, opening the door to dangers of remote deletion, alteration, or even device failure if an iPad or Kindle is dropped and breaks. Someone even gave a Ted Talk claiming that paper dictionaries aren't needed anymore since they're too old fashioned, which is a dangerous road to go down.[879] Society is on a strange course, making us more vulnerable to fake news, not less, and many question whether there is even a solution at all.

Microsoft's social media researcher Danah Boyd said, "No amount of 'fixing' Facebook or Google will address the underlying factors shaping the culture and information wars in which America is currently enmeshed."[880] She continued, "The short version of it all is that we have a cultural problem, one that is shaped by disconnects in values, relationships, and social fabric. Our media, our tools, and our politics are being leveraged to help breed polarization by countless actors who can leverage these systems for personal, economic, and ideological gain."[881]

The stress of daily life, mixed with the constant bombardment of bad news about the latest death tolls from local crime and national tragedies, makes it appealing for many to completely check out of current events and the political process and get lost in a world of entertainment. Wasting countless hours clicking through

---

[879] Ted-Ed "Redefining the dictionary" speech by Erin McKean (December 28th 2012)

[880] BackChannel.com "Google and Facebook Can't Just Make Fake News Disappear" by Danah Boyd (March 27th 2017)

[881] Ibid.

social media threads or arguing about pop culture with complete strangers online is way too easy and should be avoided in exchange for meaningful discussions with friends and family and personal study.

We should stay away from the dangers of only getting news from following certain Twitter accounts or Facebook pages because we like what they post. The risk of being stuck in an echo chamber where only news and commentaries that reflect your own opinions, attitudes and interests, could keep you completely in the dark about important events you should be aware of, and can often present only one side of an issue.

When I was a kid, my friends and I had to ride our bikes to the local video store to rent a VHS tape for $3 or $4 which had to be returned by 5pm the next day. Today we can all watch Netflix, Hulu, Amazon Prime, or any number of other streaming services for just a few dollars a month and have access to endless movies and TV shows with the push of a button. So I thank you for taking the time and effort to tune out the millions of distractions clamoring for your attention and ignoring the endless alerts, notifications, likes, comments, and posts on social media for a while to focus on the information I've assembled and analyzed in this book.

I hope you'll write a brief review and rate it on Amazon or whatever e-book store you downloaded it from if that's how you're reading it, and I encourage you to check out some of my other books as well, as this is not the only one I have written. I will conclude with a final quote from one of the best films about mass media which brilliantly conveyed the dangerous power wielded by the corporations which control it. In *Network* (1976), news anchor Howard Beale 'sees the light' about the sinister nature of the very business he's been a part of for decades and decides to blow the lid off it, live on the air. His epic rant, even though over forty years old now, is timeless, and perhaps even more powerful today than when he first made it in 1976 when the film was released.

The character, played by Peter Finch — who won the Academy Award for best actor for the role — begins by telling the audience, "Television is not the truth. Television's a god-damned amusement park. Television is a circus, a carnival, a traveling troupe of acrobats, storytellers, dancers, singers, jugglers, sideshow freaks, lion tamers, and football players. We're in the boredom-killing business. So if you want the Truth, go to God! Go to your gurus. Go to yourselves! Because that's the only place you're ever gonna find any real truth. But, man, you're never gonna get any truth from us."

He continues, getting more passionate with every sentence, "We deal in illusions, man! None of it is true! But you people sit there day after day, night after night, all ages, colors, creeds. We're all you know. You're beginning to believe the illusions we're spinning here. You're beginning to think that the tube is reality and that your own lives are unreal. You do whatever the tube tells you. You dress like the tube, you eat like the tube, you raise your children like the tube. You even think like the tube. This is mass madness. You maniacs! In God's name, you people are the real thing! We are the illusion! So turn off your television sets. Turn them off now. Turn them off right now. Turn them off and leave them off! Turn them off right in the middle of this sentence I am speaking to you now! Turn them off!"

# Also by Mark Dice:

-*Liberalism: Find a Cure*
-*The Illuminati in Hollywood*
-*Inside the Illuminati*
-*The Illuminati: Facts & Fiction*
-*The New World Order: Facts & Fiction*
-*The Resistance Manifesto*
-*Big Brother: The Orwellian Nightmare*
-*The Bilderberg Group: Facts & Fiction*
-*Bohemian Grove: Facts & Fiction*

# Connect with Mark on:

*Facebook.com/MarkDice*
*Twitter.com/MarkDice*
*Instagram.com/MarkDice*
*YouTube.com/MarkDice*
*MarkDice.com*